THE
ROYAL
WOMEN
WHO MADE
ENGLAND

THE
ROYAL
WOMEN
WHO MADE
ENGLAND

THE TENTH CENTURY IN
SAXON ENGLAND

M.J. PORTER

PEN & SWORD HISTORY

AN IMPRINT OF PEN & SWORD BOOKS LTD.
YORKSHIRE – PHILADELPHIA

First published in Great Britain in 2024 by
PEN AND SWORD HISTORY
An imprint of
Pen & Sword Books Ltd
Yorkshire – Philadelphia

ISBN 978 1 39906 843 7

Typeset in Times New Roman 11.5/14 by
SJmagic DESIGN SERVICES, India.
Printed and bound in the UK by CPI Group (UK) Ltd.

Pen & Sword Books Limited incorporates the imprints of Archaeology, Atlas,
Aviation, Battleground, Digital, Discovery, Family History, Fiction, History,
Local, Local History, Maritime, Military, Military Classics, Politics, Select,
Transport, True Crime, After the Battle, Air World, Claymore Press, Frontline
Publishing, Leo Cooper, Remember When, Seaforth Publishing, The Praetorian
Press, Wharncliffe Books, Wharncliffe Local History, Wharncliffe Transport,
Wharncliffe True Crime and White Owl.

For a complete list of Pen & Sword titles please contact:

PEN & SWORD BOOKS LIMITED
George House, Units 12 & 13, Beevor Street, Off Pontefract Road,
Barnsley, South Yorkshire, S71 1HN, England
E-mail: enquiries@pen-and-sword.co.uk
Website: www.pen-and-sword.co.uk

or

PEN AND SWORD BOOKS
1950 Lawrence Rd, Havertown, PA 19083, USA
E-mail: uspen-and-sword@casematepublishers.com
Website: www.penandswordbooks.com

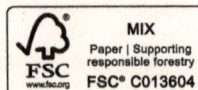

MIX
Paper | Supporting
responsible forestry
FSC
www.fsc.org   FSC® C013604

Contents

Introduction

The decision to write this book stems from my frustration when researching many of these women to offer fictionalised accounts of their lives. I consulted many secondary sources, often with only single chapters of relevance, if not only a sentence, and hunted down primary sources, which, again, might have offered only a few lines or words, some of them only available in Latin and with no translation. It is not easy to find a single title that covers this period even for the male rulers of Wessex and what would become England: Kings Alfred, Edward the Elder, Ælfweard, Athelstan, Edmund, Eadred, Eadwig, Edgar, Edward the Martyr and Æthelred II. It is impossible to find one where the focus is exclusively on the women of the same period, other than Elizabeth Norton's monograph on Elfrida, England's first crowned queen. However, readers might be more aware of Queen Emma and Queen Edith of the eleventh century, as they have both been the subject of extensive study.

Even with an acknowledged dearth of information, it must still be possible to cast a light on these women and to highlight how they, just as much as the royal men, shaped England throughout the tenth century.

That said, and as has been most eloquently stated by Wragg in *Early English Queens, 650–850*, 'Working with later sources often tell us more about the needs and concerns of the community writing these sources, rather than the individuals and circumstances of their setting.'[1] This is a particular problem for the royal women of the tenth century. The writings which are available to us are rarely, if ever, contemporary. The happenstance of survival is entirely that. Nothing that is known about Saxon England in general, and the tenth century certainly falls into that category, even with the writing of the *Anglo-Saxon Chronicle* throughout the period, has survived just by chance. Everything has some sort of bias attached to it, propaganda, if you will. This means travellers to this period must be aware of more than just what could be deemed as established 'facts'. There is not a single *fact* that could not be disputed.

It is as important to know about the sources consulted when writing this as it is to know about what the sources themselves say.

Essentially, the sources for the tenth century must be mined, not just for what they can tell us, but for *why* they've told us that. I have spent some time with the sources for the period, but only further through the book. First, it is important to meet these royal women.

Stafford eloquently sums up the dearth of information for these royal sisters and daughters:

> Were it not for the prologue to Æthelweard's Latin translation of an *Anglo-Saxon Chronicle*, we would know of only six tenth-century royal daughters or sisters from early English sources and the names of only four of them. Three of these named ones are nuns or abbesses. Only Ælfwynn, the daughter of Æthelflæd and Æthelred of Mercia, and the two daughters of Edward/sisters of Athelstan who married Otto I and Sihtric of York, appear in the witness lists of charters, though Eadburh, daughter of Edward the Elder, is a grantee of a charter of her brother Athelstan.[2]

And yet, these women, we know, existed, lived their lives, and were remembered, at least by some, after their deaths, even if that was only their children or their parents, should they have predeceased them. Yet:

> Queens only feature in the historical records when they serve a distinct purpose, whether as a family connection, as progenitors or mothers, or actors in key events. Even then, they tend to occupy the margins, even when, after a careful investigation, they may have been a key agent in major cultural or political shifts.[3]

The seeming stability of the Wessex royal house at this time is worthy of mentioning:

> When Æthelwulf [Alfred's father] succeeded his father Ecgberht to the throne of Wessex in 839, he was the first son to follow his father directly to power since 641 yet, after him his sons succeeded him in turn, followed by his youngest son's son, grandsons and great grandsons.[4]

And yet, as will be seen, this is only a veneer, and one that covers much political intrigue, as well as a huge number of early deaths, some of them violent, although none, as we know it, actually in battle against Wessex and England's enemies. This, in and of itself, is a fascinating realisation.

And so, the royal women of the long tenth century is an opportunity to delve into what is known about these women and the time in which they lived and ensure that their story is told, as well as that of their slightly better-known male counterparts. It is also an opportunity to place them into this context of seeming stability and to assign them a part other than that of mothers and grandmothers to the next generation in the proceedings of this long and turbulent period, although, admittedly, it is as mothers and grandmothers that they seem to have truly discovered their abilities to govern.

There is no surviving contemporary image of any of the royal women of the tenth century. These women are not only difficult to 'find' in the written sources, but they are also entirely faceless, apart from in the words of their contemporaries or near contemporaries. But, as far as is known, there are only images of King Athelstan that survive, in manuscript 183, folio IV Cambridge, Corpus Christi College,[5] and also King Edgar, in London, British Library Cotton Vespasian A.viii, fol. 2v.[6] And we seem to have only one physical item associated with these women: priestly vestments which may well have been stitched by Lady Ælfflæd's hands (the second wife of Edward the Elder) and that survive in Durham as part of the collection of items linked with the tomb of St Cuthbert, the Northumbrian saint associated with Lindisfarne.

Notes

Naming conventions – I have opted for those names that I have encountered most often, and most, if not all, will be the way these names appear on PASE (The Prosopography of Anglo-Saxon England), an online resource, if they do appear. Notable exceptions are Wynflæd (Wynnflæd on PASE) and Athelstan (Æthelstan on PASE, equally Alfred should be Ælfred). I have kept the spellings as offered in sources I have consulted and quoted from, but with the addition of the name used throughout the rest of the book if it is not immediately obvious.

Family Tree

Kings of Wessex, The Anglo-Saxons, and England (The House of Wessex)

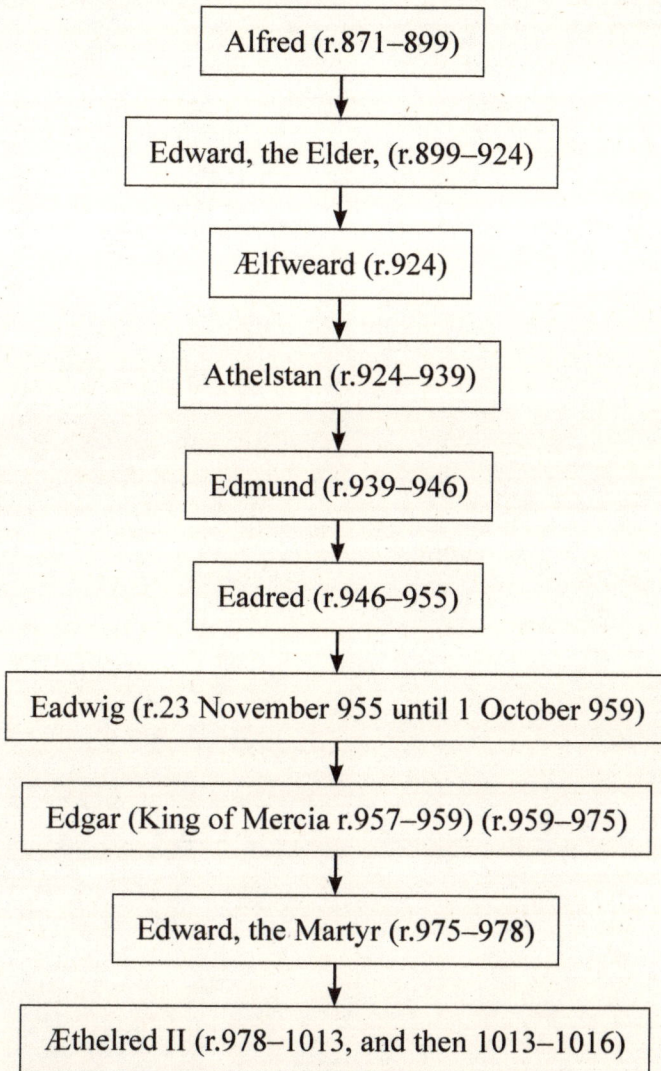

Alfred (r.871–899)

↓

Edward, the Elder, (r.899–924)

↓

Ælfweard (r.924)

↓

Athelstan (r.924–939)

↓

Edmund (r.939–946)

↓

Eadred (r.946–955)

↓

Eadwig (r.23 November 955 until 1 October 959)

↓

Edgar (King of Mercia r.957–959) (r.959–975)

↓

Edward, the Martyr (r.975–978)

↓

Æthelred II (r.978–1013, and then 1013–1016)

Kings of Wessex, The Anglo-Saxons, and England (The House of Wessex)

Chapter 1

The Long Tenth Century and its Kings

The tenth century, running from the death of King Alfred in October 899 to the marriage of King Æthelred II to Lady Emma of Normandy in 1001/1002, saw huge change, and also very little change in Saxon England. (I have chosen this end date of 1001/2 as Lady Emma of Normandy, and her influence, really belongs to the eleventh century. It also marks the death of Lady Ælfthryth/Elfrida, Æthelred's mother.)

At the death of King Alfred, the menace from the Viking raiders[1] appears to have been halted, if not averted. By the beginning of the eleventh century, the Viking raiders were back. Events throughout the eleventh century would be catastrophic for Saxon England and its rulers, resulting in the well-known events of 1066 which saw Saxon England come to an end, but also the earlier events of 1013 and 1016 when England was likewise conquered by men of Norse descent.

But 'England' would be born throughout the 900s. King Alfred (r.871–899) was termed the king of the Angles and Saxons (in a charter from 889 known as S346),[2] by 16 April 928, King Athelstan (r.924–939), his grandson, would be termed as the king of the English,[3] and indeed overlord of the British.[4] By the reign of King Æthelred II (r.978–1016), his mother would have been consecrated as England's first queen on her union to King Edgar (r.959–975), who might have been consecrated himself on two such occasions, on his accession and also in 973, during his thirtieth year in imitation of Christ being baptised during his thirtieth year.

Despite these developments, the kingship was not secure. Not one but two kings would be murdered, others would die at a young age, a child would be named as king on four occasions, and there would be some very complicated marriages for husbands and wives to negotiate.

And here, a slight detour. Throughout this book, the concept of marriage will be encountered, and that of concubinage. It is difficult

1

to truly determine a difference in these unions other than that marriage was sanctioned by the Church and gave both the wife and the children a sheen of legitimacy, which is missing from that of concubinage. And yet, both unions were evidently entirely acceptable, other than where the succession was concerned. Even then, it was perhaps merely a weapon in the war of words that would ensue when matters of the succession reared their ugly heads.

'England' would also, for much of the period, be termed as being on a military footing. There were wars and battles, and enemies aplenty. Sadly, the little-known but far-reaching Battle of Brunanburh in 937, which saw King Athelstan overawe almost every reigning king in Britain at the time, as well as a few others as well, has become lost behind the better-known events of 1066 and the Norman Conquest. And yet, as far as we know, no Wessex/English king died in battle. This is worth stressing.

Without the steadying hands of the Wessex royal women, slowly coming into prominence as the century progressed, it could be argued that this appearance of stability would not have been maintained. Certainly, it is doubtful that a child would have been proclaimed as England's king, even when there was so little alternative. 'It was as queen-mothers that both Eadgifu (919–964) and Ælfthryth [Elfrida] (964–1001/2) enjoyed their highest standing.'[5]

Who then were these royal women of the Wessex ruling family, who held tight, firstly to Wessex, and then to England, and ensured it survived the tribulations of the tenth century, a period of not constant, but near-enough constant military expeditions, so much so that King Edgar's (959–975) reign saw him titled 'The Peaceable', so rare was it to be at peace?

'His'tory

The tenth century begins with the death of King Alfred on 26 October 899.[6] We are told that, 'He was king over all the English race except that part which was under Danish control, and he held that kingdom twenty-eight and a half years. And then Edward, his son, succeeded to the kingdom.'[7] This is important to remember. Alfred was not king of all England. He was a member of the Wessex royal family who claimed their descent from Cerdic, and so the family is also known as the Cerdicings.

Alfred was the fourth brother to rule after their father, King Æthelwulf (r.839–858), and grandfather, King Ecgberht of Wessex (r.802–839). His brothers, Æthelbald (r.858–860), Æthelberht (r.860–865), and Æthelred (r.865–871), all died without leaving known children, apart from Æthelred, who left two sons. England, at the time of Alfred's death, did not yet exist. If Alfred had died following such a short reign as his brothers, it is curious to consider what might have happened and whether England, as we now know it, would have truly formed.

Edward is believed to be Alfred's second-born child, who in time would come to be known as Edward the Elder, when one of his grandsons, who became king, shared his name later in the century. Edward, born *c.*874 would die on 17 July 924, at Farndon, Cheshire.[8] He would rule from 899 until 924. This was a not insubstantial amount of time. Perhaps, the years of his rule, with their consistent attempts to drive back the aggression of the Viking raiders, as well as Wessex's other enemies, the extremely long-lived king of the Scots, Constantine II (r.900–943, seemingly forced to abdicate, as his death is recorded in 952), to name but one, and to attempt to form some sort of superiority over these other kingdoms in the British Isles, did much to lay the foundations upon which his eldest born son, Athelstan, would formally be recognised in the charters of the time as the king of the English, and on occasion, as Emperor of Britain.

> Edward the Elder is perhaps the most neglected of English kings. He ruled an expanding realm for twenty-five years and arguably did as much as any other individual to construct a single, south-centred, Anglo-Saxon kingdom.[9]

Athelstan (r.924–939) was not meant to become king after his father. Instead, that honour was supposed to go to Ælfweard, Edward's eldest son, with his second wife, Lady Ælfflæd. Sadly, Ælfweard died only a short time after his father, as the D text of the *Anglo-Saxon Chronicle* tells us: 'Here King Edward died at Farndon in Mercia; and very soon, 16 days after, his son Ælfweard died at Oxford; and their bodies lie at Winchester. And Athelstan was chosen as king by the Mercians and consecrated at Kingston.'[10]

While no mention is made of foul play, the death of Ælfweard was serendipitous for Athelstan, as well as other interested parties. Whether foul play should be suspected, there are no later suggestions that Ælfweard was murdered to clear the way for Athelstan to claim Wessex as well as Mercia. This is worthy of remembering.

Ælfweard had a brother, Edwin. No mention is made of an intention to allow Edwin to rule following the death of his brother and father. Instead, it was to Athelstan that the crown passed. It is curious that Athelstan was named as king by the Mercians first. It is to be supposed that there were some negotiations to undertake following the death of Edward and Ælfweard. While the Mercians may have wanted Athelstan, raised at the Mercian court, and associated with his aunt, Lady Æthelflæd, Lady of the Mercians (*c.*880–918), the people of Wessex may have had their doubts about the suitability of a Mercian raised king in Wessex, even if he was Wessex born. Perhaps they championed the other son, Edwin, and we simply do not know about it. Athelstan was certainly accepted as the king of the Mercians before becoming king of Mercia and Wessex. 'He [Alfred] arranged for the boy's education at the court of his daughter, Æthelflæd and Æthelred his son-in-law, where he was brought up with great care by his aunt and the eminent ealdorman for the throne that seemed to await him.'[11]

Athelstan, unlike his father, was not to enjoy as long a reign. While his consecration as king of the Mercians and Wessex only took place in 925, he ruled until his untimely death on 27 October 939, having beaten all England's enemies at the famous Battle of Brunanburh, variously believed to have taken place either in the north-east of England (as shown on a seventeenth-century map by Robert Morden), or, as is becoming increasingly accepted, on the Wirral.[12]

The symmetry of the death of King Athelstan and King Alfred, his grandfather, is noted in the *Anglo-Saxon Chronicle* A text, '40 years all but a day after King Alfred passed away'.[13] This entry is not contemporary to the *Anglo-Saxon Chronicle* A. It already speaks of our knowledge of the period being based on annal entries, which were not written contemporarily with the events they describe.

Athelstan, unlike his predecessors, did not marry. Instead, from early on, it seems to have been accepted that on his death, one of his half-brothers would claim England's crown. And indeed, it was Edmund, the oldest son of the union between King Edward the Elder and his third wife, Lady Eadgifu, who was proclaimed as England's king in 939 on Athelstan's death.

Edmund was probably no more than a toddler at the death of his father, Edward the Elder. He would have been too young to rule then, especially with a country at war with the Viking raiders. When Athelstan died, Edmund is said to have only been 18 years old. His accession was relatively calm, but this may have had more to do with the repercussions of the Battle of Brunanburh. The alliance of Norse, Scots and the kingdom of Strathclyde, was already rising against the supremacy of the 'English'. What the English needed, at Athelstan's premature death, was an acknowledged and supported king. This may account for Edmund's easy acceptance as king rather than a desire to continue the ruling line of the dominant Wessex family.

The relationship between Edmund and Athelstan deserves consideration. With his father dying so young, Edmund likely had few, if any, memories of his father. For Edmund, it would have been his older half-brother, Athelstan, who would have filled the space in his life and been like a father to him. Certainly, much is made of their close relationship in the *Anglo-Saxon Chronicle*, where they are mentioned as 'Edward's sons'.[14]

Alas, Edmund was to have a tragically short reign, and much of it was filled with strife and heartbreak. His first wife, Ælfgifu of Shaftesbury, died young, giving him two sons, Eadwig and Edgar (Eadgar). She was revered as saintly following her death. His second wife, Æthelflæd of Damerham, would have no children with him and became a widow very soon after her marriage to King Edmund when he was assassinated.

The D text of the *Anglo-Saxon Chronicle* writes for 946:

> Here King Edmund passed away on St Augustine's Day [26 May]. It was widely known how he ended his days, that Liofa stabbed him at Pucklechurch. And Æthelflæd of Damerham, daughter of Ealdorman Ælfgar, was then his queen. And he had the kingdom six and a half years; and then after him, his brother, the ætheling Eadred, succeeded to the kingdom.[15]

The reason for Edmund's assassination is much debated. Was it political reprisal by the enemies of England? Was it purely an unfortunate occurrence? It would be intriguing to know if retaliations were taken against Liofa, and whoever arranged the death of Edmund, but sadly there is no further information. Neither, it seems, was Edmund sainted following his death. This is interesting. Many members of the Wessex ruling family who died young were later revered as saints.

Once more, England could have been left with a toddler as the king of England, either Eadwig, the first-born son, or Edgar, the second-born son, but there was, luckily, a final son of King Edward the Elder and his third wife, Lady Eadgifu, still living. Eadred (r.946–955), born *c*.922, was to enjoy a slightly longer rule than his brother, but just as Athelstan, his older half-brother, determined not to marry, leaving the future rule of England for one of his two nephews.

Eadred ruled until 955. 'Here King Eadred passed away, and Eadwig, son of Edmund, succeeded to the kingdom',[16] is how the *Anglo-Saxon Chronicle* E writes of these events, but the D text has a slight variation on this. 'And Eadwig succeeded to the kingdom of Wessex and his brother Edgar succeeded to the kingdom of Mercia; and they were sons of King Edmund and St Ælfgifu.'[17]

The B and C texts read similarly. They inform, under 956 that 'Eadwig succeeded to the kingdom.'[18] And under 957 that, 'Here the ætheling Edgar succeeded to the kingdom of Mercia.'[19]

These terse words offer a very different interpretation of what was happening in England at the time. Had the kingdom been split along lines similar to when Edward the Elder and Æthelflæd of Mercia ruled? Or was this merely the action of a brother who wanted to share the rule of the kingdom with his brother, perhaps by offering him a role as an under-king? This had happened in the past – most notably, King Ecgberht of Wessex had installed his son as King of Kent on claiming that territory from Mercia during the 820s.

The entry for the *Anglo-Saxon Chronicle* B and C text, when it records Eadwig's death, perhaps hints at a similar division.

Whatever was happening, it did not last long. Eadwig was forcibly divorced from his wife by Archbishop Oda in 958. 'Here in this year Archbishop Oda divorced King Eadwig and Ælfgifu because they were related.'[20] None of the other chronicles refer to this divorce, but in 959 we are told, 'Here King Eadwig passed away, and Edgar, his brother, succeeded to the kingdom both in Wessex and in Mercia, and in Northumbria; and he was then 16 years old.'[21]

Edgar (r.959–975), like his grandfather, was to enjoy a longer reign than some of his other male relatives. And also, like his grandfather, was to potentially have three wives. Certainly, the four children that are known to have been his were born to three different women. And it is his third wife, Lady Ælfthryth/Elfrida, who is acknowledged as the first consecrated queen of the English. The Wessex royal line had finally, after many centuries, come to realise that a queen to rule alongside her king was to be an advantage. Yet, Edgar still died a young man.

The Anglo-Saxon Chronicle D for 975 reads: '8 July. Here departed Edgar, ruler of the English, friend of the West Saxons, and protector of the Mercians.'[22] Once more, it is illuminating that the chronicle makes mention of the split kingship, specifically mentioning Wessex and Mercia when recording Edgar's death.

Edgar, like his grandfather before him, left sons from two different unions. Edward, was his older son, and acknowledged as such. His younger sons, Edmund (who predeceased his father), no doubt named for his father, and Æthelred, were the children of England's first consecrated queen, Lady Elfrida.

King Athelstan suffered from the stigma of having been born before his father, Edward the Elder, was proclaimed king. This was used against Athelstan, as some believed the son of an anointed king, and therefore the sons from Edward the Elder's second marriage, were worthier to rule. This could explain why Edward the Elder married again once he became king. Equally, this might just have been later propaganda used against Athelstan. However, it must be assumed that whenever Edward the Martyr was born, it was after 959, as there were no such difficulties surrounding his assumption of the kingship after his father, despite his youth. Not yet.

'And here Edward, Edgar's son, succeeded to the kingdom.'[23] The D text breaks off after the full entry until the year 1016, which is the year that Edgar's son, who ruled as Æthelred II, died.

We are not told why Edgar died, but we can assume it was a peaceful death as England is not recorded as being at war. But events in England during the next three years were clearly difficult. And then, in 978, comes news of something befalling the young man, Edward the Martyr (r.975–978).

'Here in this year King Edward was martyred, and his brother, the ætheling Æthelred, succeeded to the kingdom.'[24] This comes from the C version of the *Anglo-Saxon Chronicle*.

The A version varies. 'Here King Edward was killed.'[25] The E version varies again, 'Here King Edward was killed in the evening-time on 18 March at Corfe passage; and they buried him at Wareham without any royal honours.'[26]

The B text ends in 977 so there is no entry. The F text has a gap between 937 and 989, and so can offer nothing further. What, then are we to believe happened to poor Edward the Martyr?

King Æthelred II, it is a true quirk that we have an Æthelred II but an Edward the Elder and an Edward the Martyr (Æthelred I of Wessex had been one of King Alfred's brother), would remain as England's king until 1016. There was a break in his kingship in 1013, when Swein, King of Denmark was proclaimed as king of England, and Æthelred II was forced to flee. He was married at least twice, once to Ælfgifu, and then to the much more widely known Emma of Normandy, although that union does fall outside the scope of this century and this book. With his first wife, he had at least four daughters, as well as many sons. Their names are only found in later sources.

This, then, is a very brief summary of the personal lives of men who would be kings of Wessex and then England. It does not reveal all but highlights the precarious nature of the continuation of the Wessex royal line throughout the tenth century. If Edward the Elder had not had more than one son, who would have ruled the country, not only after his death but then also after the deaths of Ælfweard, Athelstan and Edmund? If Edmund had not had two children and a spare brother again, then who would have ruled after his assassination? The questions should perhaps stop there, for if Edgar had only had one son, perhaps the eldest of his sons would not have been assassinated.

This then was a perilous time for the lives of these royal men, and that is not even factoring in the raging warfare that sporadically cropped up with the Norse invaders. It is, perhaps, pure happenstance that the ruling family of Wessex survived the long tenth century. This is where the royal women of the tenth century should take precedence, despite the dearth of information regarding them in the *Anglo-Saxon Chronicle* and other near-contemporary surviving sources.

Chapter 2

The Royal Women

In the online resource, The Prosopography of Anglo-Saxon England (PASE), a database of every known name from the period, 33,981 male names are listed. There are only 1,460 female names for the 600-year period of Saxon England, so only 4 per cent of entries are women. Twenty-one (possibly twenty-two)[1] of these belong to the royal women of the tenth century. Beginning with King Alfred and his family, they are his wife, Lady Ealhswith,[2] and their daughter, Æthelflæd,[3] Lady of the Mercians, and her daughter, Ælfwynn;[4] Æthelgifu,[5] Alfred and Ealhswith's second daughter, the abbess of Shaftesbury; and Ælfthryth,[6] the Countess of Flanders, their third daughter.

King Alfred's son, Edward, would marry, or rather, have children with, three different women. Ecgwynn[7] (if that was her name), mother to King Athelstan, and an unnamed daughter, given the name of Ecgwynn/Edith[8] in later sources, was Edward's first union. Ecgwynn may have died or been deemed an unsuitable consort when Edward succeeded his father to the kingdom of Wessex in 899. His second wife, Lady Ælfflæd,[9] had many children. Six of them were daughters, Æthelhild,[10] Eadgifu,[11] Eadflæd,[12] Eadhild,[13] Eadgyth[14] and Ælfgifu,[15] who all survived to adulthood. Edward's third wife, Lady Eadgifu,[16] clearly much younger than her husband, had two sons, and a daughter, Eadburh,[17] and possibly another daughter. More of this later.

King Athelstan, Edward the Elder's oldest son, never married, and on his death the kingdom passed to King Edmund, the son of Lady Eadgifu and King Edward the Elder, his half-brother. King Edmund would marry twice, firstly to Ælfgifu[18] of Shaftesbury, whose mother Wynflæd[19] is named, and secondly to Æthelflæd[20] of Damerham. King Edmund was murdered having fathered two sons. Such small children could not become England's king and so their uncle, King Eadred, ruled until his death, at which point, first the older son, Eadwig became king, and then the second, Edgar. Eadred did not marry.

Eadwig would have a union with another Lady Ælfgifu,[21] although no children were born, or survived to be written about. Edgar, when he became king, would marry, or have children with no fewer than three women, just like his grandfather – Æthelflæd,[22] Wulfthryth[23] and Elfrida/Ælfthryth.[24] From these unions, only one daughter was born, Edith/Eadgyth,[25] who spent her life in a nunnery, although whether she was a vowess is uncertain. It was Lady Elfrida's son who became king of England at the young age of perhaps only 12 – older than his uncle Eadwig would have been, had he succeeded to the kingdom after the death of his father, but certainly much younger than those who had preceded him. He, too, would marry twice, to Ælfgifu[26] and then Lady Emma of Normandy, and father many daughters, at least four with his first wife, Ælfgifu, a daughter (also called Ælfgifu),[27] Eadgyth[28], Wulfhild[29] and Ælfthryth,[30] and one with his second wife, Gode,[31] but only some of that is pertinent to the tenth century.

Throughout this period, a number of women appear in official documents, more often than not charters confirming land grants. There are several ways that these charters have been recorded. The now accepted version is that of the Sawyer catalogue. As such, all charters are listed as S and then their number. (Older catalogues are also available, and can be easily cross-referenced using the online Electronic Sawyer.) Ælfwaru,[32] named as Ælfgifu's (married to King Eadwig) sister, or possibly her sister-in-law. Ælfflæd,[33] married to Ealdorman Byrhtnoth, and her daughter, Leofflæd,[34] might just be the most well known, as she was the sister of Æthelflæd of Damerham, King Edmund's second wife. There are also two Æthelflæd's,[35] both wives to ealdormen, one to Ealdorman Æthelweard, and if not his wife then his sister by marriage – it is not made clear – and one to Ealdorman Æthelwine, an Ælswyth,[36] wife to ealdorman Ælfheah and a number of potentially royal women in nunneries who were the beneficiaries of royal charters. Several legal documents showing women taking action against those who claimed their land or leaving wills can also be named: Wulfwaru[37] and her daughters, Gode[38] and Alfwaru,[39] as well as the legal problems encountered by another Wynflæd,[40] and Eadgifu. At the beginning of the tenth century, a charter is confirmed for Æthelgyth.[41]

But this is really only a part of the story.

Life for a royal woman

While it is difficult to find faces and facts for the royal women of the tenth century, it is equally as difficult to determine how they spent their time, and what it was actually like to be a woman, let alone, a royal woman, in the tenth century.

However, some information can be gleaned. Perhaps, most importantly, we need to understand that these royal women did not live a settled life. Their lifestyle was peripatetic. While Winchester is often seen as the capital of Wessex, and therefore also England, throughout this time period, there were also many other royal sites.

It is perhaps easier to consider these women living in one place, but that is not the case. While it is impossible to provide a record for each day or even year for these women, some idea of the nature of their lives can be determined by following the movements of the royal council, the Witan; more often than not, the location of these meetings is mentioned in charters witnessed on those occasions when the royal court met.

As such, for King Athelstan, the following can be said of his years as king. In 925, he was possibly in Tamworth at some point (Tamworth was the capital of Mercia so this makes sense). On 4 September 925, he underwent his coronation at Kingston upon Thames. On 30 January 926, he was at Tamworth for the marriage of his sister to Sihtric. In 926, he was in Abingdon, where he met the embassy sent on behalf of Hugh, Count of the Franks. On 12 July 927, he was in York and then travelled to Eamont in Cumbria to meet with the northern kings. Later that year, he was in Hereford and Cornwall. In April 928, he was in Exeter. In 930, he visited Lyminster in Sussex. In March 931 he was in Colchester, on 20 June 931 he was at King's Worthy, and in November 931 in Devon. In 932 he was in Exeter once more. He spent Christmas that year at Amesbury. In January 933 he was in Wilton and Chippenham. In May 934, he was at Winchester before travelling to Chester-le-Street and then Scotland. In September, he was in Buckingham, and spent Christmas 935 at Dorchester. In 936, he was at York; in 937 he fought at Brunanburh and he died at Gloucester on 27 October 939.[42] This then, is not a great deal of geographical knowledge for over fourteen years, and Athelstan would no doubt have travelled a great deal more than his female counterparts, who perhaps were more closely tied to the royal sites in Wessex.

So where then might these sites have been? Winchester, of course, was a major centre for the Wessex royal family. Its royal mausoleum was based there, both the Old and the New Minster providing places of burial for the family members. We are also told that Alfred was born at Wantage, and so that must also have been a royal site. If we turn to Alfred's will, we find other places mentioned: Lambourn and Edington were both left to his wife, alongside Wantage; Wellow was left to his daughter, Æthelflæd; Kindclere and Candover to his second daughter, Æthelgifu; and Wellow, Ashton and Chippenham to his third daughter, Ælfthryth. The wives of kings often seem to have been gifted the same land during their tenure, and so it is possible that royal land was provided for the wives of the kings as part of their dowry. Amesbury, given to Alfred's son Æthelweard, and Wantage, given to his wife, both appear in later sources as land held by Lady Eadgifu, the third wife of Edward the Elder. She was gifted the land by her son, Eadred, and deprived of it by her grandson, Eadwig.

Equally:

> Tenth- and eleventh-century English queens often held land on which communities of men and women were established. The king's wife was provided for in this way, but the royal family as a whole were involved in the holding of religious communities and their lands. Damerham was held by Ælfflæd and Æthelflæd; Reading by Æthelflæd; Minster in Kent by Eadgifu, then Ælfthryth [Elfrida] held it. Some of these communities were of women but, not necessarily all … The nature of the relationships between the communities and these lay holders is not always clear and need not always have been the same. Queens may have been lay abbesses, and may have held all or only part of the lands and revenues attached to the communities.[43]

This then would be how they could afford to live their lives, but the day-to-day events are more difficult to determine. They must, of necessity, have attended church regularly, and been involved in the maintenance of the king and his palaces. Some of them will also often have been with child, or recovering from the birth of their children. It is highly likely that they spent at least some of their time employed in embroidery, and were, perhaps, involved more in the running of the country. But much of what we know about them is through surviving land charters, either theirs to gift, receive, or to witness, and a few scant sources, most notably, the Latin *Chronicon* of Æthelweard, a later tenth-century translation of a version of the *Anglo-Saxon Chronicle*.

Chapter 3

The Mercian Royal Women

Lady Ealhswith, wife to King Alfred

Ealhswith, *c*.850–d.902 daughter of Ealdorman Æthelred Mucel (of Mercia) and Eadburh

m. 864 Alfred of Wessex (before he became king)

> Æthelflæd, Lady of the Mercians
> Edward the Elder, king of the Anglo-Saxons
> Æthelgifu, the abbess of Shaftesbury
> Ælfthryth, Countess of Flanders
> Æthelweard, nobleman

Lady Ealhswith,[1] the wife of King Alfred, was the daughter of a Mercian nobleman, Æthelred Mucel. We are told by Asser, that Alfred 'married a wife from Mercia, of noble family, namely the daughter of Æthelred "who was known as Mucil [Mucel]", ealdorman of the Gaini. The woman's mother was called Eadburh, from the royal stock of the king of the Mercians.'[2] It is possible, but cannot be confirmed that Ealhswith's father was ealdorman in Mercia from the 820s onward when a man named Mucel is listed as attesting the surviving charters.[3] The location of the tribal region of the Gaini has yet to be ascertained. Mercia was composed of many tribal regions; the most familiar being the Hwicce and the Mægonsæte, both on the western borders with the Welsh kingdoms.

Whether Eahlswith's mother was actually a member of the Mercian ruling family is difficult to conclude. Yorke[4] determines she was related to King Coenwulf (796–821) and Coelwulf (821–823), two brother kings who ruled in the first quarter of the ninth century. It is impossible to confirm this either way due to a lack of available information. Mercia endured a string of kings throughout the ninth century, some more successful than others, and none of them able to offer the consistency and longevity that had been prevalent in the earlier eighth century during the long reigns of Æthelbald (716–757) and Offa (757–796).

Her possible father, Æthelred Mucel, witnesses two charters in the year of the marriage, S340,[5] surviving in one manuscript, and S1201,[6] surviving in two manuscripts, as well as S337,[7] surviving in four manuscripts, in 867 and S349,[8] surviving in two manuscripts, but deemed spurious, in 895.

What is known is that the union between Lady Eahlswith and Alfred was part of an arrangement with Mercia whereby Alfred's sister, Æthelswith,[9] married the then king, Burgred, and Ealhswith married Alfred. Little is known of Mercia's King Burgred (852–874), other than that he fled from Mercia in the wake of sustained Viking raider aggression in the year 874.

'Here the raiding-army went from Lindsey to Repton and took winter-quarters there, and [874] drove the king Burhred [Burgred] across the sea 22 years after he had the kingdom, and conquered all that land.'[10]

He is said to have died in Rome, alongside his wife, King Alfred's sister. Burgred's relationship to the earlier Mercian kings is difficult to unpick. Historians are left gathering together the rulership of Mercia in the ninth century in terms of the first initials given to their kings. There is a 'B' dynasty and a 'W' dynasty, as well as a 'C' dynasty. It was quite common practice for royal families to give their children names that began with the same letter. As such, when we look to the tenth century, we should see Ælfred (Alfred) and Æthelstan (Athelstan). And equally, Eadmund (Edmund), Eadred and Eadwig.

At the time of the union between the future King Alfred and his Mercian wife, Wessex was ruled by Alfred's brother, Æthelred. As the youngest of four brothers, there was no expectation that Alfred would ever be king. Yet, already, two of his brothers had died.

The purpose of this double union occurring in 868 is intriguing.

The Viking raiders had scored a victory over the Mercians and were currently holding the settlement of Nottingham. The Great Heathen Army, a later name for the events of the 860s, saw many battles. It is possible that the Mercian and Wessex royal families may have been attempting to construct a treaty of mutual defence against further attacks. If that was what they were trying to do, it was more successful for Wessex than for Mercia.

It is intriguing to think of what a young Ealhswith might have thought of her husband, and her new kingdom, but little to no information survives about the years of their marriage. Ealhswith is not even mentioned by name in the Latin Life of King Alfred, *De rebus gestis Ælfredi regis,* written by the king's biographer, Asser, in 893, the only contemporary account of a pre-conquest king. It survived in only manuscript, which was unfortunately lost in the Cotton Library fire of 1731. The version that survives is a sixteenth-century copy.[11]

It is known that five children were born to the union, three daughters, Æthelflæd, Æthelgifu and Ælfthryth, and two sons, Edward and Æthelweard.

The Anglo-Norman writer, William of Malmesbury, gives a somewhat muddled account of the children born to Ealhswith and her husband.

> By Æthelswith (Eahlswith), daughter of Ealdorman Æthelred, he had children. Æthelswith and Edward who succeeded him, Æthelflæd, who married Æthelred ealdorman of the Mercians, Æthelweard, who is said to have become a man of great learning, Ælfflæd and Æthelgifu who never married.[12]

As often happens, the career of Ealhswith comes into sharper focus once her husband died in 899. Ealhswith was never proclaimed as queen of Wessex, the Saxons or the Angles, or the Anglo-Saxons, as her husband was. There are no surviving charters from the years of her marriage. She is mentioned, as the mother of the king (Edward the Elder), in charter S363, dated from 901, which survives in four manuscripts.[13] This is the only surviving charter to name Ealhswith, and also makes mention of Edward's second wife, Ælfflæd. To put this into some context, the later Lady Elfrida, the first consecrated queen of England, is named in thirty-eight charters in total, twenty-two during her husband's lifetime and sixteen during that of her son, who ruled as Æthelred II of England.[14] Equally, Offa's queen, Cynethryth, from the eighth century, and a Mercian, appears as a witness in twenty-five surviving charters,[15] and, as has been mentioned above, the charter that names Æthelred Mucel is promulgated by King Burgred's queen, Æthelswith, and she is named on ten surviving charters.[16]

King Alfred's will survives. A rare occurrence. Only one other will of a king survives from the Saxon period, let alone from the tenth century, that of King Eadred (946–955), Alfred's grandson. In her husband's will, Ealhswith is mentioned by name and not title and is left 'the estate at Lambourn, at Wantage, and at Edington',[17] as well as a £100, the same amount of money he left to his three daughters. The vast majority of the property goes to her oldest son, Edward, who was proclaimed king after the death of his father. Edward and his brother are also left £500 each.

Wantage was the place of Alfred's birth. The other two locations gifted to Ealhswith were sites of victories over the Viking raiders.

Ealhswith's brother, Æthelwulf, is named in four charters: S219 dated 884 (in which he is in receipt of the charter) and which survives in only one manuscript, which is now lost; S220 dated 888 surviving in two manuscripts; S1441 dated 896 and S1442 dated 897, both surviving in two manuscripts.[18] These charters show him witnessing or receiving land on behalf of Æthelred of Mercia, and his niece, Æthelflæd. It seems he remained in Mercia after his sister's marriage to the future Wessex king.

Lady Ealhswith also appears in the *Anglo-Saxon Chronicle* after 899, but never with a title, only her name. In 901, the A text of the *Anglo-Saxon Chronicle* records, 'Here, Ealdorman Æthelwulf, the brother of Ealhswith died.'[19] The D text offers, 'Here departed Ealdorman Æthelwulf, the brother of Ealhswith, the mother of King Edward.'[20]

Ealhswith is known for founding a nunnery in Winchester, which would become known as the Nunnaminster to differentiate it from the two monasteries also in Winchester, and would be where her granddaughters and other female descendants spent their lives.[21] It must be assumed that Ealhswith was also involved in founding Shaftesbury nunnery, alongside her husband, over which her daughter was abbess. However, she is not specifically named to have done so.

Ealhswith died on 5 December 902, having only outlived her husband by three years. Ealhswith's death is marked in the A and C text of the *Anglo-Saxon Chronicle*. The A text, under 904 writes, 'And Ealhswith departed the same year.'[22] The C text reads under the year 902, 'Here Ealhswith passed away.'[23]

Sadly, Ealhswith's will does not survive. It is, therefore, perhaps, unsurprising that her accomplishments after her husband's death are less than for others of the royal women of the tenth century, who outlived their husbands by many years, in one case, by nearly forty. Two of Ealhswith's daughters are less obscure than their mother, and Æthelflæd, Lady of the Mercians, is perhaps the most well known of all the royal women of the tenth century.

Lady Æthelflæd, Lady of the Mercians

Æthelflæd, daughter of Alfred and Lady Ealhswith *c.*866–12 June 918

m. Æthelred of Mercia d.911

    Ælfwynn *c.*880s–918/960?

Æthelflæd,[24] said to be the oldest of the children of King Alfred, and his wife, Lady Ealhswith, was born around 866, the exact details are unknown, although the date of her death is well attested as 12 June 918.[25]

She was married to Lord Æthelred of the Mercians at some point during the 880s, although an exact date cannot be given. The first mention of this union occurs in a charter dated to 887,[26] although the date may not be reliable. There is also little information about who Lord Æthelred might have been, and his subsequent military successes should not be dismissed, as they often are. Lord Æthelred is assumed to have been a nobleman from Mercia, and one with enough of a reputation to secure the marriage alliance with the Wessex royal family (and it must be assumed, unrelated to her mother's birth family, and also her father's family through his sister's union to Burgred). This would not be the first time that Wessex and Mercia had united through marriage.

Lord Æthelred's identity is perplexing. As far as it is known, the rulers of Mercia, King Burgred, and his successor, King Coelwulf II (874–879?), had no children. This would mean that Æthelred's origins might need to be found even further back. Perhaps he was related to one of the Mercian kings who ruled during the more contested years from about 825 to Burgred's accession in 852. It must be imagined that as with Lady Æthelflæd's mother's marriage to a Wessex ætheling, the alliance was to someone of importance and was also to the advantage of Wessex, if not to Mercia.

Their marriage was a success, and yet there was only one child, a daughter, Ælfwynn, born to the union, perhaps quite soon after the marriage occurred.

Lady Æthelflæd is mentioned in her father's will as receiving the estate at Wellow, perhaps in Hampshire.[27] She also, alongside her mother and two sisters, received £100. Æthelflæd's husband is also named in her father's will when he is bequeathed a sword 'worth 100 mancuses'.[28] It has been noted that the fact Æthelred is not simply mentioned alongside the other Wessex ealdormen in Alfred's will perhaps points to his special relationship with Alfred. This might have been a political relationship. Equally, it might simply have been because he was the husband of Alfred's daughter. It would be intriguing to know Alfred's true thoughts about Mercia.

During her lifetime, Æthelflæd's name appears on fifteen surviving charters. These are a real collection, some promulgated by her father, her brother, her husband and then, in her name alone. The earliest to feature her name is S223 dated to 884x9, so between 884 and 889, which survives in two manuscripts, and discussed the building of the burh at Worcester:

> To Almighty God, the True Unity and the Holy Trinity in heaven, be praise and honour and thanksgiving for all the benefits which he has granted us. For whose love in the first place, and for that of St Peter and of the church at Worcester, and also at the request of Bishop Wærferth and their friend, Ealdorman Ethelred and Æthelflæd ordered the borough at Worcester to be built for the protection of all the people, and also to exalt the praise of God therein. And they now make known, with the witness of God, in this charter, that they will grant to God and St. Peter and to the lord of that church half of all the rights which belong to their lordship, whether in the market or in the street, both within the fortification and also that they may more easily help the community to some extent; and that their memory may be the more firmly observed in that place for ever, as long as obedience to God shall continue in that minster.
>
> And Bishop Wærferth and the community have appointed these divine offices before that which is done daily, both during their life and after their death; i.e. at every matins and at every vespers and at every tierce, the psalm *De profundis* as long as they live, and after their death *Laudate Dominum*; and every Saturday in St. Peter's church thirty psalms and a Mass for them, both for them living and also departed.
>
> And moreover Ethelred and Ætheflæd make known that they will grant this to God and St. Peter with willing heart in the witness of King Alfred and of all the councillors who are in the land of the Mercians; except that the wagon-shilling and the load-penny at Droitwich go to the king as they have always done. But otherwise, land-rent, the fine for fighting, or theft, or dishonest trading, and contributions to the borough-wall, and all the [fines for] offences which admit of compensation, are to belong half to the lord of the church, for the sake of God and St. Peter, exactly as it has been laid down as regards the market-place and the streets. And outside the market-place, the bishop is to be entitled to his land and all his rights, as our predecessors established and privileged it.

And Ethelred and Æthelflæd did this in the witness of King Alfred and of all the councillors of the Mercians whose names are written hereafter. And they implore all their successors in the name of Almighty God that no one may diminish this charitable gift which they have given to that church for the love of God and St. Peter.[29]

It is interesting that this charter is granted in the presence of King Alfred, who was not the king of Mercia at this time. Perhaps, adding his name to the charter was a means of securing it.

In S217, dated 880 for 887, Æthelflæd acts as a witness to a grant by her husband:

To the bishopric of Worcester; grant of 6 hides (mansiones) at Brightwell Baldwin and 8 at Watlington, Oxon., to pertain to the church at Readanoran (i.e. Pyrton, Oxon). With a list, in English, of six serfs formerly belonging to the royal vill at Bensington, Oxon.[30]

S220, dated to 888, and surviving in two manuscripts, is a further charter in which Æthelflæd witnesses a grant made by her husband, Æthelred.

In S346, dated to 889, surviving in a Worcester cartulary, Æthelflæd's father and husband make a grant together.

Alfred, king of the English and the Saxons, and Æthelred, *subregulus et patricius Merciorum*, to Wærferth, bishop of Worcester; grant of land at *Hwætmundes stane* in London, with commercial privileges.

Æthelflæd is once more a witness. The use of the titles of her father and husband are worthy of note, Alfred is king of the English and the Saxons, Æthelred is a subking of Mercia.

S1441 is dated to Gloucester in 896, and reads as follows:

In the reign of our Lord Christ the Saviour, when eight hundred and ninety-six years had passed since His birth, and in the fourteenth Indiction, – in that year Earl Aethelred [Æthelred] summoned together at Gloucester all the Mercian council, the bishops and the earls and all his nobility; and this he did with the cognisance and leave of King Alfred. And then they deliberated there how they could most justly govern their people, both in spiritual and temporal matters, and also do justice to many men, both clerical and lay, with regard to lands and other things in which they had been wronged. Then Bishop Werferth [Wærferth] informed the council that he had been robbed of nearly all the woodland belonging to Woodchester, which King Æthelbald had given to Worcester, [handing it over] to Bishop Wilferth for mastland and woodland, and as a perpetual gift for the good of his own soul. And Werferth [Wærferth] said that part of it had been abstracted at Bisley, part at Avening, part at Scorranstan and part at Thornbury, as far as he knew. Then all the council declared that justice should be done to that church as well as to [any] other.

Thereupon, Æthelwald said that he would not dispute the claim, and stated that Aldberht and Bishop Alhhun had formerly been occupied with this very matter; and he added that he was always ready to accede to the claims of every church to the best of his ability (?), and so very generously restored it to the bishop. And he ordered his geneat, whose name was Ecglaf, to ride with a priest from Worcester, Wulfhun by name; and Ecglaf led Wulfhun along all the boundaries, as Wulfhun read out from the old charters, how they had been determined of old by the grant of King Æthelbald.

Then, however, Æthelwald requested of the bishop and the community, that they would graciously allow him to have the use of the land as long as he lived, and also Alhmund his son; and they would hold it on lease of the bishop and the community; and neither he nor his son would ever deprive the bishop of the swine-pasture at Longridge, which he had granted him for as long as God should give it to him. And Æthelwald then declared that whosoever held this land would hold it under God's displeasure, except it be the lord of the church, to whom he had given it, with a reservation in favour of Alhmund; and this reservation, moreover, was to stand only for as long as Alhmund maintained the friendship which his father had had with the bishop. If, however, it should come to pass that Alhmund would not maintain his friendship, or if there should be proved against him a charge which disqualified him from holding land, or thirdly, if he died before [his father], then the lord of the church should take possession of his estate, as the Mercian council declared in this assembly, and as the charters of the estate directed him (or them).

This was done with the cognisance of Earl Aethelred [Æthelred] and of Aethelfled [Æthelflæd], and of Earl Aethelwulf, Earl Aethelferth, Earl Alhhelm, Eadnoth, Alfred and Werferth [Wærferth], and of the priest Aethelwald, and his own kinsmen Aethelstan and Aethelhun, and also of Alhmund his own son. And the following are the boundaries that the priest from Worcester rode over, and Aethelwald's geneat with him. First to Gemythleg, and then to Rodborough itself, then to Smececumb, then to Sengetleg, then to Heardanleg, otherwise called Dryganleg, and so to the lesser Nægleseg and then to Aethelferth's land. In this manner, Aethelwald's man showed him the boundaries, as the old charters directed and indicated to him.[31]

This charter is a record of a land dispute, and will be far from the last one encountered. This is one of the charters witnessed by Æthelwulf, Æthelflæd's uncle. The king mentioned, Æthelbald, had ruled Mercia from 716–757, showing just how long memories could be where land was concerned.

In S221 dated to 901 (which survives in one manuscript), Æthelred and Æthelflæd jointly grant a charter as the rulers of Mercia:

> To the community of the church of Much Wenlock; grant of 10 hides (cassatae) at Stanton Long and 3 hides (manentes) at Caughley in Barrow, Salop., in exchange for 3 hides (manentes) at Easthope and 5 at Patton, Salop. They also grant a gold chalice weighing 30 mancuses in honour of Abbess Mildburg.[32]

In 903, three charters survive, promulgated by Edward the Elder, Æthelred and Æthelflæd in unison, S367, S367a and S371, all requested by Ealdorman Æthelfrith. S367, which survives in one manuscript, is a request by Ealdorman Æthelfrith that a grant by Æthelwulf to his daughter Æthelgyth be renewed concerning land at Monks Risborough, Buckinghamshire, the original having been burned.[33] It seems that Ealdorman Æthelfrith was married to Æthelgyth, and this was land given to her by her father.[34]

In S367a, which survives in two manuscripts, Ealdorman Æthelfrith again asks for a charter to be renewed of a grant by Coenwulf, king of Mercia, to Beornnoth, *comes*, of 10 hides (cassati) at Islington, Middlesex.[35] Coenwulf was king of Mercia from 796–821:

> Ruling forever and governing the kingdom of the world as the offspring of the Father seated on high, Who regulates heavenly and earthly things together. In the year 903 of His incarnation, in indiction 6, it happened to Æthelfrith, dux, that all his deeds of title perished in the destruction of a fire. Therefore impelled by such a necessity, the aforementioned dux asked King Edward, also Æthelred and Æthelflæd, who then held rulership and power over the Mercian people under the aforementioned king, also all the *senatores* [? members of the Witan], that they should permit him and give authorisation for the rewriting of replacement charters for him.
>
> Then they all unanimously with devout intent agreed that other [i.e. replacement] charters be written for him in the same way as the previous ones had been written insofar as he was able to recall them from memory. If indeed he was not able to remember these, then this document can be an aid and confirmation for him, so that no one might prevail in assailing him in a law suit with other charters, neither a relative nor a stranger, although another man might present one of the old charters that he had removed deceitfully, either in the hour of the fire itself or at another time by theft. We also know that all things that customarily take place in this world, sometimes somewhat slowly, sometimes rather more quickly, pass from the failing memory of mortals into oblivion, unless they are recorded in written documents. Wherefore, in this charter we have caused to make known that it is accepted and pleasing and very appropriate concerning that land of ten hides, namely at Islington, which

Cenwulf [Coenwulf], the celebrated king of the Mercians, gave to his faithful comes, Beornnoth, to be free for himself and for his heirs in perpetuity 'after him', to be held with every appurtenance, and he strengthened his grant with the mark of the nourishing cross and faithfully confirmed it, to be possessed in perpetuity with woods, meadows and marshes and all appurtenances.[36]

In S371, surviving in three manuscripts, a further charter is reinstated. 'King Edward, with Æthelred and Æthelflæd, renews a landbook destroyed by fire for Æthelfrith, dux; confirmation of 20 hides (cassati) at Wrington, Somerset.'[37] Athelstan and Ælfweard, the sons of King Edward the Elder, with his first and second wife also witnessed this charter.

Keynes writes of these three documents:

> One such charter might be an exception; two might be a coincidence; but three, from separate archives, look to me like a conspiracy. There can be no doubt that the charters are authentic, and that they emanated from a gathering in 903 attended by the king [Edward], Ealdorman Æthelred, the Lady Æthelflæd, their daughter Ælfwynn, a range of bishops (from Kent, Sussex, and Mercia, though not from Wessex) and some members of the Mercian nobility.[38]

His argument, concerning three separate land grants, in Buckinghamshire, Somerset and Middlesex, and overseen by Edward the Elder is an acknowledgement that Edward may have been acting as king over Mercia as well as Wessex – as king of the Anglo-Saxons. Yet, it should be noted that Æthelfrith was a landholder and ealdorman in Somerset. It is equally possible that the lands he wished to have confirmed in Mercia needed the agreement of Æthelred and Æthelflæd, as opposed to being seen as Edward's to gift. Perhaps, here, we see a Wessex ealdorman, making a Mercian marriage, perhaps in imitation of that of Æthelflæd and Æthelred, and being keen to ensure the holding of lands in both those kingdoms.[39]

S361 and S1280 are both dated 904. S361, surviving in one manuscript, sees King Edward confirming 'the sale by Hungyth to Wigferth of 5 hides (manentes) at Water Eaton, Oxon., the earlier landbook having been lost'. Æthelred is named as the ealdorman of Mercia. Æthelflæd is given no title but attests next to her husband.

S1280, which survives in two manuscripts, can be quoted in entirety in translation:

> The agreement of Æthelred and Æthelflæd with Bishop Werfrith [Wærferth]. It is known and manifest to all the wise that the words and deeds of men frequently slip from the memory, through the manifold agitations caused by wicked deeds, and as the result of wandering thoughts, unless they are preserved and recalled to mind in the form of words and by the precaution of entrusting them to writing. For this reason, in the year of the incarnation of our Lord 904 and in the first Indiction, we have ordered this document to be written for the sake of the memory of posterity, namely that Bishop Werfrith [Wærferth] and the community at Worcester give and grant by charter to Æthelred and Æthelflæd, their lords, the messuage within the town wall at Worcester which is 28 rods in length from the river itself along the north wall eastwards and thence southwards 24 rods in breadth and then westwards to the Severn 19 rods in length. And likewise they grant them the meadow-land west of the Severn, on a level with the messuage, [extending] west along the bishop's dyke from the river, until it comes out at the moor-dyke, and then north until it comes out on a level with the water-course, and then eastwards until it comes back below the water-course to the Severn. They likewise grant them Barbourne, and in addition 60 acres of arable land south of Barbourne and another 60 acres to the north, and likewise, very generously, 12 acres of very good meadow-land in addition; and they graciously grant them this, towards the community and towards the church, and desire to earn it from them always, day and night, by their divine services, as best they can. And Æthelred and Æthelflæd shall hold it for all time, both within the town wall and without, uncontested by anyone as long as they live. And if Ælfwyn survives them, it shall similarly remain uncontested as long as she lives; and after the death of the three of them, it shall be given back without dispute to the lord of the church for the souls of the three of them,

endowed as it is then, if it be God's will that they may endow it. To those who increase and uphold this shall be added the reward of eternal bliss in heaven. Those who diminish and break it shall be confounded by eternal punishment, unless they have made due amends. All the community, both young and old, have confirmed this agreement with the symbol of the cross of Christ, and twelve of their names are recorded hereafter in writing, and likewise the names of the friends whom we selected as witnesses... + The agreement of Æthelred and Æthelflæd with Bishop Werfrith and the community at Worcester.[40]

This charter names Æthelred, Æthelflæd and their daughter, and this *haga* in Worcester has been reconstructed.[41] In this format of the charter, no titles are given for Æthelred, Æthelflæd or Ælfwynn.

S1446,[42] surviving in two manuscripts, with a known lost original, is dated 903, and sees a land dispute being settled between Bishop Wærferth over some land in Sodbury, Gloucestershire. As a resolution, Æthelred and Æthelflæd made it clear that they believed the land should be conceded to Eadnoth, then in another session, finding against Bishop Wærferth, which is interesting, since Bishop Wærferth was an ally of theirs.[43]

Charter S1282,[44] surviving in one manuscript, is dated 907 and deemed spurious as it includes Alfred's name, and he had died in 899.

There is then a space of some years where no charters have survived. When Æthelflæd's name appears once more, she is the sole promulgator of charters, her husband no doubt having already died. It is believed he died in 911. S224 and S225 date to 914 and 915.

S224, surviving in one manuscript, reads, 'Æthelflæd, Lady of the Mercians, to her faithful friend Alchelm, for sixty swine and 300 solidi, 2 manentes in Stantune.'[45]

S225, also surviving in one manuscript, names Æthelflæd as the ruler of Mercia. It reads: 'Æthelflæd, ruler of the Mercians to Eadric minister; grant of permission to acquire ten hides (manentes) at Farnborough, bought from Wulflaf. The original landbook, granted by King Offa to Bynna, Wulflaf's great-great-great-grandfather (*abavus*) had been destroyed in a fire.'[46]

It is interesting to consider how many of these landbooks were misplaced, lost, stolen, or burned by mistake. No doubt house fires were a frequent problem.

Throughout Æthelflæd's marriage, her husband and brother were often at war with the Viking raiders. Constant mention is made of the battles won and lost in the *Anglo-Saxon Chronicles*. The overriding impression is that it was a time of war. Indeed, Stafford has noted that the *Anglo-Saxon Chronicles* for these years are really a record of military endeavours and very little else.[47]

As with her mother, it is after the death of her husband that Lady Æthelflæd thrived, although the exact date of Æthelred's death must be assumed, as it is not noted in the sources. From 911 until her death in June 918, Æthelflæd was the Lady of the Mercians and was named as such in the *Anglo-Saxon Chronicle*.

She is mentioned by name, or by her title, in ten different occurrences in the *Anglo-Saxon Chronicle*. These all occur after the death of her husband, although some of them are clearly copies of other entries.

In 909, the D text states, 'And the same year Æthelflæd built *Bremesburgh*.'[48] The C text records this as occurring in 910 'And the same year Æthelflæd built the stronghold at *Bremesbyrig*.'[49]

In 912, the C text records, 'Here, on the eve of the Invention of the Holy Cross, Æthelflæd, Lady of the Mercians came to *Scergeat* and built a stronghold there, and the same year, that at Bridgnorth.'[50]

In 913, the C text further records, 'Here, God helping, Æthelflæd, Lady of the Mercians, went with all the Mercians to Tamworth, and then built the stronghold there early in the summer, and afterwards before Lammas that at Stafford.'[51]

In 913, the D text states, 'Here Æthelflæd built Tamworth and also Stafford stronghold.'[52]

In 916, the C text records, 'Æthelflæd sent an army into Wales and broke down Brecon More and there took the wife of the king as one of thirty-four.'[53]

In 917, the C text writes, 'Here, before Lammas, God helping, Æthelflæd, Lady of the Mercians took possession of the stronghold which is called Derby, together with all that belonged to it.'[54]

Æthelflæd's death, like that of her mother, is recorded in the A and C editions of the *Anglo-Saxon Chronicle* and also in the E version of the *Anglo-Saxon Chronicle*, even if only in passing. 'Here Æthelflæd, Lady of the Mercians, passed away.'[55]

A text states: 'and then when he [Edward] was settled in the seat there, his sister Æthelflæd at Tamworth, died 12 days before midsummer

... and all the nation of the land of Mercia which was earlier subject to Æthelflæd turned to him.'

The C text of 918 offers:

> Here in the early part of this year, with God's help, she [Æthelflæd] peaceably got in her control the stronghold at Leicester and the most part of the raiding-armies that belonged to it were subjected. And also the York-folk had promised her – and some of them granted so by pledge, some confirmed with oaths – that they would be at her disposition. But very quickly after they had done that, she departed, twelve days before midsummer, inside Tamworth, the eighth year that she held control of Mercia, with rightful lordship; and her body lies inside Gloucester in the east side-chapel of St Peter's Church.[56]

Æthelweard's *Chronicon* mirrors this information in saying that 'her body was buried in the fortress of Gloucester.'[57]

It is fairly evenly split in the *Anglo-Saxon Chronicle* between those entries which call her Æthelflæd only (six), and those that name her as both Æthelflæd and assign her the title of Lady of the Mercians (four) – whereas only one merely refers to her as 'she'. (One of the entries names her as Æthelflæd twice.) None of these references speaks of her as someone's wife or daughter, although, there is a reference to her being the king's sister in the A text. Unlike her mother, Æthelflæd is regarded as ruling in her own right and, as such, is given her title. This is, perhaps, a result of the Mercian Register, or *Æthelflæd Chronicles*,[58] said to have been used to compile this section of the *Anglo-Saxon Chronicle* and found in the C and D text versions of the chronicles. Still, the one entry which could be independent of the Mercian Register, the E text, does name her as both Æthelflæd and Lady of the Mercians.

William of Malmesbury, the later, Anglo-Norman writer, offers the following about Æthelflæd:

> London, the capital of the kingdom of the Mercians, he [Alfred] gave to a leading noble called Æthelred in fealty to himself, together with his daughter, Æthelflæd.[59]
>
> At the same time we must not overlook the king's [Edward] sister, Æthelflæd, Æthelred's widow, who carried

no small weight in party-strife, being popular with the citizens and a terror to the enemy. She was a woman of great determination who, after having difficulties with the birth of her first, or rather her only, child, abhorred her husband's embraces ever after, declaring, that it was beneath the dignity of a king's daughter to involve herself in pleasures which would be followed in time by such ill effects. She was a virago, a very powerful influence and help in her brother's policy, and no less effective as a builder of cities; it would be hard to say whether it was luck or character that made a woman such a tower of strength for the men of her own side and such a terror to the rest. She died five years before her brother, and was buried in the monastery of St Peter of Gloucester, which she herself and her husband Æthelred had built with such exertions, translating to it the bones of St Oswald from Bardney.[60]

John of Worcester adds the following details:

> Æthelflæd, Lady of the Mercians, built two towns, namely Chirbury and Weardyrig, after Christmas, and a third, Runcorn, before Christmas.[61]

Further:

> While these things were taking place his sister Æthelflæd, Lady of the Mercians, distinguished by her prudence and justice, a woman of outstanding virtue, in the eight years after that in which she began to rule on her own the kingdom of the Mercians with vigorous and just government, died on the nineteenth day before the calends of July, leaving Ælfwynn, her only daughter by Æthelred, the under-king, as heiress to her kingdom.[62]

It seems highly probable that Æthelflæd's death, when it came, was unexpected, occurring in the middle of an advance into the Danelaw and the Five Boroughs (Derby, Nottingham, Lincoln, Stamford and Leicester). The knowledge that she only had one child that lived to adulthood should be considered. While attempts were made to reconcile this in later sources, it is possible that there was either an impediment to her having more children or that she suffered stillbirths, and these details have not survived. Alternatively, as William of Malmesbury comments, perhaps she did not like her husband. In this scenario, the suggestion that Alfred intended for Athelstan, Æthelflæd's nephew, to become king of Mercia should perhaps be considered.

Ælfwynn, second Lady of the Mercians

Ælfwynn, daughter of Æthelred of Mercia and Lady Æthelflæd
b.*c.*880/890–918/*c.*960 (unknown)

Ælfwynn,[63] the daughter of Æthelflæd of Mercia and her husband, Æthelred, was born at some point in the late 880s or early 890s. It is believed that she was an only child, although it does appear (in the later accounts of William of Malmesbury) that her cousins, Athelstan, and Edith/his unnamed sister were sent to Mercia to be raised by their aunt when Edward remarried on becoming king in 899. There is a suggestion that it might have been Alfred's decision to do this and that Athelstan was being groomed to become king of Mercia. As such, Ælfwynn might have had close links to her Wessex cousins.

Ælfwynn is mentioned in three charters. S367, surviving in one manuscript, dates to 903, where she witnesses without a title, and is a request by Ealdorman Æthelfrith that a grant by Æthelwulf to his daughter Æthelgyth be renewed concerning land at Monks Risborough, Buckinghamshire, the original having been burned.[64] S1280, surviving in two manuscripts, dated to 904 reads in translation:

> Wærferth, bishop, and the community at Worcester, to Æthelred and Æthelflæd, their lords; lease, for their lives and that of Ælfwynn, their daughter, of a messuage (haga) in Worcester and land at Barbourne in North Claines, Worcs., with reversion to the bishop. Bounds of appurtentant meadow west of the [River] Severn.[65]

This haga has been reconstructed in Worcester.[66]

In S225, surviving in one manuscript, dated to 915, Ælfwynn witnesses below her mother. Hers is the second name on the document.[67]

This could be significant, as she would certainly have been an adult by now. As her father was now dead, having passed away in *c*.911, was she already prepared as the heir to Mercia on her mother's death? Athelstan does not witness these charters, although he does witness S371 dated to 903. However, this might not be significant as Ælfweard, his half-brother also witnesses S371.[68]

Ælfwynn is named in the *Anglo-Saxon Chronicle* in the C text under 919. 'Here also the daughter of Æthelred lord of the Mercians, was deprived of all control in Mercia, and was led into Wessex three weeks before Christmas; she was called Ælfwynn.'[69]

And from there, we hear nothing more of Lady Ælfwynn, the second Lady of the Mercians. Even though this is the first record of a ruling woman being succeeded by her daughter.

There is no further mention of Ælfwynn in the *Anglo-Saxon Chronicle*. It has been assumed that she became a nun, and she might well be referenced in charter S535, surviving in one manuscript, and which Eadred granted at the request of his mother, dated to 948, which reads, 'King Eadred to Ælfwyn, a religious woman; grant of 6 hides (mansae), equated with 6 sulungs, at Wickhambreux, Kent, in return for 2 pounds of purest gold.'[70] Bailey has suggested that, 'In view of its close association with the women of the royal family, and of Eadgifu's patronage of Ælfwynn (in S535), I would venture to suggest that it is possible she too may have ended her days at Wilton.'[71]

King Eadred would have been Ælfwynn's cousin if this is the same person. King Eadred gave behests such as this to a number of religious women during his reign, as did his brother, Edmund, but more of this later.

This would mean that rather than ruling as her mother would have wanted her to, reference the charters she witnessed, Ælfwynn was overridden by her uncle, who essentially stole her right to rule Mercia as soon as he possibly could on her mother's death. It must be said that he might have later paid for this with his life if he was indeed putting down a Mercian rebellion in Farndon when he died.

Alternatively, there is another beguiling theory that Ælfwynn might not have become a nun but was, in fact, married to Athelstan, an ealdorman of East Anglia, known as the 'Half-King', because of the vast control he had in East Anglia.[72] It has long been believed that this label might well have resulted from the fact that Athelstan was an extremely powerful and well-landed nobleman who was much beloved by the Wessex royal family and its kings. However, it might well be because he was indeed married to the king's cousin (under Athelstan, Edmund and Eadred). If this is the case, and it is impossible to prove, then Ælfwynn, as the wife of Ealdorman Athelstan, had four sons, Æthelwold, Æthelwine, Æthelsige and Ælfwold, and these sons would be friends and enemies of the kings of England in later years. She might also have been given the fostering of the orphaned, and future King Edgar, which would also have made these men the future king's foster brothers:[73]

> He [Athelstan Half-King] bestowed marriage upon a wife, one Ælfwynn by name, suitable for his marriage bed as much as by the nobility of her birth as by the grace of her unchurlish appearance. Afterwards she nursed and brought up with maternal devotion the glorious King Edgar, a tender boy as yet in the cradle. When Edgar afterwards attained the rule of all England, which was due to him by hereditary destiny, he was not ungrateful for the benefits he had received from his nurse. He bestowed on her, with regal munificence, the manor of Weston, which her son, the Ealdorman, afterwards granted to the church of Ramsey in perpetual alms for her soul, when his mother was taken from our midst in the natural course of events.[74]

If this identification is correct, 'This would explain why she was considered suitable to be a foster mother to the ætheling Edgar. It may even explain why Edgar was considered in 957 suitable to rule Mercia.'[75]

If Lady Ælfwynn did survive beyond the events of 919, it seems highly likely she would have continued her friendship with her cousin, Athelstan, when he became king of Mercia, and then Wessex and then England. It is also highly likely that she might have rallied support for him in Mercia.

It is also possible that she could have been forced to become a nun by her uncle but that her cousin had warmer feelings toward her. Equally, she may have simply slipped into obscurity or, perhaps, not only moved into a nunnery but subsumed herself in the quest for knowledge as did her mother's sister, the Abbess of Shrewsbury, Æthelgifu, and her cousins, the daughters of King Edward the Elder and his second wife, Lady Ælfflæd. Certainly, the first known occurrence of a woman succeeding a woman in Saxon England ended in obscurity for Lady Ælfwynn.

Edith/Eadgyth/Ecgwynn/unnamed daughter

Edith/Eadgyth/Ecgwynn/unnamed daughter of Edward the Elder, and his unnamed first wife (Ecgwynn?) *c.*890s–937?

m. Sihtric, king of York in 925, repudiated by 927 when Sihtric died

Edith[76] is believed to be the biological sister of Athelstan, and, therefore, the daughter of King Edward and his first wife, possibly named Ecgwynn. Edith is unnamed in the *Anglo-Saxon Chronicle*, but her marriage is mentioned in both the D and the C texts.

The C text records that in 924, 'Athelstan was chosen as king by the Mercians, and consecrated at Kingston, and he gave his sister.'[77] And here the text, rather enigmatically, comes to a halt until 954.

The D text, is rather more helpful, under 925 stating that, 'Here Athelstan and Sihtric, king of Northumbria, assembled at Tamworth on 30th January, and Athelstan gave him his sister.'[78]

This, therefore, refers to the union between Athelstan's sister and Sihtric, a Norse king of Jorvik or York, a grandson of the mighty Viking raider, Ivarr, who was so instrumental in the wars of the 860s, when 'The Great Heathen army' descended on Saxon England. The union is intriguing. It does seem to be the only occasion that a marriage union was enacted between the Viking raiders and the Wessex royal family. This could potentially be because the union was a failure, either Sihtric died (which he did in *c.*927), or he repudiated his bride before his death and sent her back to Mercia. (I do not think it worth highlighting the union of King Cnut and Queen Emma here as, essentially, Queen Emma's position was as the consort of a member of the Wessex royal family. She was not a birth member of the dynasty.)

There is the suggestion that Edith may have become a nun on her return to Mercia. She is associated with the nunnery at Polesworth by traditions recorded at Bury in the twelfth century. Following the death of her husband, she is said to have returned to Mercia and 'founded a nunnery at Polesworth, near the Mercian royal centre at Tamworth. There she remained a virgin, practising fastings and vigils, offering prayers and alms to the end of her life, and dying on July 15.'[79]

However, Thacker goes on to state that, 'it must be admitted that it [the cult] was not a very successful one. Her feast day (15 July) occurs in only three relatively late (i.e. post-Conquest) calendars, and it is impossible to identify her in any of the surviving Anglo-Saxon litanies.'[80]

What might have happened had the marriage to Sihtric been a success is fascinating to consider. While York was claimed by King Athelstan in 927 as a direct result of the failure of the marriage and the death of Sihtric, had sons been born to the union, had Sihtric lived, and had Athelstan been unable to claim York at this time, it is possible that many of the problems faced by the House of Wessex, throughout the later 920s to the 950s, could have been avoided. Edith/Ecgwynn is not the first royal woman of the tenth century about whom we know so very, very little.

Chapter 4

The Wives of Edward the Elder

Ecgwynn, first wife of King Edward the Elder

Ecgwynn m. King Edward the Elder (*c.*874–17 July 924), son of King Alfred and his wife, Lady Ealhswith.

Athelstan *c.*892–939

Unknown daughter/Edith/Eadgyth/Ecgwynn *c.*890s–937?

Almost nothing is known of the woman who was King Edward the Elder's first wife. Her name is believed to have been Ecgwynn.[1] But all that can be said with any certainty is that she did exist, as her son, Athelstan, later king of the English, most certainly existed and was not claimed by either of King Edward's second and third wives as belonging to them. Athelstan was invested by King Alfred during his lifetime, and this, more than anything, proves that the marriage was deemed as legitimate and that Alfred believed Athelstan would one day rule in his stead.[2]

It is believed that Ecgwynn's family may have had roots in the west of the country. The pair had married by *c.*893. A later reference in the *Vita S Dunstani* suggests the possibility that she may have been related to Archbishop Dunstan's family.[3] William of Malmesbury describes her as an *illustris femina*, 'noble lady'.[4] Alternatively, she may have been a Mercian by birth.

There has been much speculation about her identity and why she is so obscure. The explanation most often offered is that she either died during childbirth or that she was unacceptable as a wife when Edward's father died and he became king of Wessex. This might be because the union was not an official one in the eyes of the church but rather a union through concubinage. To explore this further, the classic view was summarised neatly by Archbishop Theodore at the Synod of Hertford, 673, reported by Bede, 'That lawful wedlock alone is permissible; that incest is forbidden; and no man may leave his wife except, as the gospel

34

provides, for fornication.' The use of the expression 'lawful wedlock' here, implies that other, less acceptable forms then existed. It is clear that concubinage and bigamy continued throughout the period. Successive ninth-century popes castigated English matrimonial behaviour at all levels ... These dicta, with an additional stress on monogamy – 'one wife, one life' – were to prove points of increasing conflict between church reformers and the secular community as the tenth century progressed.[5]

Alternatively, it was perhaps deemed politically expedient for Edward to ally himself with a more powerful noble family, and his second wife, Lady Ælfflæd was certainly better connected than the obscure Lady Ecgwynn, as is apparent because Ælfflæd's name is known, as – we believe – is that of her father, Ealdorman Æthelhelm.

Yorke has made a valid argument that the slurs regarding Ecgwynn and her marital status:

> should be seen in the context of the disputes between the sons of Edward the Elder following his death in 924, rather than something which was an issue in the 890s.[6]
> Alfred's investiture of Ecgwynn's son Athelstan implies that he regarded the marriage as completely legitimate, and that it had produced a future king.[7]

Alternatively, the suggestion has been made that Alfred's acceptance of Athelstan as a future king was intended to be for Mercia, not Wessex, and this could perhaps connect with her being a Mercian by birth.

Equally, the new king might have needed the powerful support of Lady Ælfflæd's father, and, as we do not know who Ecgwynn's father was, that family may have lacked the political clout required for a man who was now hoping to be king. Edward's succession was not uncontested. His cousin, Æthelwold, the son of his father's older brother, who ruled as Æthelred I (865–871), believed he had as much right to the kingdom as Edward did. It seems possible that an agreement was even forged between the two brothers, Alfred and Æthelred, to ensure Æthelred's sons would have a landed base necessary to claim the kingship, but that Alfred constantly reneged on his promises. The issue was not successfully resolved until the death of Æthelwold in 902/3. Many years later, the matter of this family would still be causing problems for the dominant Wessex ruling family, most notably when Eadwig (955–959) seems to have married into it.

In the charters that have survived, and they are few and far between for Athelstan, he does not refer to his birth mother. It is possible he had no recollection of her if she died while he was still young.

The truth about whether or not Athelstan, and his sister, were sent to the Mercian court once Edward remarried cannot be ascertained. Certainly, Dumville, is at pains to emphasise that this idea stems from the later writings of William of Malmesbury and that no contemporary reference exists. 'It does not authorise us to accept William of Malmesbury's unconfirmed statement, repeated as a fact in almost every modern account, that Athelstan was fostered at the Mercian court of Æthelred and Æthelflæd.'[8]

Athelstan's mother is one of the most obscure of these royal women of the tenth century. The fact she was the mother of one of the most successful kings of the period should not mean she is overlooked.

Lady Ælfflæd, second wife of King Edward the Elder

Ælfflæd, (*c.*875–*c.*922) daughter of Ealdorman Æthelhelm of Wiltshire (who died in 897)

m. King Edward the Elder (*c.*874–17 July 924). She 'retired' to Wilton Nunnery when Edward remarried in 917/8/9

> Ælfweard (*c.*901–d.924)
> Edwin d.933
> Æthelhild
> Eadgifu *c.*900–d.951
> Eadflæd
> Eadhild d.937
> Eadgyth
> Ælfgifu

Edward may have remarried before he became king (899) or when he was king. The date of the union is unknown. His second wife was the daughter of an ealdorman, and it is believed that this ealdorman was Æthelhelm of Wiltshire.[9] The ealdorman's death is recorded in the *Anglo-Saxon Chronicle* under 897,[10] but whether the marriage took place before or after his death is unknown, as are the reasons for the second marriage. It has been argued that once Edward became king, he needed a new wife so that he could father an heir, an ætheling, who would be deemed worthy because he was the child of an actual ruling king. Alternatively, his first wife may have died, perhaps in childbirth.

It has been suggested that Ælfflæd[11] was the niece of Æthelwold, Edward's cousin, and granddaughter of Æthelred I (865–871), Alfred's older brother, and this union might have been decided upon to prevent Æthelwold from claiming the kingship as his own.[12] Perhaps it was intended as a means to unify the family, even though the marriage would have caused problems as it was within the prohibited degrees sanctioned by the church.

When Edward became king, Æthelwold, the son of Alfred's older brother, Æthelred I, had a better claim to the kingship than Edward, being the son of the older brother. Until Æthelwold's death in 902/3, some may have thought to proclaim him as the king of the Anglo-Saxons. As such, Edward may well have needed to make a stronger marriage union, with a family directly linked to the heartlands of Wessex, as it appears the family of Ælfflæd's was. If it was the intention, it failed. This perhaps suggests that the union was not between the two branches of the same family. Another argument that seems to prove this was that royal sons were not made ealdormen, and Ælfflæd's father is named as an ealdorman.

This union between Edward and Ælfflæd produced at least two sons and six daughters. There is some confusion regarding the daughters born to Edward's second and third wives, which might be due to a problem with the transmission of the information. Those children that can be named as being Ælfflæd's children are: Ælfweard (reigned 924 only), king for a few days after his father's death and before his own; Edwin, who died in 933; Eadgifu, Eadhild, Eadgyth, Æthelhild, Eadflæd and possibly an Ælfgifu. Foot has stated that 'William of Malmesbury counted one daughter of Edward the Elder too many',[13] to account for the problems with an additional daughter, who may, or may not have existed. Edward would go on to have two sons and possibly two daughters with his third wife, Eadgifu, although it is normally accepted that Eadgifu was the mother of two sons and one daughter.

As to Ælfflæd herself, she is mentioned in one of the surviving charters from Edward's rule that of S363,[14] surviving in four manuscripts, dated to 901, in which she is described as *conjux regis*, 'wife of the king', and is named as is the king's mother, Lady Ealhswith. Edward attests first, and then his mother, and then his wife. This priority to Ealhswith, as 'mother of the king', as opposed to the king's wife, would also be mirrored by Edward's descendants later in the century. It is unknown if Ælfflæd was consecrated as queen. Edward's coronation took place on 8 June 900, but Ælfflæd never attests a charter as queen.[15] Edward 'was crowned with the royal crown on Whitsunday, having been elected by the chief men, (900) when the hundredth one of the years was passing, from when his great-grandfather Ecgbyrht [Ecgberht] enjoyed royal authority in his own person'.[16] As only one charter survives with her attestation, this may not prove that she was never consecrated queen.

However, her sons, and it is unknown when they were born, began to attest charters from 901 (S365, surviving in two manuscripts, and S366, surviving in only one manuscript). Ælfweard, the firstborn son, attests as *filius regis* where he is named above Athelstan, his older half-brother, but behind his uncle, Æthelweard, Edward's younger brother. Æthelweard and Athelstan are also termed as *filius regis* in both charters, which would be correct as they were both the children of a king, Æthelweard being the son of Alfred, Athelstan, the son of Edward. Athelstan does attest to more of his father's charters (eleven)[17] than Ælfweard does (eight),[18] but again, the number is still small and so may not be representative. Added to which, many of these surviving charters are deemed to be either suspicious or spurious. In fact, only three of the eleven charters that Athelstan witnesses under his father are deemed to be authentic,[19] and only one of those witnessed by Ælfweard,[20] which is dated to 901. This would have been very early in Edward's reign, when his cousin, Æthelwold, was still alive and contesting the rulership of Wessex.

Lady Ælfflæd is not mentioned in the *Anglo-Saxon Chronicle*. This is perhaps not surprising, as at this time the *Anglo-Saxon Chronicle* is almost a record of military endeavours, with little mention of anyone other than Edward, and in the *Æthelflæd Chronicles*, of Æthelflæd.

For all her success in producing children for the king, Edward placed his second wife in the nunnery at Wilton so that he could marry for the third time in *c.*919.[21] This third union was a political one so that Edward could be assured of support from the south-east while he was away in Mercia, fighting or stealing his niece's right to rule as the second Lady of the Mercians.[22]

There is one further written mention of Ælfflæd, embroidered on a stole (a strip of silk worn round the neck of a priest, and hanging to the knees) and maniple (a strip worn over the left arm) from St Cuthbert's Tomb opened in 1827, which read *Ælfflæd fieri precepit*, 'Ælfflæd had this made', *pio episcopo friedestano*, 'for the pious bishop Frithestan'.[23] Frithestan was bishop of Winchester from 909 to 931, but he may never have taken possession of the items, due to a falling out with the Wessex ruling family.[24] As such, these items were not intended for Cuthbert's tomb but may have made their way there, no doubt, gifted by King Athelstan on his pilgrimage during his journey to the lands of the Scots in the early summer of 934, as we are told by the *Historia de sancto Cuthberto*:

> Therefore, while King Athelstan was leading a great army from the south to the northern region of Britain, taking it to Scotland, he made a diversion to the church of St Cuthbert and gave royal gifts to him, and then composed [a] signed testament and placed it at Cuthbert's head.[25]

If Ælfflæd made these, the survival of these items is a unique physical link to the royal women of the tenth century.

Ælfflæd's daughters made a variety of marriages or chose to live their lives in a nunnery, either taking vows or as a lay sister. Ælfflæd may have joined some of these daughters at Wilton if she did not die before being set aside by her husband. It is believed that she was buried at Wilton. Mention of her sons is relevant here. Ælfweard was the oldest of her sons. He attests charters from either 899 or 901 (it is not possible to date two of these charters any more closely than during Edward's reign, and the vast majority of the available charters are deemed spurious in some way). Only one charter attested by Ælfweard, S365, surviving in two manuscripts, dated to 901 is deemed to be 'substantially authentic'.[26] In this, he attests alongside Athelstan, his older half-brother.

Ælfflæd's oldest son, Ælfweard, was declared king on the death of his father in Wessex. He was not to enjoy the kingship for long. The *Anglo-Saxon Chronicle* D states he died sixteen days after his father in 924.[27] Ælfflæd's other son, Edwin, has his death recorded in 933 in the *Anglo-Saxon Chronicle*, E text, 'Here the ætheling Edwin drowned at sea.'[28] Edwin's fate is one of almost ignominy. Certainly, there's no mention that Edwin appeared alongside Athelstan at the treaty of Eamont in 927, and his death in 933 means he could not have taken part in either the journey to Scotland or in the Battle of Brunanburh.

It is to be assumed, as we have no other information, that Ælfflæd died before her sons. If she did not, we do not know if she had any part to play in the dynastic difficulties of 924, following the death of Edward, and whether she tried to have Edwin replace his dead older brother as king of Wessex. We do not know what killed Edward or Ælfweard. The *Anglo-Saxon Chronicle* C records the deaths as follows: 'Here King Edward died at Farndon in Mercia, and very soon after that his son Ælfweard died at Oxford; and their bodies lie at Winchester.'[29]

The fate of Ælfflæd's daughters will be examined in detail below.

William of Malmesbury, in his *Gesta Regum Anglorum*, provides much detail about Ælfflæd and her family and children:

Edward's second son was [Ælfweard] by Ælfflæd daughter of Ealdorman Æthelhelm ... By the same wife he had Edwin ... He also had by the same wife six daughters; Eadflæd, Eadgifu, Æthelhild, Eadhild, Eadgyth, Ælfgifu. The first and third took a vow of virginity and spurned the pleasures of earthly marriage, Eadflæd took the veil and Æthelhild in lay attire; both lie at Wilton, buried next to their mother. Eadgifu was given in marriage by her father to King Charles, as I have said, Eadhild by her brother Æthelstan [Athelstan] to Hugh; Eadgyth and Ælfgifu were sent by the same brother to Henry emperor of Germany, who married the second of them to his son Otto and the other to a certain duke near the Alps. He also had by a third wife called Eadgifu two sons Edmund and Eadred, who both reigned after Æthelstan and two daughters Eadburh and Eadgifu. Eadburh became a nun and lies at Winchester; Eadgifu was a famous beauty, and was given in marriage by her brother Æthelstan to Louis prince of Aquitaine.[30]

The king, having many daughters, gave Eadgifu in marriage to Charles king of the Franks, who was son of Charles the Bald; whose daughter, as I have said more than once, King Æthelwulf had married on his way back from Rome ... His first-born son was Æthelstan [Athelstan], born of a noble lady called Ecgwynn, together with a daughter whose name I do not find accessible in written records; she was given in marriage by that same brother to Sihtric king of the Northumbrians.

Hugh married one of Edward's daughters.[31]

> With Sihtric, king of the Northumbrians, he [Athelstan] made a lasting peace, giving him one of his sisters in marriage.[32]

And a little later advising that Sihtric was:

> Rewarded with the hand of Æthelstan's sister.[33]
> Henry I, Conrad's son (for there were many men of that name), king of the Teutons and emperor of the Romans, asked for the hand of the king's sister for his son Otto.[34]

Ælfflæd replaced a wife, and was, in her turn, replaced by another wife of Edward the Elder. The nature of these interactions would be intriguing to know more about. It is tempting to imagine that Ælfflæd went from believing herself invincible to being coldly discarded. Sadly, this will never be known. Alternatively, having carried to term so many children, she may have been exhausted and welcomed the opportunity to retire to a nunnery. It is impossible to know with any surety, but the very real emotions she must have endured, whatever happened, should be considered.

Eadgifu, third wife of King Edward the Elder

Eadgifu, (*c.*902–964/6) daughter of Ealdorman Sigehelm of Kent, who died at the Battle of the Holme in 902/3

m. Edward the Elder (his third wife, her only husband)

    Eadburh *c.*919–952
    Edmund *c.*921–946
        m.1. Ælfgifu of Shaftesbury
            Eadwig *c.*940–959
            Edgar *c.*942–975
        m.2. Æthelflæd of Damerham
    Eadred *c.*923–955

Eadgifu[35] lived a long life, unlike many of the kings of Wessex and then England that she would have known throughout her life. It is said that Eadgifu was the daughter of yet another ealdorman, Sigehelm of Kent,[36]

41

who must have died either not long after her birth or even just before it at the devastating Battle of the Holme in 902/3, when Edward fought for his kingship against a coalition of his disgruntled cousin, Æthelwold, and the Danes. The *Anglo-Saxon Chronicle* A for 905, corrected to 903, reads:

> Here Æthelwold enticed the raiding-army in East Anglia into hostility, so that they raided across the land of Mercia until they came to Cricklade and there went over the Thames, and took all that they could grab, both in Braydon and round about there, and then turned back homewards. Then King Edward went after them as quickly as he could gather his army, and raided across all their territory between the Dykes and the Wissey, all as far north as the Fens. Then when he wanted to go back out from there, he ordered it to be announced through all the army that they all go out together; then the Kentish remained behind there against his command, and he had sent out seven messengers to them. Then they were surrounded there by the raiding-army, and they fought there. And there were killed Ealdorman Sigewulf, and Ealdorman Sigehelm, and Eadwold the king's thegn, and Abbot Cenwulf and Sigeberht, son of Sigewulf, and Eadwold, son of Acca, and many others in addition to them though I have named the most distinguished. And on the Danish side were killed their king Eohric and the ætheling Æthelwold, who had incited him to that hostility, and Beorhtsige, son of the ætheling Beornoth, and Hold Ysopa and Hold Oscytel, and very many others in addition to them whom we cannot name now; and on either hand there was great slaughter made, and there were more of the Danish killed, although they had possession of the place of slaughter.[37]

This is a long entry in the *Anglo-Saxon Chronicle*, no doubt a testimony to the importance of this battle and the fact that Ealdorman Sigehelm died defending his kingdom from the enemy, which consisted not just of the Viking raiders but also a member of the Wessex royal family.

There is much about Eadgifu that is unknown. But what can be envisaged is this – throughout the middle years of the often-overlooked tenth century – Lady Eadgifu was a dominant force at the court of the

Wessex/English kings. She 'almost' embodies, as an individual, the years that are so rarely studied – those from the death of King Alfred in 899 to the beginning of the reign of the much-maligned King Æthelred II, her great-grandson.

Eadgifu was titled the king's mother in the surviving charter evidence.[38]

Despite the marriage union not taking place until *c*.917–919, and with Edward's death coming in 924, Eadgifu was the mother of two sons, and at least one daughter, possibly two (see previous discussion regarding Ælfflæd, Edward's second wife). Edmund, Eadred and one certain daughter, Eadburh, were born in perhaps the space of no more than five years. It would be easier if the dates of birth were known. It is written that Edmund was 18 at the time of his accession,[39] in 939. This means he would have been born around 920–921. Edmund does seem to have been the oldest son, as he was acclaimed as the king of England on the death of Athelstan in 939, with Eadred only becoming king after Edmund's murder in 946. However, it is possible that Eadburh was the oldest child.

What the relationship was like between the older king and his young wife is impossible to determine. Certainly, she did not attest to any charters while the king's wife, but equally, there is a dearth of surviving charters from the end of Edward's reign, so that does not necessarily mean that she did not. There is only one charter from *c*.921, that of S379, surviving in two manuscripts, but it is believed to be an authentic charter of 933, with the details changed to show Edward the Elder as the grantor of the charter, as opposed to Athelstan. It is unknown if Eadgifu was consecrated as queen of the Anglo-Saxons alongside her husband.

Equally, we do not know what happened to Eadgifu when her husband died, followed by her stepson, Ælfweard, in the same year (924), allowing Athelstan, another stepson, but a man who could have been older than her, to become king of Mercia and Wessex. It must be imagined that Edward the Elder's death was a surprise, but perhaps the accession of Ælfweard was not unexpected. Eadgifu's children would have been far too young to inherit after their father. Here, it would be good to have some of Edward's charters for the later years of his reign. It is unknown if he classed all his male children as 'æthelings' (throne-worthy), if he perhaps gave precedence to his older sons, but not Athelstan, away in Mercia (if William of Malmesbury is to be believed), or if, had he lived until Edmund was older, it would have been Edmund who would have become king after his father's death. A beguiling suggestion by Jayakumar is that Athelstan might have been marked to succeed by his grandfather Alfred in Mercia, not in Wessex.[40]

It has been suggested that Eadgifu became a lay associate at Shaftesbury Abbey after the death of her husband. If this is the case, it seems she did not remain there for long.[41]

Did Eadgifu have a good relationship with her stepson, Ælfweard, when he became king? Did she fear for her sons once her husband was dead? What was her relationship like with her stepdaughters, some of whom might have been older than her? Was she relieved by the death of Ælfweard and content to strike up a relationship with Athelstan? What did she think of Edwin, Ælfweard's single surviving full-brother, and his chances of claiming the kingdom of Wessex after the deaths of Edward the Elder, and Ælfweard? Did she, perhaps, play a part in Athelstan, already proclaimed as king of Mercia, becoming acceptable to the Wessex Witan? Certainly, there was over a year's gap between the death of Ælfweard and Athelstan's coronation at Kingston upon Thames in September 925.[42] This might not have been unusual. Possibly Athelstan was forced to subdue the rebellious Mercians who had forced Edward to journey to Farndon in the first place.

As the stepmother of Athelstan, it is possible that Eadgifu attained some greater influence as the mother of the king's successor when Athelstan decided not to marry (although some believe she was absent from court during this period because she did not witness any of Athelstan's charters), 'nor is it surprising that Eadgifu, as the consort of the previous king, served little role in her stepson's court.'[43] Perhaps because Athelstan:

> the new king wanted to avoid Eadgifu and her sons becoming the locus for an opposing faction. To counter this, he may have encouraged his stepmother to withdrawn from public life ... The sum of this evidence suggests an arrangement between the king and the queen-dowager whereby, in return for Eadgifu's absence from, and support for, his court, Æthelstan [Athelstan] would ensure the throne passed to her sons.[44]

Athelstan decided that his half-brother, the oldest son of Eadgifu, should become king after his death. Indeed, it appears as though the relationship between them all was somewhat close, with Eadgifu being given responsibility for raising her children, the king's heirs, at the royal court. Yorke has commented that, 'the enhanced position [of Lady Eadgifu] may also have been developed specifically for the widowed Eadgifu as part of an alliance with her stepson Æthelstan [Athelstan] in which she supported his position and he recognised her sons as his heirs.'[45]

Edmund began to attest Athelstan's charters from at least 931 (S414, surviving in one manuscript) as the king's brother (it is impossible to specifically date some of the charters that Edmund attests). Eadred also attests to this charter. So, it is possible that from at least 931, Edmund and Eadred, and by association, their mother, were members of Athelstan's court, potentially as a means of securing Athelstan's control of Wessex when he was away on his numerous expeditions to the north. In 934, Athelstan is known to have travelled to Scotland via Chester-le-Street.[46] In 937, he was at the Battle of Brunanburh, which is thought to have taken place in the north of England.[47]

Eadgifu's position, and that of her sons, during Athelstan's reign, is difficult to determine. If the poem, *Brunanburh*, found in the A version of the *Anglo-Saxon Chronicle* for the year 937, is deemed to be contemporary, it reads as follows:

> Here King Athelstan, leader of warriors,
> ring-giver of men, and also his brother,
> the ætheling Edmund, struck life-long glory
> in strife round Brunanburh, clove the shield-wall,
> hacked the war-lime, with hammers' leavings,
> Edward's offspring, as was natural to them
> By ancestry, that in frequent conflict
> They defend land, treasures and homes,
> Against every foe.[48]

This would present Athelstan, and his oldest half-brother with his father's third wife, standing shoulder to shoulder in the shield-wall, defeating the combined forces of the Dublin Norse, the Scots under Constantine, the men of Strathclyde, as well as a whole host of others in the alliance against the advances Athelstan had made in extending the territory of the English kingdom during his reign.

However, it is believed that this poem, one of only four entries in the *Anglo-Saxon Chronicle* which occurs in verse,[49] is a later, retrospective, addition.[50] That is not to say that Edmund and Athelstan did not fight together at Brunanburh, but perhaps it was not in the spirit of brotherly love. Or perhaps it was?

Athelstan's death would have once more thrown the ruling family into disarray. Edmund, having fought at Brunanburh with his brother, was suddenly king at the age of 18. And what a kingdom he could claim. England had been truly born, but England also had, thanks to the Battle of Brunanburh, made some powerful enemies. I find it important to highlight that while the House of Wessex had suffered a number of fatalities amongst its young men (Edward the Elder was to be the most long-lived of their rulers, (*c.*874–924) until Æthelred II, (*c.*966–1016; r.978–1013 and 1014–1016) the kingdom of the Scots, under Constantine was to enjoy the rule of a single monarch for over forty years (900–943), and indeed, Constantine's rule might have ended in 943, but he lived until 952.

It is only on the accession of her son, Edmund, in 939 that Eadgifu's name is found on the surviving charters. Again, this could be due to the survival rate of Athelstan's charters, but many more do survive from his reign (sixty-six)[51] than his father's (twenty-eight),[52] so this might not be a relevant argument.

From 940, Eadgifu often attests to her oldest son's charters. There are fifty-six surviving charters issued in Edmund's name.[53] Eadgifu attests twenty of these as the 'king's mother'. Of these twenty, two of them are taken to be spurious by academic scholars of the period,[54] and so I accept that there are eighteen genuine charters attested by Eadgifu during Edmund's reign, including a charter which was issued to Edmund's 'mother'.[55] As such, her name appears in eighteen of the king's charters, dated from 940 to 945, although one is dated 942/6, which means it may have been issued later than 945.[56] For eleven of these charters, she attests second only to the king.[57] For a further five, she attests after the king and then Eadred, her second-born son.[58] And for one of the surviving charters, she attests after the archbishops and then Eadred, so she is fifth on the list of attestations.[59]

It would be tempting to state that early in Eadgifu's son's reign, she attests second, but as Edmund's rule stabilises, there is an acknowledgement that should anything befall Edmund, it is to Eadred, and not Edmund's young sons, that the kingship would pass, but unfortunately, it is not quite so clear cut. The charters in which she attests after Eadred are dated 944 and 945, but S493 is dated to 944 as well, and in this, she attests second, only after Edmund. Equally, the dating of the charters is not always reliable, and while some are dated, for some, the date has to be interpreted based on the witness lists. For instance, if someone attests the charter and it is known they were dead by that date, then the date of the charter must be before their death.

Following the death of Edmund, who was murdered, according to the *Anglo-Saxon Chronicle*,[60] Eadgifu once more regularly attested to the charters issued in her second son's name. There are sixty-three surviving charters from Eadred's reign (946–953). Not all of these are deemed authentic in the format they have survived. It is possible that some are forgeries. They are usually deemed spurious. Of these charters, over half of them (thirty-three) were witnessed by Eadgifu.[61] Of these thirty-three, four are deemed to be spurious.[62] Of the remaining twenty-nine, Eadgifu's name appears second only to her son on twenty-two of the charters.[63] She appears after the bishops but before her grandchildren, Eadwig and Edgar.[64] Eadwig and Edgar begin to attest from 953/5.[65]

Eadgifu is also the recipient of S562, dated to 953, where she is named and also designated as the king's mother.

It would seem that Eadgifu may have been more important during the reign of Eadred, than even during the reign of Edmund. This is worth considering in more detail. Eadred did not marry, like Athelstan, and unlike his older brother, Edmund. Was this a purposeful decision? As Athelstan before him, did Eadred intend his nephews to rule after him? If this were the case, then Eadgifu, as both mother of the king and grandmother of future kings, would have been a much-needed steadying force, especially after the unexpected murder of King Edmund in 946. Edmund would only have been about 25 years old. He could have been expected to live much longer. And while he had a brother to succeed him, despite Edward the Elder fathering five sons, only Eadred now remained.

It is unknown for what reason Edmund was murdered, but, certainly, the House of Wessex would have been shaken by the event. While no mention is made of the perpetrator being punished, it must be assumed that he was.

During the reign of her son, Eadred, Eadgifu asked her son to issue a grant to a royal woman, living in a nunnery. This is charter S535 and may be the one which mentions our 'lost' Ælfwynn, the second Lady of the Mercians.[66] Equally, this may have been another royal woman. Even amongst those that are known, there are many that remain unknown. Archbishop Dunstan claimed to be related to the royal family, but it is unsure how, although it has been suggested that this relationship was to Lady Ælfflæd, second wife of King Edward the Elder as opposed to the Wessex ruling family.

Eadgifu appears in the surviving will of her second son, Eadred. In this, it is written, 'Then I grant to my mother the land at Amesbury and Wantage and Basing and all the booklands which I have in Sussex and Surrey and Kent and all those which she held before.'[67]

Eadwig became king on the death of his uncle. It is unknown what caused Eadred's early death, at no more than 32, but there are some later accounts, which suggest he had some sort of problem with his stomach, perhaps not unlike his grandfather, Alfred.[68] Eadwig, in 955, can have been no older than 17, perhaps only 15. Eadwig was the youngest man to become king of England, at that time. Sadly, Eadwig's reign was marred by conflict between the ruling family of Wessex and also the ealdormanic families. This discord resulted in Mercia and Wessex being split. From 957, Edgar was labelled the king of Mercia, and granted charters using the title 'king of Mercia'.[69]

It is difficult to tell at such a distance just how 'split' England was under Eadwig and his brother. While the charter evidence clearly presents Edgar as king of the Mercians, and then the Northern Territories, it is possible that this was a way of acknowledging Edgar as Eadwig's heir and not a true split of the kingdom, especially as Eadwig is termed king of the English during the period, and Edgar appears to continue to attest Eadwig's charters. It is intriguing to consider what happened during those brief four years between 955–959, and just what part Eadgifu played in them. Certainly, she fell foul of Eadwig, as did Bishops Dunstan and Cynesige, her allies, and that is interesting in and of itself.

It was another of Eadgifu's acknowledged allies, Archbishop Oda, who divorced Eadwig and his wife, Ælfgifu, potentially against the wishes of both young people. Ælfgifu may have been the sister of the later Ealdorman Æthelweard, who wrote the *Chronicon* and in which he claims to be descended from Æthelred I, King Alfred's older brother 'King Æthelred, from whose root I spring'.[70] She might then have been a member of the family who tried to take the kingdom from Edward the Elder, the descendants of Æthelred I, Alfred's brother. If this was the case, then Eadgifu may have had a very personal reason for not wanting anything to do with Eadwig's wife – her father died at the Battle of the Holme, which would never have occurred if not for Æthelwold's attempts to claim the kingship from Edward the Elder.

If Ælfgifu and her mother were at the Wessex royal court during the first few years of Eadwig's rule, then it is possible that Eadgifu was deprived of her role as the main supporter of the Wessex royal family. Her position may have been taken by a woman she entirely despised. 'It is no coincidence that Eadgifu's discomfiture and Dunstan's flight and exile from court coincide with Ælfgifu's rise and that of her supporters.'[71]

It is under her grandsons that Eadgifu was first punished by one, Eadwig, and then restored to her position by the other, Edgar. Charter S1211 (which survives in one manuscript) informs that Eadgifu was deprived of all her land by Eadwig. The only person that we know who did so was her oldest grandson, Eadwig, and he did not live long once he became king. While there is no evidence that his death was anything less than natural, Eadwig was very young when he died. It is possible that not everything was quite as fortuitous and by chance as it might seem.

Although Eadwig's reign was brief, eighty-seven charters survive, and seventy-one of those are to named individuals as opposed to religious establishments. To put this into context, his uncle, Eadred, ruled for nine years. Sixty-seven charters survive for the entire period, and fifty-five of those were to named individuals. While the percentage of charters to individuals whom the king must have felt needed rewarding for some actions is the same, Eadred did rule for twice as long. To Eadwig's reign, the advance of a number of important individuals throughout the second half of the tenth century, must be assigned. These included, Ealdorman Ælfhere of Mercia; Æthelweard, who would become an ealdorman, and is believed to be the same who wrote the *Chronicon*; and Ealdorman Byrhtnoth of Essex. Byrhtnoth's marriage to the sister of Lady Æthelflæd of Damerham, the second wife of Eadwig's father, Edmund, must have taken place before Byrhtnoth's advancement.

In 959, no doubt, as soon as Edgar was declared as king on the death of his brother, the following document was written regarding land owned by Eadgifu's father, and then her, and which others sought to take from her. It shows, perhaps in only one document, the fluctuations Eadgifu experienced during her long life. It reads:

> Eadgifu declares to the archbishop and the community of
> Christ Church how her estate at Cooling came [to her].
> That is, that her father left her the estate and the [land]

book, just as he legally acquired them and his ancestors had bequeathed to him. It happened that her father borrowed thirty pounds from Goda, and entrusted the estate to him as security for the money. And [Goda] held it for seven 'winters'. When it came about, at around this time, that all the men of Kent were summoned to the battle at the Holme, Sighelm [Sigehelm], her father, did not want to go to the battle with any man's account unpaid, and he repaid Goda the thirty pounds and he bequeathed the estate to his daughter Eadgifu and gave her the [land]book. After he had fallen in the battle, Goda denied the repayment of the money, and withheld the estate until six years later. Then Byrhsige Dyrincg claimed it unceasingly for so long, until the Witan of that time commanded Eadgifu that she should purge her father's possession by [an oath equivalent to] that amount of the money. And she produced the oath in the witness of all the people at Aylesford, and there purged her father's repayment by an oath of thirty pounds. Then she was still not able to possess the estate until her friends obtained from King Edward [the Elder] that he prohibited him [Goda] the estate, if he wanted to possess any [at all]; and so he gave it up. Then it happened in the first place that the king so strongly blamed Goda that he was deprived of all the [land] books and property, all that he owned. And the king then granted him and all his property, with [land] books and estates, to Eadgifu to dispose of as she wished. Then she said that she did not dare before God to pay him back as he had deserved of her, and she restored to him all his land except the two sulungs at Osterland, and she refused to give back the [land] books until she knew how loyally he would treat her in respect of the estates. Then, King Edward died and Æthelstan [Athelstan] succeeded to the kingdom. When Goda thought it an opportune time, he sought out King Æthelstan and begged that he would intercede on his behalf with Eadgifu, for the return of his [land] books. And the king did so. And she gave back to him all except the [land] book for Osterland. And he willingly allowed her that [land] book and humbly thanked her for the others. And, on top of that as one of twelve he swore to her an oath, on behalf of those born and [yet] unborn, that this suit was for ever settled. And this was done in the presence of King Æthelstan and his Witan at Hamsey near Lewes [Sussex]. And Eadgifu held the land with the landbooks for the days of the two kings, her sons [i.e. Edmund and Eadred]. When Eadred died and Eadgifu was deprived of all her property, then two of Goda's sons, Leofstan and Leofric, took from Eadgifu the two afore-mentioned estates at Cooling and Osterland, and said to the young prince Eadwig who was then chosen [king] that they had more right to them than she. That then remained so until Edgar came of age and he [and] his Witan judged that they had done criminal robbery, and they adjudged and restored the property to her. Then Eadgifu, with the permission and witness of the king and all his bishops, took the [land] books and entrusted the estates to Christ Church [and] with her own hands laid them upon the altar, as the property of the community for ever, and for the repose of her soul. And she declared that Christ himself with all the heavenly host would curse for ever anyone who should ever divert or diminish this gift. In this way this property came to the Christ Church community. S1211[72]

To explain:

Dating to around 959, the document provides the ownership history of an estate at Cooling in Kent. Eadgifu had inherited this land from her father, who had mortgaged it for a loan of £30, which he repaid before going on the campaign on which he died. However, Goda, the man who had made the loan, claimed not to have received payment and proceeded to take practical ownership of the estate. While Eadgifu retained the landbook, or freehold record, and tried various means of asserting her ownership, it was not until Edward the Elder intervened, presumably after their marriage, that the matter was resolved to some degree. Edward seized not only the estate in question but all Goda's lands, handing their ownership and administration over to Eadgifu. The charter indicates that Eadgifu acted magnanimously, giving almost all of these back to Goda, though her primary consideration was likely to avoid creating a powerful political enemy. Sensibly, however, she retained possessions of the landbooks to ensure Goda's loyalty, as well as a small estate at Osterland, in addition to her hereditary holdings at Cooling. The matter was fully resolved in Æthelstan's (Athelstan) reign when the king interceded with Eadgifu on Goda's behalf. Eadgifu returned the landbooks, but retained the estates at Osterland and Cooling, while Goda swore an oath in Æthelstan's presence declaring that he considered the matter to be closed ... Eadwig seized his grandmother's landholdings and, in the case of the Cooling and Osterland estates, turned them over to Goda's sons ... After Eadwig's death in 959, Edgar restored his aging grandmother's possessions.[73]

Unlike Eadwig, Edgar ruled well when he became king of England, and earned the epithet Edgar the Peaceable, but perhaps he was just lucky to live a longer life than his older brother and that of his father and uncle and to inherit an England at peace with its neighbours, and more importantly, with itself.

Under Edgar's rule, Eadgifu is mentioned in four charters, and one (S811, surviving in one manuscript) of these is worth mentioning, a charter to her. 'King Edgar to Eadgifu, his grandmother; renewal of a charter concerning 65 hides (mansae) at Meon, Hants., the old landbook having disappeared while in Edgar's custody.'[74] While this is far from the only charter to be a reissue of an earlier charter, it is tempting to consider how Edgar approached the conversation with his formidable grandmother.

Shortly before her death, Eadgifu witnessed, perhaps as her final royal duty, the refoundation charter of the New Minster, Winchester, in 966 (S745 surviving in three manuscripts). She would therefore have met both Edward and Edmund, the oldest two of Edgar's children, who also witness the charter, but perhaps not the future king, Æthelred. It is impossible to say if she met Edith before she went to Wilton nunnery with her mother. It is feasible that Eadgifu may have been supplanted by Elfrida, who would ensure the House of Wessex endured throughout the final thirty-four years of the tenth century. Lady Elfrida, or Ælfthryth, witnesses the refoundation charter above Lady Eadgifu.[75] What Eadgifu's part was in the marriage of Edgar to Ælfthryth/Elfrida would be interesting to know, especially as it was Edgar's third marriage.

There is some thought that Eadgifu may have remarried later in life, perhaps allying herself with a powerful Mercian family to aid Edgar in his bid to become king of Mercia.

William of Malmesbury, in his *Gesta Regum Anglorum*, provided information about Eadgifu:

> He also had by a third wife called Eadgifu two sons Edmund and Eadred, who both reigned after Æthelstan [Athelstan] and two daughters Eadburh and Eadgifu. Eadburh became a nun and lies at Winchester; Eadgifu was a famous beauty, and was given in marriage by her brother Æthelstan to Louis prince of Aquitaine.[76]

It is to William of Malmesbury that the confusion surrounding the number of daughters Eadgifu gave birth to is assigned. Foot has argued that William of Malmesbury counted an extra daughter.[77] Others argue that there were more daughters.

In his *Gesta Pontificum Anglorum* William mentions Eadgifu's role in keeping Bishop Æthelwold in England. 'It was Eadred's mother, Eadgifu, a woman famous throughout the whole land of Britain for the praises paid to her religion, who took up Æthelwald's [Æthelwold] case and persuaded her son to keep him.'[78]

This information may have originated from Ælfric's *Life of St Æthelwold*:

> At length, when a time had passed after he had received monastic orders, he determined to go to lands across the sea, to train himself more perfectly in sacred books and monastic discipline but the venerable Queen Eadgifu, King Eadred's mother, prevented his attempts, advising the king not to let such a man depart from his kingdom. It then pleased King Eadred by his mother's persuasion to give to the venerable Æthelwold a certain place, Abingdon by name, in which a little monastery was situated in ancient days; but it was then waste and deserted, consisting of poor buildings and possessing only 40 hides.[79]

Chapter 5

The Religious

A surprising number of the royal women of Wessex spent their lives behind the walls of cloisters. This, perhaps, seems strange; surely, the royal women were important as potential wives to create alliances for the kinship group. And yet, this option was possibly never presented to them. Many of these women came to be revered as saints after their deaths, and 'royal monasteries' emerged; Wilton, the Nunnaminster and Shaftesbury. This requires some unpicking.

The information for some of these women is that they were always destined for a monastic life. This is especially true of Alfred and Ealhswith's daughter, Æthelgifu, abbess of St Mary's, Shaftesbury, and Eadburh, the (probably) only daughter born to Edward the Elder, and his third wife, Eadgifu. But they were not alone. Two more of Edward the Elder's daughters spent their lives in a nunnery, and possibly a third, the natural sister of Athelstan, following the breakdown of her marriage and subsequent death of her husband, Sihtric of York. Equally, it is postulated that Athelstan's mother, if she did not die, may have retired to a nunnery, as did Edward the Elder's second wife, Ælfflæd, and indeed potentially, Edgar's first and second wife, as well as his daughter, with his second wife, Edith. Both Wulfthryth, Edgar's second wife, and Edith, their daughter, were revered as saints after their death, as too was Æthelred's murdered brother, Edward the Martyr. Yet, this focus on the religious does seem to have run its course by the reign of Æthelred II. All his daughters seem to have made matches with the ruling men in England at the time, apart from one.

What then was causing this outpouring of religious conviction?

Firstly, a word of caution: some of these women may not have taken their vows. Some of them may simply have been living in religious institutions as the very means of avoiding marriage, or may have still been living in their homes but having adopted the veil of the religious. Others, it appears, may have chosen a lifetime of study and religious reflection. Other than the religious houses of England, there was no other environment where these women could become scholars if that were their calling.

Æthelgifu, the abbess of St Mary's, Shaftesbury

Æthelgifu, abbess of Shaftesbury, daughter of Alfred and Ealhswith

It is believed that Æthelgifu[1] was the third born child of Alfred and Ealhswith. Certainly, Æthelgifu was younger than Æthelflæd.[2] Æthelgifu, for whatever reason, was always destined for a religious life. Asser writes, 'Æthelgifu, devoted to God through her holy virginity, subject and consecrated to the rules of the monastic life, entered the service of God.'[3]

Further, Asser adds:

> King Alfred ordered the other monastery to be built near the east gate of Shaftesbury as a residence suitable for nuns. He appointed his own daughter Æthelgifu, a virgin consecrated to God; and many other noble nuns live with her in the same monastery, serving God in the monastic life.[4]

When the abbey at Shaftesbury was built is unknown, and indeed, the surviving foundation charter for the nunnery, known as charter S357 (two versions of the charter survive, in the same manuscript, one in English and one in Latin), is believed to be spurious. It is suggested by Keynes and Lapidge that the nunnery was built between 880 and 893 when Asser wrote his biography of Alfred.

Æthelgifu, like her mother and brothers, is mentioned in her father's will but not by name.

> And to my eldest daughter the estate at Wellow; to the middle one that at Kingsclere and at Candover.[5]

> to my eldest daughter, to the middle one, to the youngest and to Ealhswith, 400 pounds to the four of them, 100 pounds each.[6]

There is a suggestion that Æthelgifu may not have survived her father, as the properties bequeathed to her in her father's will never formed part of the land owned by Shaftesbury Abbey.

Of significance is that Ælfgifu, the first wife of King Edmund and the mother of his two sons, was buried at Shaftesbury on her death in 944. Later in the century, the body of Edward the Martyr was translated to Shaftesbury in 979. Shaftesbury Abbey was an important religious site to the Wessex royal family. But no more of Æthelgifu is known.

The religious daughters of Edward the Elder

King Alfred and Ealhswith had three daughters who survived to adulthood. Of these three, two made prestigious marriages, arguably both marrying for the security of the heartland of the Wessex kingdom. One daughter became a nun and later an abbess. It is possible that Edward the Elder planned on copying much of this, only he had many more daughters. And so, while four of them made continental matches which enhanced the prestige of their father and half-brother, not one, not two, but three of Edward the Elder's daughters chose, or were forced, to take up holy orders, although one daughter was a lay sister and never a vowess.

Æthelhild

Æthelhild, daughter of Edward the Elder, and his second wife, Lady Ælfflæd

The birth order of Edward the Elder's children is unknown. Therefore, we do not know why Æthelhild[7] became a lay sister at Wilton Abbey. Could it be because it was her choice, her father's, or mother's, or that of her half-brother, Athelstan?

Wilton Abbey was strongly associated with the Wessex royal family. Her sister Eadflæd became a nun, and the two sisters were joined by their mother. Their younger half-sister also became a nun at the Nunnaminster. Nothing further is known of Æthelhild. She is not mentioned in the *Anglo-Saxon Chronicle*, or in any of the surviving charter evidence. We do not know her date of birth, or her date of death.

William of Malmesbury's *Gesta Regum Anglorum* tells us more (see section on Lady Ælfflæd in Chapter 4).[8]

Eadflæd

Eadflæd, daughter of Edward the Elder, and his second wife, Lady Ælfflæd

Eadflæd[9] became a nun at Wilton Abbey. And she is named in a charter issued by Athelstan (S438, surviving in one manuscript) granting land to St Mary's, Wilton dated 937, the year of the Battle of Brunanburh. Provided the dating is secure, and the charter is authentic, this points to Eadflæd still being alive at this date. The absence of her sister's name, Æthelhild, may mean she had predeceased her sister. Again, Eadflæd is mentioned by William of Malmesbury in his *Gesta Regum Anglorum*, 'Eadflæd took the veil'.[10] Note should be made here of the distinction between the two types of religious women. It is, as Foot has discussed, unhelpful to name these women as 'nuns' for that term did not mean the same as it does now, instead referring to an older woman. Rather, it is believed that there were lay sisters and also those who wore the veil. Both could have been attached to a nunnery, although, aside from the Nunnaminster, no religious establishment is specifically termed as a monastery for women.

Eadburh

Eadburh, *c*.919–952 daughter of Edward the Elder and his third wife, Eadgifu

William of Malmesbury in his *Gesta Pontificum Anglorum* tells the story of Edward the Elder's youngest daughter, Eadburh,[11] being consigned to the Nunnaminster in infancy as she showed such signs of devotion:[12]

> There had been a convent on this spot before, in which Eadburg [Eadburh], daughter of king Edward the Elder, had lived and died, but by then it was almost in ruins. When she was barely three, Eadburg had given a remarkable proof of her future holiness. Her father had wanted to find out whether his little girl would turn towards God or the world. He set out in the dining room the adornments of the different ways of life, on this side a chalice and the Gospels, on the other bangles and necklaces. The little girl was brought in by the nurse and sat on her father's knees. He told her to choose which she wanted. With a fierce look she spat out the things of the world, and immediately crawling on hands and knees towards the Gospels and chalice adored them in

girlish innocence … Her father honoured his offspring with
more restrained kisses and said, 'Go where heaven calls
you, follow the bridegroom you have chosen and a blessing
be upon your going.' … Countless miracles during her life
and after her death bear witness to the devotion of her heart
and the integrity of her body.[13]

William later adds that 'Some of the bones of Eadburg [Eadburh] the
happy are buried',[14] at Pershore.

Aside from the later William of Malmesbury, Eadburh is the recipient
to land in one charter, that of S446, dated to 939 and surviving in one
manuscript. 'King Athelstan to Eadburh, his sister; grant of 17 hides
(mansae) at Droxford, Hants.'[15] Perhaps, Athelstan was ensuring
his sister's future with this charter. Maybe he knew he was dying.
Perhaps this was a means of guaranteeing the survival of the religious
establishment in which she lived.

Edith/Eadgyth

Edith/Eadgyth daughter of King Edgar, and his second wife, Wulfthryth
　　　c.962–*c*.984 (date is given as 16 September 983 in her *Vitae*)

Lady Eadgyth/Edith[16] was the daughter of King Edgar and his second
wife, Wulfthryth. She died while young and is mentioned in charter
S1449 (surviving in one manuscript) and the Newminster *Liber Vitae*.
She spent her life at Wilton Nunnery, where she was later revered as
a saint, having died around 984. It is probable that her mother played
some part in her daughter's sainthood.

William of Malmesbury in his *Gesta Pontificum Anglorum*, has much
to say about Edith/Eadgyth:

being the resting place of the sweet remains of the bones
of the blessed Eadgyth, the daughter of king Edgar, who
cherishes it with her love. Wilton is a sizeable town,
situated above the river Wylye, and so famous that it gives
its name to the whole county. There Eadgyth, consecrated
to God from her infancy, won the favour of God by her
unspoilt maidenhood, and the favour of men by her careful

service, eliminating any pride in her birth by the nobility of her mind, though I have heard from my elders that there was one thing about her which men regarded as a grave offence, namely that she tricked their sight by her splendid golden clothes. She would process, decked with garments more *haute couture* in appearance than was demanded by the sanctity of her profession. St Æthelwald [Æthelwold] openly criticised her for it, but it is said that she made an apt and witty reply, 'It is only men's conscience that waits for God's true and irrefutable judgement, for, as Augustine says, pride can exist in miserable rags as well. So I think that the mind can be pure when clad in these garments of gold as in your tattered skins.'[17]

This continues, with St Dunstan having a vision predicting Eadgyth's death:

Eadgyth struck to her noble purpose, and before her youth had ended she breathed her last on the day predicted, when she was just twenty-three ... And as the miracles at her tomb increased in number as a result, the order was given that the maiden's body should be taken out.[18]

The tale of Eadgyth's uncorrupted body continues and then time moves forward, and William's words tell of King Cnut who 'burst into a frightful peal of laughter against the virgin herself: he would never believe that the daughter of king Edgar was a saint, seeing that the king had surrendered himself to his vices and was a complete slave to his lusts'. Cnut demanded that the tomb was opened 'and the dead girl, with a veil spread in front of her face, rose out of the grave up to her waist, and seemed to make an attack on the contumacious king'.[19]

William confirms that St Edith's feast day is still celebrated and adds the following about her mother:

Her mother Wulfthryth lies buried in the same church. She was not actually a nun, as popular opinion crazily supposes. She had merely put on a veil as her own idea in her sudden fear of the king, before, as the story continues, the king snatched away the veil and dragged her to his bed. Because he had touched a woman, who had been a nun, if only potentially, he was reproved by St Dunstan and made to do penance for seven years. Also, when Eadgyth had been born, Wulfthryth did not develop a taste for repetitions of sexual pleasure, but rather shunned them in disgust, so truly is she named and celebrated as a saint.[20]

Ælfthryth, a daughter of Æthelred II and his first wife, Ælfgifu

A daughter of Æthelred II and his first wife, is named as the Abbess of Wherwell under Edward the Confessor (who would have been her half-brother) but no further information is known about her, and this does fall outside the tenth-century royal women, but is worthy of note.

Chapter 6

English Wives

Ælfgifu of Shaftesbury, and her mother, Wynflæd

Ælfgifu of Shaftesbury, d.c.944 daughter of unknown and Wynflæd

m. Edmund, King of England (939–946)

    Eadwig b.c.940–959
    Edgar b.c.942–975

There is little information about Ælfgifu.[1] It is unknown who her father was, but her mother, Wynflæd, is known. Ælfgifu died by or during the year 944. She was Edmund's first wife, and their children were acknowledged as legitimate, for all in the only surviving charter to show her name, she is called *concubina regis affui*.[2] However, this charter, S514, which survives in two manuscripts, dated from 942 to 946 may not be authentic. As such, her witnessing the charter twelfth, behind her husband, brother by marriage, mother-in-law, and the archbishops and bishops, may not be relevant, nor might her title. It is unknown when the marriage between Ælfgifu and Edmund took place. There is the possibility that they were married before the death of Athelstan in 939, although it would perhaps be expected that Edmund, as Athelstan's acknowledged heir, might have made a grandiose marriage. Which, it is possible, this was. Certainly, her mother appears to have owned much land and was a wealthy woman, even if the identity of her father is unknown.

Æthelweard's *Chronicon* informs that:

> Queen Ælfgifu died, the wife of King Eadmund [Edmund], and afterwards she was held to be a saint. And at her tomb, with the help of God, down to the present day, very many miracles take place in the monastery known by the common people at Shaftesbury.[3]

61

Shaftesbury was the abbey also associated with King Alfred's daughter, Æthelgifu, who had been abbess there, until her death, the date of which is unknown.

While we know very little about Ælfgifu herself, her mother, Wynflæd, is worthy of consideration, and it is interesting to think about the royal women who might well have surrounded Ælfgifu's young sons as they were growing up. While it is often said that Lady Eadgifu, the third wife of King Edward the Elder, had the raising of the two children, there was also Wynflæd, a maternal grandmother, who must have had some sway with the children and would certainly have felt she deserved a position at the king's court.

Wynflæd is also 'probably the same Wynflæd ... who was the beneficiary of a charter of King Eadmund's [Edmund] dated 942, which granted her land at Cheselbourne and Winterbourne in Dorset'.[4] This charter named her as a religious woman, a *nunne*, but the word *nunne*, so recognisable to the modern reader, did not in fact, as Foot argues, mean what we think it does. Two terms *mynecena* and *nunne* appear to have been used, with *nunne* actually meaning a lay sister. Instead, Wynflæd may have been a religious woman, living on her own estates, having adopted the veil of a widow and determined to live a chaste life.[5]

She is also believed to be the same woman who left a will:

> Her will begins with bequests to an unnamed church, including a gift of two silver cups 'to the refectory' for the benefit of the community, and a monetary gift to each servant of God; this establishment was apparently distinct from Wilton, which is identified as the recipient of a separate gift, but is probably Shaftesbury, which house Wynflæd named later in her will. Wynflæd was obviously close to this congregation and her bequests included her *nunscrude*, her 'nun's clothing', but she was not necessarily a cloistered *mynecenu*. She had clearly in widowhood retained control of her landed estates and their stock as well as a number of valuable personal possessions; since she made mention of her untamed and tame horses, she would further appear to have been breeding and training horses.[6]

She left one of her black tunics and her best holy veil and headband to Ceolthryth, and a gown, cap and headband to Æthelflæd the White. Afterwards Æthelflæd was told to supply from Wynflæd's *nunscrude* the best she could for Wulfflæd (freed earlier in the will on condition that she would serve Wynflæd's daughter) and for Æthelgifu (a seamstress who was not freed, but given to the testatrix's granddaughter) and to supplement the gift with gold so that each of them should have sixty pennyworth.[7]

A veil was 'a mark of entry to the communal religious life, widows taking vows were distinguished by their clothing as having taken vows of continence, their distinctive dress being conferred at the time of their consecration to religion'.[8] The discussion of the veil does not necessarily mean that Wynflæd was cloistered. She may have lived as a chaste widow on her estates.

The cult of St Ælfgifu was in existence by the 970s, when Lantfred of Winchester writes of it,[9] and Wynflæd appears to have been associated with the nunnery at Shaftesbury as well. And indeed, the *Anglo-Saxon Chronicle* reports that, 'Here King Eadred passed away, and he rests in the Old Minster. And Eadwig succeeded to the kingdom of Wessex, and his brother succeeded to the kingdom of Mercia; and they were sons of King Edmund and St Ælfgifu.'[10] But this annal entry may not have been contemporary to events, and so does not necessarily mean the cult sprang up immediately after her death.

Ælfgifu is also mentioned in the *Liber Eliensis*, A History of the Isle of Ely, where she is named as Edith. 'Edmund's queen, Edith, bore him two sons, Edwy [Eadwig] and Edgar. And when she gave birth to Edgar, St Dunstan heard voices of heavenly beings singing psalms and saying, "Peace of the English in the time of the boy now born and of our Dunstan".'[11] Further on, she is also called Edmund's 'saintly queen, Edith'.[12] The *Liber Eliensis* was compiled in the twelfth century.

William of Malmesbury in his *Gesta Pontificum Anglorum* offers the following:

Ælfgifu, the wife of Edmund, who was Alfred's great-grandson, built the nunnery, and her bodily remains were placed there after her death. She was a woman always intent on good works. She was so pious and loving that she would even secretly release criminals who had been openly condemned by the gloomy verdict of a jury. For her the expensive clothes, which entice some women to cast shame aside, were material for munificence, and she would give away the costliest dresses to some poor woman, the moment she had seen her. With Ælfgifu even the envious could only praise her physical beauty and her skill in handiwork, as there was nothing they could criticise. I have spoken elsewhere of the grace of prophecy which God poured on her. In her lifetime she performed the works of virtue, but after her death miracles glittered. I once composed these verses about them:

She bore sharp pain for several years,
Then gave her soul, refine, to God.
Her blessed remains, their journey done,
God's mercy marked with countless sign.
The blind and deaf, who worship them,
Restored to health, attest her work.
The lame who come walk upright home,
The rich return made wise, the crazed made sane.[13]

Æthelflæd, second wife to King Edmund

Æthelflæd (of Damerham), daughter of Ealdorman Ælfgar (unknown–*c.*962–991)

>   m.1. Edmund, king of the English d.946
>   m.2. Athelstan Rota, ealdorman

Æthelflæd[14] is described in the *Anglo-Saxon Chronicle* texts D, E and F when recording Edmund's murder, under 946 as Edmund's queen, so she may have been consecrated after their marriage. 'And Æthelflæd of Damerham, daughter of Ealdorman Ælfgar, was then his queen.'[15]

Before Edmund's death, her name appears in charter S513, surviving in three manuscripts. 'King Edmund to Æthelflæd, his wife; grant, for life, of 100 hides at Damerham and Martin, Hants., and Pentridge, Dorset; with reversion to St Mary's, Glastonbury.'[16] This charter is dated to between 944 and 946. However, apart from this occurrence, she does not attest to any of Edmund's charters, and the secure dating of their marriage is not possible. It must, by necessity, have occurred after the death of his first wife and before his death in 946, but how long the union lasted is unknown.

Named in the *Anglo-Saxon Chronicle* as the daughter of Ealdorman Ælfgar, his will is listed in S1483, surviving in two manuscripts:

> Will of Ælfgar, including bequests of land at Cockfield, Suffolk; Fen Ditton, Cambs.; Lavenham, Suffolk; Baythorn, Essex; Monks Eleigh, Suffolk; Colne, Tey, Peldon, (West) Mersea, Greenstead, Tidwoldingstone (Heybridge near Maldon) and Totham, Essex; Ashfield and Rushbrook, Suffolk; the beneficiaries including St Edmunds *Bedericesworth*; the community at Stoke (probably Stoke-by-Nayland, Suffolk); Barking, St Mary's; Canterbury, Christ Church; and London, St Paul's.

Specifically, Æthelflæd is to have use of the land at Peldon and Mersea, and Greenstead, Essex. She is bequeathed land at Cockfield with reversion to St Edmunds *Bedericesworth* – as well as land at Fen Ditton, Cambridgeshire to be left by her to a holy foundation; at Lavenham, Suffolk, to pass to her child if she has one and if not to the holy community at Stoke; and land at Baythorn, Essex, to pass to her child if she has one, if not to Barking, St Mary's.[17]

Ealdorman Ælfgar is said to have been the ealdorman of Essex. He does not begin witnessing charters until 943, S493 surviving in one manuscript,[18] perhaps on the marriage of his daughter to the king. He attests to one of Edmund's charters and then continues to hold his position, under Eadred, witnessing twenty-two charters and also one of Eadwig's before his death. Ælfgar, it seems, did not have any sons, but his two daughters made advantageous marriages, Æthelflæd to King Edmund and Ælfflæd, to Byrhtnoth, who would become Ealdorman of Essex in place of his father by marriage in 956, when he was advanced to the position by King Eadwig, Æthelflæd's stepson.

As with King Edgar's third wife, it is not possible to say whether Ælfgar became the ealdorman on his daughter's marriage to the king or whether he was already an ealdorman.

Following Edmund's death, Æthelflæd's fate is difficult to determine. She may well have remarried an ealdorman known as Athelstan Rota.

If that is the case, the union was once more childless. Note of this union may be mentioned in the *Liber Eliensis*:

> Her sister [Lady Æthelflæd's], moreover, the wife of Ealdorman Athelstan, whose name was Æthelflæd [recte Ælfflæd], was a very wealthy woman by virtue of her estates, her marriage-portion and the inherited patrimony of her family. Hence she seemed the noblest among her kinfolk. However, while she seemed to cling to the uncertain riches of the World, she was devoutly scrupulous about the observance of holy religion and, after the death of her husband, remained perpetually in widowhood ... [Moreover] she gave them [the monks] Ditton and Hadham and Kelshall, and in her will in English she had these things confirmed, except that she made the proviso that her sister, Ælfflæd, who has been mentioned earlier; should keep the *vill* of Ditton while she lived.[19]

In charter S1795, surviving in one manuscript and dated 969, King Edgar, Æthelflæd's second stepson, allows her to grant forty hides at Hadham in Hertfordshire to St Paul's church. In the charter, she is named as both a widow and a nun:[20]

> Here I, Edgar, king of the English, enthroned on the inviolable royal seat of the kingdom of whole of Britain through the favour of the All-Accomplishing One, have bestowed as a perpetual inheritance for the sake of the reward of eternal life and the companionship of the denizens of heaven a certain parcel of land, namely, 40 hides, to wit, in a place that is called by rustics and by the known name of this people Hadham, on a certain widow who, being a nun dedicated with the veil on account of [her] love for the eternal and heavenly Bridegroom, once was joined in lawful matrimony to my father, namely, King Edmund, up to the end of his life, and from her birth has been called by the noble name Æthelflæd, so that during her life, having been granted her prayer, she may enjoy [it] with all its appurtenances [that] the supreme benignity of the Ruler has produced on the surface of the earth and after the passing of

her life she may bequeath it by handing it over in perpetuity to whichever heirs coming afterwards she wishes. This she had granted to the church of [St] Paul's. May it be, therefore, saith the king, that the aforementioned land be free of the whole yoke of earthly service, released from royal tribute, these three being excepted, namely, a share of military service, [and] the restoration of bridge and fortress.

Again, we may find that as with Wynflæd, the mother of Edmund's first wife, our idea of the religious woman may not correctly describe Æthelflæd's position later in life. She may, once more, have adopted the veil of the widowed woman.

Æthelflæd's own will survives in charter S1494, surviving in two manuscripts, dated 962–991:

Will of Æthelflæd, including bequest of land at Lambourn, Cholsey and Reading, Berkshire, to the king; at Damerham, Hants., to Glastonbury; at Hamme to Christ Church, Canterbury; at Woodham, Essex, to Ealdorman Beorhtnoth [Byrhtnoth] and her sister for life, with reversion to St Mary's, Barking; at Hadham, Herts., to the same, for life, with reversion to St Paul's, London; at Fen Ditton, Cambs., to Ely Abbey; at Cockfield and Chelsworth, Suffolk, to the same for life, with reversion to St Edmunds, Bedericesworth [Bury]; at Fingringhoe, Essex, to the same for life, with reversion to St Peter's, Mersea; at Polstead, Suffolk, to the same for life, with reversion to Stoke [Stoke-by-Nayland, Suffolk?]; at Withermarsh, Suffolk, to Stoke; at Stratford St Mary, Lavenham, Balsdon, Suffolk, and at Peldon, Mersea and Greenstead [near Colchester, Essex], to Ealdorman Beorhtnoth [Byrhtnoth] and her sister for life, with reversion to Stoke; at Elmsett, Suffolk, to the same for life, with reversion to Edmund; at Thorpe [Morieux, Suffolk?], to Hadleigh, Suffolk; at Wickford, Essex, to Sibriht, her kinsman; at Hadham, Herts., to Ecgwine, her reeve; at Donyland, Essex, to Beorhtwald, her servant, to Ælfwald and Æthelmær, her priests, and to Ælfgeat, her kinsman; and at Waldingfield, Suffolk, to Crawe, her kinswoman.[21]

Through these few documents, it is possible to trace Æthelflæd's landholdings, and also to see that to a large extent, she did carry out the requests placed upon her both by her husband and her father. The 100 hides at Damerham, is indeed returned to Glastonbury. The land at Cockfield, which her father requested she bequeath to St Edmunds, is bequeathed to her sister and husband, with the instruction that it should then be returned to St Edmunds. Lavenham is treated in a similar way, to be reverted to the community at Stoke. And the land granted to her by King Edgar is in turn gifted to Ecgwine, her reeve. Her will, though, does also show that she held more land than can be shown to have been gifted to her by her husband or father. Æthelflæd of Damerham was a wealthy member of the nobility.

The exact date of Æthelflæd's death is unknown. As such, it is not possible to determine how much influence she might have enjoyed during Edgar, her stepson's, reign.

Lady Ælfgifu, wife of King Eadwig

Ælfgifu, d.*c*.966–975, daughter of unknown father and Æthelgifu
   m. King Eadwig (23 November 955 until 1 October 959), divorced in 958

Ælfgifu[22] was the daughter of Æthelgifu, although the identity of her father is unknown.

King Eadwig was proclaimed as king on the death of his uncle on 23 November 955. But Eadwig only ruled for nearly four years, although it was a time of intense political factionalism, potentially, embodied in the identity of his wife, Ælfgifu. It is worth mentioning here that despite the near-constant military annals that form most of Edmund and Eadred's entries in the *Anglo-Saxon Chronicle*, there is no mention of any warfare in the entries from 955 to 959. And this is no doubt because two ruling factions made the English king look only at his kingdom and no further afield, and when these entries were added to the manuscripts, at a later date, it was only this that was remembered of Eadwig's reign.

It is the *Anglo-Saxon Chronicle* D entry for 958 that sheds some light on what was happening in England at this time. 'Here in this year Archbishop Oda divorced King Eadwig and Ælfgifu because they were related.'[23]

This terse entry follows others, informing that Eadwig has been proclaimed king, and then one which also states his brother, Edgar, was proclaimed king of Mercia. 'And Eadwig succeeded to the kingdom of Wessex, and his brother Edgar succeeded to the kingdom of Mercia.' The *Anglo-Saxon Chronicle* D[24] and the *Anglo-Saxon Chronicle* texts A and E make no mention of any divide between Wessex and Mercia, whereas the B and C manuscripts seem to go one further, recording Eadwig's succession in 956, while under 957, we are told, 'Here the ætheling Edgar succeeded to the kingdom of Mercia.'[25]

Much has already been made of the Wessex and Mercian divide. It is impossible to determine from such a distance in time how much these documented divides were merely a show of administrative division or whether it was a real and true one. Beginning with Æthelflæd and then Athelstan, Mercia was to be governed either by someone sympathetic to the Mercians, or someone specifically associated with Mercia. Why then might Edgar, and not Eadwig have been suitable to the Mercians, and what did all this have to do with Ælfgifu?

It is believed that Ælfgifu, whose mother is named Æthelgifu in S1292, surviving in two manuscripts, is the sister of Æthelweard, whose *Chronicon* has already been cited and who is identified as the ealdorman of the Western Provinces from *c.*975. If the identification is sound, then Ælfgifu, as Æthelweard does in his *Chronicon*, could claim descent from Æthelred I, through his son, Æthelwold, the same Æthelwold who so worried Edward the Elder at the start of his reign, until his death at the Battle of the Holme in 902/3. She was therefore descended from the very family close to the Wessex ruling family that Alfred had gone to such extremes to exclude from the succession on his death.

'Ælfred was the son of Æthelwulf, from who we are descended. Five sons followed him. Of these, I am descended from King Æthelred and you from King Alfred, both sons of King Æthelwulf.'[26] So writes Æthelweard in the introduction to his *Chronicon*. It seems that not only did this mean that Eadwig and Ælfgifu were related (third cousins once removed),[27] but that Eadwig was making it clear that this family was to be reunited with the current ruling, although younger, half of the family. This, it seems, did not please everyone, and no doubt accounts for why eighty-five charters of Eadwig's survive from his time as king. He was prolific in trying to build himself a faction to support what might have been a contested kingship.

From Æthelweard's *Chronicon*, written at a time when Eadwig's brother's son was king, comes the only, and brief, positive statement about Eadwig. 'He for his great beauty got the nickname "All-fair" from the common people. He held the kingdom continuously for four years and deserved to be loved.'[28]

Ælfgifu witnesses S1292 during the reign of her husband. S1292 is dated 956/7, and survives in two manuscripts. It is a memorandum in the vernacular from Abingdon. In it, Ælfgifu is titled the king's wife, not queen. S1292 is a charter not included in the charters issued by Eadwig for he is a witness to the charter between Bishop Beorhthelm and Abbot Æthelwold in which the two exchanged lands with one another. As such, Ælfgifu seems to attest to none of the king's charters, although, if Æthelweard was her brother, then he and another of their brothers did attest to the king's charters. Æthelweard attests S594, S672, S630, S616 in 956 and S658, S660 and S586 in 959, his brother attesting S616 next to him.[29]

Here, we must turn to a saint's life, that of Saint Dunstan, written by someone only known as B, for more information. This, of course, is a biased source. After all, its intention was to cast Dunstan in as holy a light as possible. Along the way, it is inevitable that Dunstan must encounter those who are deemed unholy:

> King Edmund's son, young in years and with small wisdom in ruling, although he had been elected to make up the line of royal names in both peoples. To him attached herself a well-born but foolish women, who together with her grown-up daughter pursued him with indecent proposals, aiming to join either herself or her daughter to him in marriage. He – and I am even now ashamed to mention it – took it in turns (so it is said) to subject them to his lustful attentions, fondling them obscenely; not that either felt any shame.
>
> When the anointed time came round, he was by common consent anointed and consecrated king by the assembled nobility of the English. On the very same day, after the king's ritual installation and anointing, his lust suddenly prompted him to rush out to caress these whores in the manner I have described, leaving the happy feasters and the seemly assemblage of great men … In the end they chose two of their whole number whom they knew to be the most

resolute, Abbot Dunstan and his relative Bishop Cynesige. They were to do what all commanded, bringing back the king willy-nilly to the seat he had left ... they went and found the royal crown, brilliant with the wonderful gold and silver and variously sparkling jewels that made it up, tossed carelessly on the ground some distance from the king's head, while he was disporting himself disgracefully in between the two women as though they were wallowing in some revolting pigsty ... Dunstan put out his hand and removed him from the couch where he had been fornicating with the harlots, put his diadem on him, and marched him off to the royal company, parted from his women, if only by force. Then this Æthelgifu (that being the name of the woman Dunstan had shamed) directed the empty orbs of her eyes in blazing fury against the reverend abbot.[30]

While Ælfgifu is not named herself in this extract, her mother is.

Ælfgifu long outlived her young husband, and at some point, she and Eadwig's brother, King Edgar, reconciled. It would be interesting to know if she retained importance at the king's court when Edgar became king, or even after her divorce from Eadwig. There is no reference to Ælfgifu becoming a nun in later life, and it must be assumed that she remained an influential member of the family, even after her husband's death.

Ælfgifu's will has survived in one manuscript.[31] This reads:

This is Ælfgifu's request of her royal lord; she prays him for the love of God and for the sake of his royal dignity, that she may be entitled to make her will. Then she makes known to you, Sire, by your consent what she wishes to give to God's church for you and for your soul. First, she grants to the Old Minster, where she intends her body to be buried, the estate at Risborough just as it stands, except that, with your consent, she wishes that at each village every penally enslaved man who was subject to her shall be freed and [she grants] two hundred mancuses of gold to that minster and her shrine with her relics. And she grants to the New Minster the estate at Bledlow, and a hundred mancuses of gold; and a paten to the Nunnery and the estate at Whaddon to Christ and St Mary at Romsey; and Chesham to Abingdon, and Wickham to Bath.

And I grant to my royal lord the estates at Wing, Linslade, Haversham, Hatfield, Masworth and Gussage; and two armlets, each of a hundred and twenty mancuses, and a drinking-cup and six horses and as many shields and spears.

And to the Ætheling the estate at Newnham and an armlet of thirty mancuses.

And to the queen a necklace of a hundred and twenty mancuses and an armlet of thirty mancuses, and a drinking-cup.

And I grant to Bishop Æthelwold the estate at *Tæafersceat* and pray him that he will always intercede for my mother and for me.

And with my lord's permission I grant the estates at Mongewell and Berkhampstead to Ælfweard and Æthelweard and Ælfwaru in common for their lifetime, and after their death to the Old Minster for my royal lord and for me. And they are to pay a two-days' food-rent every year to the two minsters, as long as they possess the estates. And to my sister Ælfwaru I grant all that I have lent her; and to my brother's wife Æthelflæd[32] the headband which I have lent her.

And to each abbot five pounds of pence for the repair of their minster.

And, Sire, with your consent, [I wish] that I may entrust the surplus to the Bishop and the Abbot for the repair of the foundation, and for them to distribute for me among poor men according as seems to them most profitable for me in God's sight. And I beseech my royal lord for the love of God, that he will not desert my men who seek his protection and are worthy of him.

And I grant to Ælfweard a drinking-cup and to Æthelweard an ornamented drinking-horn.[33]

Ælfweard and Æthelweard would have been her brothers. Notably, she gifts much to the king but also to the queen and the ætheling, perhaps pointing to the reconciliation that must have taken place between them all. It is probable that the queen was Lady Elfrida, although it cannot be determined whether the ætheling was Edward, Edgar's oldest son or Edmund, his oldest son with Elfrida. This would depend on the date of the will, which, as it stands, can only be dated through a handspan of years. It would be tempting to use this as evidence that Ælfgifu was well known to the king, queen and their son, and that they enjoyed a personal relationship. Obviously, it is impossible to say this with any certainty.

Ælfgifu's brother, Æthelweard would become an important nobleman in the reign of Æthelred II, and without his *Chronicon*, written to a distant relative in Germany, Abbess Matilda, we would know much less than we do about events in tenth-century England, and certainly, a lot fewer of the names of the royal women.

Æthelflæd, first wife to King Edgar

Æthelflæd (Eneda), said to be the daughter of Ealdorman Ordmær (see below)

m. *c.*958 King Edgar of Mercia, later England

   Edward b.*c.*960–978

Æthelflæd[34] may have been the name of King Edgar's first wife, and with whom he had one child, a son named Edward, who would be king after Edgar's premature death in 975. The marriage may have occurred while Edgar was king of Mercia, and as such, she might have been from a Mercian ealdormanic family. We are told that her father was Ealdorman Ordmær, but there is no record of an Ealdorman Ordmær in any of the sources for the period. It is possible there may be some confusion between Æthelflæd and Edgar's third wife, Elfrida, whose father was Ealdorman Ordgar. It has also been suggested that Æthelflæd and Elfrida may have been cousins.[35] Equally, there is a thegn in Mercia called Ordmær,[36] so it might have been a misunderstanding with the title, not the name of the father.

This Ordmær is mentioned in the *Liber Eliensis*. Under Book II, 7 we are told how King Edgar gave Hatfield to St Æthelthryth, (she founded the monastery):

> The glorious King Edgar, just as he had promised, set about venerating and enlarging the place and, wishing to fulfil his vow, made an offering to God and St Æthelthryth, with a charter of forty hides of land in the district which is called Hatfield which a certain powerful man called Ordmær and his wife Æalde bequeathed to him on their death.[37]

The *Liber Eliensis* then goes on to discuss the dispute that arose concerning this land, and therefore explaining why it mentions Edgar at all, and why it traces the history of the land granted to Ely.

Æthelflæd is not named in any contemporary sources. We only have her name from the later, Anglo-Norman, sources of William of Malmesbury and John of Worcester.

William of Malmesbury tells the tale of Edgar violating a nun and the story whereby he was tricked into spending the night with a noblewoman's daughter's slave as opposed to the woman herself. William names Æthelflæd 'also called Candida, daughter of the powerful ealdorman Ordmær, he begat Edward'. [38]

This does not mean that Æthelflæd may not have been her name, but rather that some caution should be exercised in assuming it is the correct name. What can be said is that a first 'wife', if that is what she was, did exist, as the birth and subsequent rule of Edward the Martyr informs us. More than that, it is difficult to say. And sadly, her son, Edward, when he did rule, did not do so for very long, and none of the surviving charters make mention of the identity of his mother. Once more, the character assassination of Edgar's first wife may have more to do with the issues surrounding his successor than any perceived difficulties at the time. Edward the Martyr, as his name implies, met an untimely end and would not rule long after his father's death.

Eneda means swan or fair, and it is been suggested that there is a reference to this Æthelflæd, in the will of Wynflæd, believed to be the mother of Edmund's first wife.[39] However, the identification is not firm enough to be stated as fact.[40] In this will, S1539, which survives in one manuscript, the following is written:

> and to Æthelflæd the White her ... gown and cap and headband, and afterwards Æthelflæd is to supply from her nun's vestments the best she can for Wulfflæd and Æthelgifu and supplement it with gold so that each of them shall have at least sixty pennyworth.[41]

If this is the same Æthelflæd, then it would appear that, like so many of the Wessex royal women, she was placed in a nunnery when her husband decided it was time for a new wife, or, as discussed for Wynflæd, determined to live a life of continence. However, this identification is not assured.

The date of her death, and any details of her relationship with her son, Edward, are therefore unknown. Like King Athelstan before him, there are no charters issued by Edward that mention his mother. It is possible he did not know her at all.

Wulfthryth, second wife to King Edgar

Wulfthryth, d.*c.*1000

m.*c.*961 Edgar, king of the English

    Eadgyth/Edith *c.*961/2–984

Wulfthryth[42] was the second wife of King Edgar, and together they had one daughter, Eadgyth/Edith. Wulfthryth and Edgar's union is mired in something of a political scandal, which is challenging to unpick. It is difficult to assign credibility to it as it comes from later, mostly post-conquest, sources, and certainly from sources whose primary purpose was not to record events in the way we might expect a 'history' to be recorded.

These scandals revolve mostly around Edgar, who developed a difficult reputation both due to the religious reforms he implemented during his lifetime and the later character of his youngest son, Æthelred II. But, first, the religious developments of the Benedictine Reformation. By necessity, these reforms were advantageous to some and disadvantageous to others. The idea behind them was to impose the strict order of Benedictine monasticism. This was not well received by everyone.

'Edgar came to be remembered, in the monastic houses which had been reformed or founded during his reign, as bringer of the stability, peace and good order that had been lost and was now craved.'[43]

Wulfstan of Winchester and Byrhtferth of Ramsey wrote in the 990s, so in the lifetime of his son, and also his third wife. Wulfstan heaped praise on the king in his *Life of St Æthelwold*, and Byrhtferth, in his *Life of St Oswald*, spoke of Edgar on his death as 'glory of leaders and ruler of the whole of Albion'.[44]

But, following the Norman Conquest, opinion about Edgar turned, as Anglo-Norman chroniclers looked for a means to portray the English as deserving of having been so fiercely conquered in 1066. Much of this blame came to be laid at the feet of Æthelred II, Edgar's son, and therefore, by association with his father and his scandalous relationships with his three wives. Edgar came to be seen as a 'womaniser'.[45]

As such, much attention was directed Edgar's way about his three marriages. While the identity of his first wife is hardly known, both Wulfthryth, and Elfrida, his third wife, have lurid tales surrounding them.

To turn to Wulfthryth. It is believed that the union was a political match, possibly with a powerful political family related to the family of the wife of Æthelred I, Alfred's brother (as is supposed for the marriage of his brother to Ælfgifu, only on this occasion to the wife's side of the family). She was the daughter of Ealdorman Wulfhere (it is the 'wulf' element of the name that is of interest). Edgar's intentions for this union were to ally with a particular family, and we are told by the *Vita* of Wulfthryth's cousin Wulfhild, abbess of Barking, written by Goscelin in the 1080s (so a long time after the Norman Conquest), that Edgar had intended to marry Wulfhild and not Wulfthryth, but that they were cousins. Wulfhild, however, was a professed nun, and despite Edgar attempting to seduce her at the house of her aunt, Edgar was eventually content to marry Wulfthryth, who had not taken her vows. As an apology for his behaviour, Edgar made Wulfhild the abbess of Barking:

> Although the attempted seduction of Wulfhild provided Goscelin with the opportunity to present Edgar in the common place hagiographical role of the powerful man who puts a saint's chastity to the test, the tone in general towards him is approving. He is a *rex strenuissimus* and praised for his generosity.[46]

However, the ire of the biographer quickly turns to Edgar's third wife. More in due course.[47]

The name of Wulfthryth is provided, by these later sources, that of Goscelin's *Vita S. Edithe*, a life of Wulfthryth and Edgar's sainted daughter. But two charters do survive in the fourteenth-century cartulary of Wilton.

S766, dated to 968, and surviving in one manuscript reads:

> King Edgar to Wilton Abbey; confirmation of land given to the church by Wulfthryth, consisting of 10 hides at South Newton, 10 at Sherrington, 20 at (Kingston?) Deverill, 3 at

Baverstock and 3 at Frustfield, Wilts; and 10 at Watchingwell in Calbourne, Isle of Wight.[48]

S799, dated to 974, also surviving in the same manuscript reads:

King Edgar to Wulfthryth, abbess, and Wilton Abbey; confirmation of privileges and land including land at Chalke, Wiltshire.[49]

Yorke believes the first of these charters, S766, 'may be evidence of a handsome settlement made to Wulfthryth when she separated from Edgar, that she had confirmed as the possession of the nunnery soon after'.[50]

It is believed that Eadgyth/Edith, Wulfthryth's daughter with Edgar, was kept with her mother at the nunnery over which Wulfthryth was the abbess. Eadgyth/Edith is said to have died in 984, and was quickly revered as a saint, as was Wulfthryth herself, on her death in *c.*1000.

The relationship between Edgar's surviving wives following his death is worthy of consideration. During the reforming movements undertaken on England's religious houses, there is a suggestion that Elfrida was made responsible for the nunneries, not just as an overseer, but as someone with a marked interest in their wealth and lands. As such, Elfrida may have found opposition at Wilton, from Abbess Wulfthryth, and also from Barking, under Abbess Wulfhild, but more of this shortly.

It is also quite ironic that both women, Wulfthryth and Elfrida, seem to have died within a year or two of each other. They were to get no relief from one another.

Ælfthryth /Elfrida, third wife to King Edgar

Ælfthryth/Elfrida, daughter of Ealdorman Ordgar *c.*945–17 November 1001/1002

m. 1. Æthelwold, the ealdorman of the East Angles (d.962)

      Ælfflæd, her stepdaughter

m. 2. Edgar, king of the English (d.975)

      Edmund *c.*966–d.971
      Æthelred II *c.*966–d.1016

As with many of the royal women of the tenth century, Lady Elfrida's[51] origins are not clear. Her father, Ealdorman Ordgar, is mentioned, but seems to have attained his ealdormany because of his daughter's marriage, and therefore, the king did not set out to marry the daughter of an ealdorman, but felt it necessary to promote her father on their marriage. This might also have been the case with Edmund's marriage to Æthelflæd, his second wife. While it is difficult to be sure of this, it does appear that Ordgar only began to witness the king's charters as '*dux*' from 964, the supposed date of the union. Prior to this, he had been a '*ministri*' during Eadwig's reign.[52] Ordgar witnesses four charters during Eadwig's reign, from 957 onwards. It would be interesting to know if Ordgar was one of Eadwig's appointees, as he attempted to develop a party to run counter to that of his grandmother, Eadgifu, and his brother, Edgar.

> Here, in this year, King Edgar took Ælfthryth for his queen;
> she was the daughter of Ealdorman Ordgar.[53]

There are later, and rather scurrilous, accounts regarding the union of Elfrida and Edgar. These stem from the fact that while she was Edgar's third wife, he was also her second husband. Her previous union had been with Ealdorman Æthelwold of the East Angles, son of Ealdorman Athelstan Half-King, discussed in relation to Ælfwynn, the second Lady of the Mercians.

It appears as though Elfrida had no children with her first husband, but that he might have had children from his first marriage, a daughter named Ælfflæd, for whom Elfrida and Edgar founded the nunnery at Romsey, where their son Edmund was later buried. By the eleventh century, Ælfflæd was venerated as a saint.[54]

We must therefore assume Elfrida was Ealdorman Æthelwold's second wife.

Ealdorman Æthelwold died in 962, having succeeded his father, Ealdorman Athelstan Half-King on his somewhat hasty retirement to Glastonbury in 956/7. It did not take long for Edgar to decide to remarry, although his second wife, Wulfthryth, had not long since given birth to their daughter, Edith. This is where the legends of Edgar's union with Elfrida begin.

A later story is told of how Edgar had determined to marry Elfrida, but he sent Ealdorman Æthelwold to discuss the arrangements with her, only for Æthelwold to fall in love with Elfrida and claim her as his wife. Edgar could only marry Elfrida's on Æthelwold's death, which William of Malmesbury in his *Gesta Regum Anglorum*, informs was actually murder on the part of the king.

'The king had given him a task respecting Ælfthryth [Elfrida], daughter of Ordgar, ealdorman of Devon, whose beauty had beguiled the eyes of all those who brought news of it, until through them its praises reached the king's ear.'

Having tricked the king and advised that Elfrida/Ælfthryth was 'a girl of ordinary everyday appearance', the king learned the truth of the rumours and determined to meet Elfrida/Ælfthryth:

> Æthelwold hastened on ahead to see his wife, begging her to think of his own survival and to dress herself to look as ugly as she could … She found the heart to break faith with her wretched lover and her first husband, and sat down at the mirror to paint her face … All happened as she intended. He [Edgar] fell in love with her at first sight so passionately that, concealing his resentment, he sent for the ealdorman to come hunting in the forest of Wherwell, and there pierced him with a javelin … To expiate the crime a monastery was built on the spot by Ælfthryth [Elfrida], which is still inhabited by a large community of nuns.[55]

There were also some difficulties regarding the legitimacy of the marriage, perhaps because Wulfthryth still lived, or perhaps because of the alleged adultery the pair had committed while Æthelwold lived, or perhaps even because Æthelflæd still lived. Gaimar reports that:

> It was not more than a month after this
> That king Eadgar [Edgar] was in London.
> In his bed he lay, he and the Queen.
> Around them was a curtain
> Delicately wrought of crimson cloth.
> Behold archbishop Dunstan
> Very early came into the room.
> Against the bedpost inlaid with vermilion,
> The archbishop leaned.
> To the king he spoke in English.
> He asked who that was
> Who lay with him in his bed.

The king answered, 'It is the queen
'Ælfthryth [Elfrida], to whom this kingdom is attached.'
Said the archbishop, 'That is false.
'Better it were that you were dead
'Than to lie thus in adultery,
'Your souls will go to torment.'[56]

These stories, as with those concerning Wulfthryth's union with Edgar, are more concerned with presenting Edgar as a womaniser than with actually recording how the two met. The passage of time between the origination of these stories and the events they portray also lend themselves to other factors at play.

It must be considered that Edgar was perhaps unhappy with his union with Wulfthryth, or maybe, and this is something that we do not tend to consider, there had been complications following the birth of Edith. Maybe Wulfthryth was believed unable to have more children. Or, it might simply have been a love match between Elfrida and Edgar. Bishop Æthelwold, a supporter of the Wulfthryth match, became a supporter of the union with Elfrida. There was no doubt a reason for this. He must have been content with the reasons behind the divorce of the Wulfthryth match. Bishop Æthelwold and Elfrida were firm allies in later years.

Elfrida then, heralded from a powerful West Country family. Her father, and specifically her brother, are associated with the foundation of Tavistock Abbey. John of Worcester informs that Ordgar founded the monastery in 961. Charter S838, surviving in two manuscripts, with some debate about its authenticity, states that it was founded by his son.[57] This information comes from William of Malmesbury, as seen previously. If the union was political, then perhaps Edgar was moving to counter a threat from that area of his kingdom. Eadwig's wife, Ælfgifu, and her family were strongly associated with the same region. Her brothers were becoming prominent at court and perhaps Edgar feared a faction developing around the divorced wife of his now dead, older brother. Æthelweard was not promoted to the ealdordom, it seems, until after Edgar's death.

It could also have been an attempt to counter the threat posed by so many of Eadwig's chosen appointees still having influence at court. Equally, losing such a valuable ally so early in his reign, through the death of Ealdorman Æthelwold, Elfrida's first husband and potentially Edgar's foster brother, may have opened up a chasm for Edgar. Yes,

Æthelwold had three brothers who would all be successful throughout Edgar's reign, but perhaps Edgar wished to make good on that loss and ensure his control of the East Anglian ealdordom (which had lost two ealdormen (Athelstan Half-King, and his oldest son) in only a short space of time)), by marrying the ealdorman's widow (if we consider Cnut's marriage to Lady Emma, after Æthelred II's death as a later example of a 'new' king taking over the legitimacy of a previous king by marrying their widow). Of course, other than the story told above about how Elfrida, Æthelwold and Edgar met, we do not know if they knew one another throughout Elfrida's first marriage. Neither do we know the identity of Æthelwold's first wife and what befell her.

The union, it appears, took place in 964. And it is believed that when the marriage occurred, Elfrida was consecrated as queen. She appears as a witness to the king's charters from 964,[58] with the designation 'queen'. She is 'the first West Saxon queen to be given such a designation in witness lists'.[59] She is England's first crowned queen, and this marks her as different from all her predecessors, even those who might have been designated as queen. They would have been queen of Wessex or queen of the Anglo-Saxons.

Of perhaps most significance for a perceived 'changing of the guard' at Edgar's court is the New Minster refoundation charter of 966.[60] By the date of this charter, Elfrida had already successfully given the king a son, Edmund, even if he was not to survive his childhood. By providing the important male heir, Elfrida had proven her worth as the king's wife. She is listed on the charter as the most senior of the royal women, even above that of Lady Eadgifu, Edgar's grandmother, and the woman who had steered England through some of its most difficult years. This would be the last attestation from Eadgifu, and she must have died soon afterwards, either having retired to a nunnery, or while still a member of the king's court. Yorke considers whether Elfrida's position was perhaps merely inherited from Eadgifu as it had 'come to be seen as necessary for the smooth running of the court. Ælfthryth [Elfrida] was succeeded in her turn by her daughter-in-law Emma of Normandy, under whom the potential for turning queenship into an office was taken further.'[61]

However, it was under Elfrida's son that her position became more exalted, just as with Eadgifu. While a wife, Elfrida may have been termed as queen in the charters that survive, she was not often in a position of great prominence, but rather to be found after the archbishops and bishops.[62]

To return to the refoundation charter of the New Minster. It is Elfrida and Edgar's son, Edmund, who witnesses in third position, after only the king and Archbishop Dunstan. Edmund was not the king's oldest son. That was Edward, born to Edgar's first wife. And yet, Edward witnesses after his younger half-brother. The document reads, in translation, 'Edmund Ætheling, the legitimate son of the aforementioned king' (*clito legitimus*).[63] After this came Edward. 'Edward Ætheling, begotten by the same king' (*clito procreates*).[64]

This difference in status between the two sons appears to have been further signalled by 'the fact that the crosses of Edmund and Ælftthryth are filled with gold, while that of Edward has been left as a painted outline'.[65] Yorke has stated that it cannot be known whether this occurred at the time of the production of the manuscript or has been added at a later date, i.e. were Elfrida and her oldest son singled out for this honour at the time, or did it occur at a later date?

In 971, the *Anglo-Saxon Chronicle* A reports, 'Here the ætheling Edmund passed away, and his body lies at Romsey.'[66] The royal couple were no doubt devastated by the loss of their son, and they chose to bury him at the nunnery where Elfrida's stepdaughter was living. This must have given some comfort.

In 973, King Edgar was consecrated as the king, for what seems to have been, a second time, although when he was first consecrated is unknown. It is the events of 973 that are mentioned, nothing earlier. It is highly likely that Lady Elfrida was either consecrated for the first time at this date or that she too underwent a second coronation.

The *Anglo-Saxon Chronicle* A records this second coronation as follows:

> Here, Edgar, ruler of the English,
> Was consecrated as king in a great assembly
> In the ancient town of Ache-man's city –
> The warriors swelling in the island also call it
> By the other terms Baths. There was great rejoicing
> Come to all on that blessed day,
> Which children of men name and call
> Pentecost Day. There were gathered,
> As I have heard, a pile of priests,
> A great multitude of monks,
> Of learned men. By then had passed
> Reckoned by number, ten hundred years,

From the time of birth of the illustrious King,
Shepherd of Lights – except there remained
Twenty-seven of the number of years,
As the writing say. Thus nigh on a thousand years
Of the Lord of Victories had run on when this befell;
And Edmund's offspring, bold in deeds and conflict,
Was nine-and-twenty years in the world when this came about,
And then in the 30th was consecrated prince.[67]

As part of the religious reforms over which Edgar presided, one of the important elements was to enhance the position not only of the king but also the queen. It has been noted when considering Athelstan, that there was some concern that he was born before his father was king, and his mother was not a queen. This made him less 'throne-worthy' in the eyes of some, at least when it came time to determine who would succeed his father.

Under Edgar and his third wife, change may have been taking place to resolve this issue. As such, the son of a consecrated father and mother was more acceptable as a future king, as one who had been born only to a consecrated father. However, 'the second coronation ordo and other references to the event emphasise her [Elfrida's] role as the king's consort and bed companion rather than granting her any position comparable to the king's.'[68]

The words from the *Regularis Concordia*, developed in the late 960s and early 970s to ensure the adoption of the Benedictine form of monasticism, state:

> And he [Edgar] saw to it wisely that his queen Ælfthryth
> [Elfrida], should be the protectress and fearless guardian of
> the monasteries; so that he himself helping the men and his
> consort helping the women there should be no cause for any
> breath of scandal.[69]

Edgar's death, when it came in 975, was unexpected. He was still a young man, no older than 32 at his death, if the entry for the coronation in the *Anglo-Saxon Chronicle* is correct. Once more, the *Anglo-Saxon Chronicle* A records the death in verse:

Here Edgar, king of the English,
Ended earthly pleasures; he chose another light,

Radiant and happy, and abandoned this poor,
This transitory life. The children of nations
Men on earth everywhere in this native turf,
Those who have been rightly trained in the art of reckoning,
Name the month that the young Edgar,
Ring-giver of his warriors, departed from life,
The month of July, on its eighth day;
And his son afterwards succeeded
To the royal kingdom, and ungrown child,
Leader of earls, whose name was Edward.[70]

It was not Elfrida's son who succeeded his father, but rather, Edward, Æthelred's oldest half-brother. Elfrida attests no charters during the brief, three-year period of her stepson's rule. Only with the death or martyring of Edward in 978 and the accession of Æthelred does Elfrida once more appear in charters, sixteen of Æthelred's charters in total,[71] during the rest of her life. She attests more charters for her husband than her son, but seems to have been more influential during the life of her son.[72]

If Edward was no more than 15 when he became king, then Æthelred was perhaps no older than 11. His name does not appear in the New Minster refoundation charter dated to 966, although his older brother's does. This perhaps points to the fact that he had not yet been born in 966.

Elfrida's part in the murder of Edward the Martyr is found in a number of sources. One of those closest to the time period is the *Anonymous Life of St Oswald, Archbishop of York*, now thought to have been written by Byrhtferth, the full text of which can be found alongside a discussion of this source. It makes mention of the queen, Elfrida, although it does not specifically lay the blame for Edward's death at her feet, but rather those staying with her.[73]

In his discussion of Shaftesbury, William of Malmesbury also lays the blame for the murder of Edward the Martyr at the feet of Lady Elfrida once more:

> He was murdered, though innocent, by a stepmother's guile, and lifted up to heaven. He was first buried at Wareham, a town near the sea, and not far from Corfe, where he was killed. His body lay there for three years. His enemies had envied his royal renown while he was alive, and after his death they begrudged him a burial in holy ground. But

God's power was at hand to raise to triumph the guiltless one by the fame of his miracles. For at his grave lights shown from the sky, the lame man walked, the dumb man used his tongue again, all illnesses alive gave way to health.

William then tells the story of how the 'murderess' of Edward the Martyr wanted to visit the gravesite of these miracles but that her animals were unable to get to it, despite being attacked with whips, and so she allowed for someone else to take command and 'the sacred remains were lifted from their ignominious grave and taken in great pomp to Shaftesbury'.[74]

This then is the story of Edward's body being moved to Shaftesbury by Ealdorman Ælfhere.

While Elfrida is not named as the murderess in this section, the very next part concentrates on Wilton and we are told that Wherwell was founded by Ælfthryth/Elfrida, 'murderess of St Edward, as an act of penance'. While Tavistock 'was started by Ordgar, earl of Devon, father of the Ælfthryth who was the wife of king Edgar'.[75]

The death of Edward ensured that Æthelred became king in his place. There does not seem to have been any opposition to his rule, and certainly, it would have been difficult to find another who had a claim to rule England.

'In this year Æthelred was consecrated as king on the Sunday, fourteen days after Easter, at Kingston; and there were at his consecration two archbishops and ten diocesan bishops,' the *Anglo-Saxon Chronicle* C records.[76]

From 996, S877, a fascinating charter survives in a single manuscript, in which Æthelred gifts land to his mother in exchange for other land at Cholsey, and which contains the details of the man the land was confiscated from:

In the name of our God and Lord Jesus Christ, in the year of our Lord's incarnation 993 … in the eighteenth year of my rule, have conceded by a grant to my venerable mother, Ælfthyrth [Elfrida] by name, certain pieces of land in different places, namely seven ploughlands, in the place which is called Brabourne, and three and a half in the same place which is called Evegate; moreover two also in the field of the citizens, and three in addition in the place which the inhabitants are accustomed to call Nackington; and also three at Chalk and one at *Wirigenn*; on condition that she is to have and possess these aforesaid lands as long as she may retain the vital spirit unextinguished in the moral flesh; and then, indeed, she is to leave it to what heir she pleases in success to her just as we have indicated above, in eternal inheritance.

Truly, these aforesaid lands a certain man, by name Wulfbald, is known to have held, and they were awarded to the control of my right by the most just judgement of all my chief men, on account of the guilt of his crime, as is found written in what follows in an account in English. And I concede to her these territories in exchange for the land which she previously gave to me, i.e. Cholsey requiting a gift with a gift, desiring to obtain the divine promise: 'Give, and it shall be given to you'.

These are the crimes which Wulfband committed against his lord: first, when his father was dead, he went to his stepmother's land, and seized there everything that he found inside and outside, great and small. Then the king sent to him and ordered him to pay back the plundered goods; then he ignored that, and his wergild was assigned to the king. Then the king immediately sent to him and made the same demand; then he ignored that, and then a second time his wergild was assigned to the king. On top of that, he rode and seized the land of his kinsman, Brihtmær of Bourne. Then the king sent to him and ordered him to vacate that land; then he ignored that, and his wergild was assigned to the king a third time. And the king sent to him yet again, and ordered him off; then he ignored that and his wergild was assigned to the king a fourth time. Then took place the great assembly at London; Ealdorman Æthelwine was there and all the king's councillors. Then all the councillors who were there, both ecclesiastical and lay, assigned to the king all Wulfbald's property, and also placed him at the king's mercy, whether to live or to die. And he retained all this, uncompensated for, until he died. Afterwards, when he was dead, on top of all this, his widow went, with her child, and killed the king's thegn Eadmær, the son of Wulfbald's father's brother, and fifteen of his companions, on the land at Bourne which Wulfbald had held by robbery despite the king. And when Archbishop Æthelfar held the great synod at London, he and all his property were assigned to the king.[77]

Elfrida is believed to have been actively involved in the raising of her grandchildren.

The Wherwell cartulary states Elfrida's death occurred on 17 November 1002 – although it might have been in 1001. After her death, in charter S904, surviving in eight manuscripts, dated to 1002 her involvement in founding the nunnery is referenced:

> Ethelred, ruler of the English, 'co-regulus' of the British Isles, to the nunnery of Werewelle [Wherwell], founded by his mother Ælfthryth [Elfrida]. Confirmation of title to 70 mansae in different places; grant of an additional 60 cassati at Æthelingedene in Sussex [East and West Dean, Sussex], which formerly belonged to Queen Ælfthryth. The property of the house is to be held free of all but the three common dues. On the death of the Abbess [Heanflæd], the community may elect her successor, with the advice of their metropolitan.[78]

This charter was witnessed by Elfrida's grandsons, Athelstan, Ecgberht, Eadmund [Edmund], Eadred, Eadwig and Eadgar. It would be interesting to know what her grandsons thought of their grandmother once she was no longer a guiding force in their life.

Lady Elfrida suffers from having acquired a later and very scurrilous reputation during the eleventh century, and it is difficult to unpick the cause of this. It was common for the Anglo-Norman writers to cast aspersion on the lost kings and queens of England. But it is possible, considering Edgar's own reputation for acquiring nuns as partners, that this was merely a reflected bias against her, the intention to cast doubt on Edgar, not his third wife or even his second.

Equally, and following the discussion by Foot in *Veiled Women*, it should perhaps be noted that 'later Anglo-Saxon ecclesiastics discouraged second marriages and were utterly opposed to the taking of more than two marital partners'.[79] Equally, 'Any widow who took a husband within the space of that year would lose her morning gift and all her inheritance from her first husband; even if remarried by force she would lose her possessions unless she left her new spouse for good.'[80] Perhaps here is a reason for the obscurity of the wives of both Edgar and Edward the Elder.

Chapter 7

The Continental Connection

Ælfthryth, the Countess of Flanders

Ælfthryth, (*c.*875–7 June 929) daughter of King Alfred and Ealhswith
m. **Count Baldwin II** (b.*c.*863–918) of Flanders
  Arnulf I (Count of Flanders (*c.*900–965 r.918–965)
  m.1. unknown (mother of children isn't known for sure.)
  m.2. *c.*934 Adela, daughter of Herbert II of Vermandois
      Baldwin III of Bolougne (Count of Bolougne and Ternois
      r.*c.*955–961) (d.961)
      m. Matilda of Saxony
          Arnulf of Bolougne (b.*c.*958–*c.*987) (Count of
Bolougne 962–*c.*987)
          Liutgarde m. Wicman II, Count of Hamaland
          Hildegarde m. Thierry, Count of West Frisia
          Unknown third daughter m. Isaac, Count of Valenciennes/
          Cambrai

  Adalulf/Adelolf (Count of Bolougne (*c.*900–933 r.918–933)
      Illegitimate son, Baldwin Balzo d.973
  m. unknown
      Adalulf d.961/2
      Arnulf I (Count of Bolougne 961–*c.*988)
  Ealhswith/Ealswith/Ealswid
  Eormenthryth/Ermengarth
      A grandson called Ecgberht (parents unknown)
  Ælfthryth?

Ælfthryth[1] was a daughter of King Alfred and Lady Ealhswith. Asser writes that, 'Edward and Ælfthryth were at all times fostered at the royal court under the solicitous care of tutors and nurses, and indeed with the great love of all.'[2] There is some discussion that Edward and Ælfthryth may have been closer in age than Edward and Æthelflæd, and this might account for them spending so much time together.[3] Asser also notes that a number of children born to Alfred and Ealhswith did not survive to adulthood. However, Asser actually leaves off from completing how many of Alfred and Ealhswith's children perished. This might also account for why Edward and Ælfthryth were kept at the court, and it must be assumed, close to their parents.

Asser describes the education given to Edward and Ælfthryth. As Yorke has commented, 'Such descriptions are rare for Anglo-Saxon princes, but even scarcer for princesses, and this seems to be the only recorded instance of a prince and princess being given the same upbringing.'[4] She goes on to note that, 'Edward and Ælfthryth acquired the courtly virtues of humility, friendliness, and gentleness and both read secular and ecclesiastical works in English – the Psalms and Old English poems are specifically mentioned.'[5]

Asser goes into some detail about the education that Edward and Ælfthryth received, contrasting it with their brother, Æthelweard, who was not educated in the same way and was not kept with the court all of the time. It is believed that Æthelweard was taught at the monastic school centred on Glastonbury. Yorke believes this was a deliberate attempt by Alfred's official biographer, Asser, to show that Edward and his youngest sister were more esteemed than their (younger) brother. It was a means of perpetuating the belief that Edward was destined to rule Wessex, which, when Asser wrote, was by no means assured, whereas Ælfthyrth was destined to make a great marriage, which she might have already done, or, negotiations might have been taking place.

This union between Ælfthryth and Count Baldwin II is believed to have taken place sometime between Asser's writing and the death of Alfred in 899. As Æthelweard's *Chronicon* informs, Ælfthryth was married to Count Baldwin II of Flanders (879–918).[6] Count Baldwin II was the son of Alfred's stepmother, Judith, through her third marriage to Baldwin, Count of Flanders, with whom she eloped in 860, against her father's wishes. Perhaps this was a love match that had been denied her before. Judith had previously been married to Æthelwulf, King of Wessex, Alfred's father, and also to Æthelbald, King of Wessex, Alfred's brother. There is no record of children born to these unions.

Judith was a daughter of Charles the Bald (823–877), who in turn was the son of Louis the Pious (773–840), a son of Charlemagne (*c.*742–814). Charles the Bald was king of the Franks from 840–877 and emperor from 875–877.

So, what exactly was Flanders, and why might it have been a suitable province to ally with the Wessex king?

> Flanders has been described as the first real territorial principality to emerge in the Frankish kingdoms, though there is some dispute about its origin. Whether or not Charles the Bald should be credited with its creation, it is clear that the Viking invasions in the years following 879 gave Baldwin II the opportunity to assert himself in the region, and it is Baldwin II who is generally accepted as the first count of Flanders.[7]

The union made for Ælfthryth might well have been to service the interests of her father, giving him a powerful ally on the other side of the Channel, but it was not to a man who seems to have been often at peace. Prior to their marriage, Baldwin had frequently been at war with the Northmen and 'even appears to have used the Northmen's raids as a cover for his incorporation of Aardenburg *pagus* to his territories'.[8] Baldwin was growing his territory. And the Northmen were far from the only potential enemy.

'The political dynamics of northern France in the tenth century revolved around the rivalry between the Robertians and the Carolingians for control of Neustria, combined with the continued difficulties with Scandinavian raiders in the first half of the century.'[9] Even after their marriage, Baldwin II remained fiercely competitive. In 900 and perhaps *c.*902 he had two of his rivals, Archbishop Fulk and Herbert, assassinated.

Although not mentioned by Asser, presumably because the marriage union took place after he had completed work on his manuscript, Ælfthryth is usually accorded the title the Countess of Flanders, but it is unknown what title Baldwin II, took, as there are no surviving charters from his reign. There is a later charter, which does describe her as *comitisse* and her sons as *comitum*, but this may be spurious.[10]

Ælfthryth is mentioned in the will of her father. Not only does she receive £100 from her father, alongside her two sisters and her mother, but she also received 'the estate at Wellow, at Ashton, and at Chippenham'.[11] It should not be deemed as strange to think that she held on to these estates even when married and living in Flanders. Lady Godifu/Gode, the daughter of Æthelred II and Lady Emma, held estates throughout her two marriages on the continent, and bequeathed the lands to her son, Ralph, which he was able to then command when he joined his uncle, King Edward the Confessor, on his return to England from exile at his uncle's court in Normandy.

Ælfthryth's children, two sons, named Adalulf (after his grandfather Æthelwulf of Wessex) and Arnulf, would be important during the reign of King Athelstan, who they knew and communicated with, as will be seen later. On the death of their father in 918, the two sons divided the territory controlled by their father. Arnulf was known as the Count of Flanders, Adalulf as the Count of Bolougne.

According to charter S1205d, dated 918 and surviving in three manuscripts, Ælfthryth and her sons granted land at Lewisham, Greenwich and Woolwich to St Peter's Abbey, Ghent.[12] That said, there is some debate about the authenticity of this charter.

Ælfthryth and Baldwin, we are told by Æthelweard's *Chronicon*, also had two daughters, Ealhswith/Ealswith, no doubt named for Ælfthryth's mother, and Eormenthryth/Ermengarth.[13] No more is known of these granddaughters of Alfred and Ealhswith. Another daughter is also mentioned, Ælfthryth (by Foot), but I can see no further mention of this elsewhere. Tanner believes that 'it is probable that Hilduin (Count of Tournai) married one of Baldwin II's daughters.'[14]

Ælfthryth may have died *c.*929. It would be interesting to know if she was involved in any of the marriage negotiations between her nieces and their continental husbands before her death, and if so, if she ever returned to Wessex after her marriage to Baldwin. It is unknown if she had any political influence after the death of her husband.

Her sons were to have several interactions with their English relatives. William of Malmesbury informs that Adalulf was involved in the embassy to Athelstan's court on behalf of Hugh the Great, when he proposed a union with Eadhild, although there is no corroboration of this from other sources. That does not mean it did not happen, merely that the only knowledge of it is based on a much later source.

'The leader of this mission was Adulf [Adalulf], son of Baldwin, count of Flanders by Æthelswith [Ælfthryth] daughter of King Edward [should read Alfred].'[15]

The story of Ælfthryth's sons, Arnulf and Adalulf will continue shortly.

The daughters of Edward the Elder and his second wife, Lady Ælfflæd

Eadgifu

Eadgifu, daughter of King Edward the Elder and Lady Ælfflæd

b.*c*.900–951

m. 1. *c*.918 Charles III of West Frankia 879–929 (King of West Frankia 898–922)

    Louis b.921/922–954 (King of West Frankia 936–954)

m. 2. *c*.951 Herbert 'the Elder' *c*.910–980/4

Eadgifu[16] was perhaps the oldest daughter of King Edward the Elder, and his second wife, Lady Ælfflæd. She is not to be confused with her stepmother, Eadgifu, but it is quite easy to do so.

The assumption that Eadgifu was the oldest daughter born to Edward the Elder and his second wife, stems from the fact that she was the first to marry. And what a union it was. While her aunt, Countess Ælfthryth, had married Count Baldwin II of Flanders, Eadgifu would be wed to Charles III, King of West Frankia (879–929), who ruled the kingdom from 898 to 922, although he co-ruled from 893 onwards. He is often known as Charles the Simple. This union is written about by Æthelweard in the prologue to his *Chronicon*: 'Eadgyfu [Eadgifu] was the name of the daughter of King Eadweard [Edward], the son of Ælfred … and she was your great-aunt and was sent into the country of Gaul to marry the younger Charles.'[17]

Events in West Frankia at this time could easily fill another book but, suffice to say, this was a union of some prestige for the granddaughter of King Alfred and one which saw her become the queen of the West Franks. She might well have thought this was quite an advancement on the role her mother and stepmother played at the Wessex court.

It is somewhat ironic that while faced with a young stepmother at home in the final years of her father's reign, Eadgifu herself would be married to a man much her senior. Charles III fathered six daughters with his wife, Frederuna[18] as well as four illegitimate sons with his concubines.[19]As such, on the death of his first wife in 917, Charles had no legitimate heir to rule after him. Charles III would have been a similar age to Eadgifu's father.

Eadgifu is not mentioned in the *Anglo-Saxon Chronicle*, but she does feature in *The Annals of Flodoard of Reims 919–966*. Foot maintains that as Eadgifu's marriage does not feature in the work of Flodoard, it must have occurred before he began writing and, therefore prior to 919.[20] Under the year 938, we are told something of the lands that Eadgifu held from her husband.

'Louis's father [King Charles the Simple] had given Tusey on the Meuse and other *villae* pertaining to it to Louis's mother [Eadgifu] as a dowry.'[21]

Yet, Charles III did not rule a quiet kingdom, far from it, in fact. It might be that the union was devised to secure Charles's kingship by allying with the House of Wessex, as well as ensuring he left a legitimate male heir. The union took place at some time between 917 and 919. Louis, Eadgifu and Charles's son, was born in 921/922, and his birth seems to have coincided with Charles losing control of his kingdom to an overpowerful nobleman, who ruled as Robert, King of the West Franks from 922 to 923 when Charles III was briefly reinstated before being deposed once more and imprisoned, where he would remain until his death in 929.

What happened next is slightly more difficult to determine for Eadgifu, but it is known that Louis was sent to the Wessex royal court, to be fostered firstly by her father and then by her half-brother, Athelstan.[22] It is likely that Louis was a similar age to Edward the Elder's younger children. If Eadgifu did not accompany her son to England, then it is possible that Louis simply exchanged one Eadgifu for another – his mother, for his mother's stepmother. If Eadgifu returned to Wessex in 923 as well, she would have been in Wessex when her father died, her full brother became king, albeit briefly, only for Athelstan, her half-brother, to become king. It would be interesting to know Eadgifu's personal thoughts on these matters, but it is impossible. There is simply no record of this.

What is known with more surety, is that on Charles's death, in 929, Eadgifu was certainly once more living in England with her son Louis. And she would do so until 936 when Louis regained his kingship, and Eadgifu returned to West Frankia as the king's mother.

Louis's reinstatement does seem to have had much to do with his uncle by marriage, Hugh of the Franks (*c*.895–956), married to his aunt Eadhild.

We are told by Flodoard:

> Louis's uncle, King Athelstan, sent him to Frankia along with bishops and others of his *fideles* after oaths had been given by the legates of the Franks. Hugh and the rest of the

nobles of the Franks set out to meet Louis when he left the ship, and they committed themselves to him on the beach at Bolougne-sur-Mer just as both sides had previously agreed. They then conducted Louis to Laon and he was consecrated king, anointed and crowned by Lord Archbishop Artoldus (of Rheims) in the presence of the leading men of the kingdom and more than twenty bishops.[23]

But all might not be quite as bland as Flodoard states. Hugh might have been married to Eadhild, Louis's aunt, but he was also an extremely powerful nobleman, brother to the previous king, Ralph. As McKitterick states, 'No doubt Hugh calculated that he would be able to exert effective power within the kingdom as the young monarch's uncle, chief advisor and supporter.'[24]

The French writer, William of Jumièges in his *Gesta Normannorum Ducum*, also offers the following account from around 1060–1070:

When Athelstan, king of the English, heard of the great reputation of the famous duke, he sent messengers to him with many gifts and begged him to make effort to restore his nephew Louis to the throne of his father King Charles – who had been caught by the snares of bishop Ascelin [here, there is an error, with new stories becoming conflated] and died in prison – and also for his sake to forgive the Breton Alan for the crimes he had committed against him. For Louis and his mother Eadgifu had sought refuge with King Athelstan, after Louis's father had been captured in an ambush by the Franks, so as not to become another victim of their cruelty.[25]

Young Louis would only have been about 16 when he was proclaimed king of West Frankia. He was also a virtual stranger to those he now ruled, having been fostered at the Wessex/English court since 923. He was known as Louis d'Outremer or Transmarinus, both meaning 'overseas'. The reason Hugh did not claim the kingship directly for himself, but determined to rule through another, is, McKitterick states, because it would have proven to be wildly unpopular, and the disintegrating kingdom of Charlemagne was already an unruly place. Equally, ruling through another might not have been new to Hugh. Hugh's sister, Emma, had been married to Ralph, who ruled after Robert, from 923 to 936, while it was their father, Robert, who had previously usurped Charles III.

Louis was consecrated on 19 June 936, but no more than a year later he abandoned his uncle's assistance and took himself to his mother at Laon where he made his own appointment to the arch-chancellorship, Artald, Bishop of Reims, and also formed an alliance with Hugh the Black of Burgundy, who was the brother of the Ralph who had ruled after the death of Louis's father, and was therefore Hugh's brother by marriage. (As in England at this time, when there are many people with similar names, the same can certainly be said of West Frankia. For now, we have Hugh the Great and Hugh the Black.)

While Louis attempted to exert some control over his nobles, he was a stranger in West Frankia. It would be interesting to know what part his mother played in securing his kingship for him. Certainly, while in exile in Wessex, she would have seen how her stepmother, Eadgifu, protected her young sons, being groomed for the kingship after the death of their uncle, Athelstan. Did Louis rule with the powerful support of his uncle in England, and mother behind him? What must the arguments have done for relationships between Eadgifu and her sister Eadhild? These, regrettably, are all matters that simply cannot be determined, but are worthy of consideration.

Eadgifu held the domain of Anthony and the abbey of St Mary at Laon, while the king's mother. This passed to her daughter-in-law, perhaps with some unhappiness, as Louis presented them to his wife, Gerberga, not long after his mother had finally remarried to Herbert, the son of Herbert II of Vermandois in 951. Eadgifu did not live long following this union, and it is curious to question why she waited so long to remarry, having been a widow since 929. Especially considering her choice of husband, who was the son of the man who had acted as her first husband's gaoler. It is not hard to determine why Louis thought to punish her by removing her lands and giving them into the hands of his wife.

The union of Louis and his wife took place against a backdrop of complex political and military manoeuvring between East and West Frankia, where another of Louis's aunts, Eadgyth, was now the wife of Otto of East Frankia, son of Henry I (d.936). Louis's wife, Gerberga, was Otto's sister, and she had already been married, but her husband had died in bitter infighting in Lotharingia.

Children born to the union of Louis and Gerberga would have been Eadgifu's grandchildren, as well as Eadgyth's nieces and nephews.

The marriage of Eadgifu and her second husband is recorded in *The Annals of Flodoard*:

> Queen Ottoberge [Eadgifu], the mother of King Louis, left Laon escorted by men of the brothers Heribert [Herbert] and Adalbert to meet with Heribert. Heribert received her and then married her, which greatly angered King Louis. The king took the abbey of Saint Mary, which she was holding in Laon, and gave it to his wife Gerberga. Moreover, he brought the fisc of Attigny under his domination.[26]

While Eadgifu is mentioned mostly in sources from West Frankia, her name does appear in *Great Domesday Book* with property recorded of 6 carucates in Denton or Wyville, Lincolnshire (in 1066), which was then held by Robert de Tosny.[27] We do not know when this land was gifted to Eadgifu, but presumably it would have been by her father or half-brother when she was living in England.

Eadhild

Eadhild, daughter of King Edward the Elder and Lady Ælfflæd
b.*c.*902–937

m. Hugh, the Great, *dux Francorum c.*895–956
    No surviving children

Eadhild,[28] perhaps the second daughter of Edward the Elder and his second wife, Lady Ælfflæd, marriage to Hugh the Great, later known as *dux Francorum,* was another continental dynastic marriage similar to that of her sister. It would be interesting to know if Eadgifu played any part in the negotiations for the marriage. Alas, no sources survive to inform us about this. Under 926, Flodoard of Reims states, 'Hugh, son of Robert, married a daughter of Edward the Elder, the king of the English, and the sister of the wife of Charles.'[29] This was not Hugh's first marriage, he had previously been married to a daughter of the Count of Maine, but the union was childless.

    There is no record of the marriage in the *Anglo-Saxon Chronicle*. However, it is mentioned in Æthelweard's *Chronicon*, 'Eadhild, furthermore, was sent to be the wife of Hugo, son of Robert.'[30] And also in Flodoard's Annals, which record, 'Hugh, [the Great], the son of Robert, married [Eadhild] a daughter of Edward [the Elder], the king of the English, and the sister of [Eadgyfu] [Eadgifu]the wife of [King] Charles [the Simple].'[31]

There is a later, really quite detailed account in the twelfth-century source of William of Malmesbury's *Gesta Regum Anglorum*. For this part of the narrative, William claims to have obtained the information from a certain very old book. Think of that what you will. He describes Eadhild as 'in whom the whole mass of beauty, which other women have only a share, had flowed into one by nature', was demanded in marriage from her brother by Hugh of the Franks.[32]

According to William of Malmesbury, during the marriage negotiations, Hugh presented to Athelstan, via Adalulf, the son of Baldwin II of Flanders, and therefore cousin to Athelstan and Eadhild:

> spices and perfumes never smelt in England before, precious jewels (including emeralds), a vase made of onyx, horses richly caparisoned and a gold crown encrusted with gems. Hugh presented Athelstan with no fewer than three priceless relics – the sword of Constantine in whose hilt one of the nails of the Passion was mounted, the Holy Lance 'which Charlemagne had won in the war against the Saracens' ... and the standard of St Maurice which Charlemagne had brought back from Spain.[33]

Athelstan is said by William of Malmesbury to have 'comforted the passionate suitor with the hand of his sister',[34] as well as equally fine gifts.

Hugh was a very wealthy individual. His family:

> commanded the region corresponding to ancient Neustria between the Loire and the Seine, except for the portions ceded to the Vikings between 911 and 933. Hugh also possessed land in the Touraine, Orleanais, Berry, Autunois, Maine and north of the Seine as far as Meaux, and held the countships of Tours, Anjou and Paris. Many powerful viscounts and counts were his vassals and deputies ... a number of wealthy monasteries were also in Robertian [the family named after his father] hands. Hugh himself was lay abbot of St Martin of Tours, Marmoutier, St Germain of Auxerre (after 937), St Denis,

Morienval, St Riquier, St Valéry and possibly St Aignan of Orleans, St Germain-des-Pres and St Maur des Fosses.[35]

Once more, we are left with no knowledge of what Eadhild thought of her marriage to Hugh. Whether she played a part in her nephew, Louis, being restored to the kingdom of West Frankia, is equally unknown. However, King Athelstan was, it seems, at the height of his powers in 936. He was able to 'interfere' in the rule of at least two, and potentially three countries (West Frankia, Brittany and Norway), ensuring his foster sons received their birthrights. The role that his sisters played in the negotiations for Louis's return to West Frankia, if they had any, have not been recorded, but it cannot be a coincidence that Louis was about 16 years old, while his aunt, married to Count Hugh, was childless at the time. Louis was young enough to need a regent if he was proclaimed as king by the West Frankish nobility.

Eadhild, died in 937, childless. What her legacy might have been can be interpreted from Hugh's marriage to his third wife, Hadwig, another daughter of Henry of the East Franks, who had six children with Hugh, one of whom, Hugh Capet (*c.*940–996) was king of the West Franks from 987 to 996. Through their son, Robert II, the Capetian kings of France claimed descent. Hugh might not have lived to see his son's success, dying in 956, but his dynasty was certainly successful.

Eadhild did not live to see the rather vicious events of the late 930s and 940s, where sister was pitched against sister, East Frankia against West Frankia, and in which her widowed, and then quickly remarried husband, was to play a huge role.

Eadgyth

Eadgyth, daughter of Edward the Elder, and his second wife, Lady Ælfflæd

m. Otto I of East Frankia in 929 or 930, son of Henry the Fowler of East Frankia

> Liudolf, Duke of Bavaria m. Ida
>> Matilda, Abbess of Essen (Æthelweard's *Chronicon* is addressed to Matilda)
>> Otto
> Liudgar m. Conrad the Red, Duke of Lotharingia
>> Otto

Eadgyth,[36] a daughter of Edward the Elder, and his second wife, Lady Ælfflæd, has her marriage mentioned in the entry for the D text of the *Anglo-Saxon Chronicle* under the year 924. Alongside Athelstan's unnamed biological sister, she is the only one of Edward's daughters to be mentioned in the *Anglo-Saxon Chronicle*. 'and he gave his sister across the sea to the son of the King of the Old Saxons (Henry)'.[37] Foot notes that in the Mercian/Æthelflæd Register section of the *Anglo-Saxon Chronicle*, this sentence in 924 is unfinished. The D text chooses to complete this sentence differently, referencing the union of Eadgyth to Otto, as opposed to the union of Athelstan's unnamed sister to Sihtric of York. This then explains why the reference occurs in the annal entry for 924, whereas the union took place in 929/30, following a Saxon military triumph over the Slavs in the late summer of 929.[38]

Foot states that such a prestigious union 'helped to establish Henry's status as king; he probably conferred royal status on Otto at about this time'.[39] This union then, benefited the Wessex royal family, as they moved towards being the kings of all England, and the Saxon family of Saxony, as they too laid claim to the kingship of East Frankia.

Æthelweard's *Chronicon* adds to our knowledge by informing his readers that Athelstan sent two of his sisters for Otto to choose the one he found most agreeable to be his wife.

'King Athelstan sent another two [of his sisters] to Otho [Otto], the plan being that he should choose as his wife the one who pleased him. He chose Eadgyth.'[40] This story is also told in Hrotsvitha's *Gesta Ottonis*. 'He bestowed great honour upon Otto, the loving son of the illustrious king, by sending two girls of eminent birth, that he might lawfully espouse whichever one of them he wished.'[41]

Bishop Cenwald of Worcester accompanied both sisters to Saxony. The account of his visit can be witnessed in a confraternity book from St Galen, where he signed his name. Eadgyth was certainly the mother of a son and a daughter, Liudolf and Liudgar.

In a later entry, reference is made to the descendants of this union between Eadgyth and Otto, when in the C text of the *Anglo-Saxon Chronicle* for 982, mention is made of the ætheling Liudolf who was the 'son of Otto the Elder and King Edward's daughter'.[42] It was to Liudolf's daughter, Matilda, the abbess of Essen, that Æthelweard's *Chronicon* was addressed in his prologue, and the very reason why so much personal information was supplied. It seems then, that only fifty years after the marriage took place, the English had lost track of some of their royal sisters.

Queen Eadgyth would die, seemingly suddenly in 946, and so would not live to see her husband become Holy Roman Emperor. It would take a devastated King Otto five years to remarry. Eadgyth was revered as a saint in her adopted country.

The unnamed sister(s) Ælfgifu or Eadgifu

As mentioned above, by both Æthelweard's *Chronicon* and Hrotsvitha's *Gesta Ottonis,* King Athelstan is said to have sent two sisters to the court of Otto of Saxony for him to determine which he would marry. This sister has vexed historians, even Æthelweard in his *Chronicon* is unsure of her name,[43] and he wrote his text much earlier than other sources available, by *c.*978 at the latest. It would be hoped that a woman who left England only forty years earlier might have been remembered. Æthelweard believed she had married 'a certain king near the Alps, concerning whose family we have no information, because of both distance and the not inconsiderable lapse of time'.[44] He held out hopes that Matilda, to whom he dedicated his work, might be able to tell him more.

Hrotsvitha does not mention whom this sister married but names her as Aldiva, by which she meant the Old English name Eadgifu. William of Malmesbury names a second daughter born to Edward and his third wife as Eadgifu, but if this is correct, she would have been young at this time, no more than perhaps 11 or 12. This sister, William informs, married Louis, prince of Aquitaine. 'Eadgifu was a famous beauty, and was given in marriage by her brother Æthelstan [Athelstan] to Louis prince of Aquitaine.'[45] William did not believe this daughter was the one that accompanied Eadgyth to Saxony, but that another daughter, Ælfgifu, did so. But he followed the *Chronicon* in saying that this sister married 'a certain duke near the Alps'.

This is all very confusing. Foot comments, 'It would be prudent, as Edouard Hlawitschka has suggested, to remove one of these (sisters – Eadgifu and Ælfgifu) from our reckoning.'[46] As such, this sister's name is unknown, although it can be determined that she married Louis, the brother of Rudolf II of Burgundy, known as the king of Arles (912–937).[47] If this identification is correct then Rudolf II's son, Conrad

(937–993) married Matilda, daughter of Louis IV, king of the West Franks, and thus Ælfgifu's nephew by marriage married her great-niece, the granddaughter of Eadgifu.

> Louis, brother of Rudolf of Burgundy, and his English wife were influential figures in that region when Rudolf died young, leaving only a child, Conrad, as heir.[48]

More than this, it is impossible to say. It is unsettling to realise that the daughter of one of the House of Wessex's kings could so easily be 'lost' to our understanding today, and indeed, to that of her descendants only forty years later. This raises the awareness that if noble women could disappear from the written records, then so too could almost anyone.

The Wessex royal family on the continent

Or, was this what Edward the Elder and Athelstan hoped to avoid by not concluding marriage for their daughters and sisters with members of the English nobility.

As has been mentioned above, King Alfred's daughter, Ælfthryth married Baldwin II of Flanders. Baldwin was the son of Alfred's stepmother who had also been his sister by marriage before her marriage to Baldwin's father. During the tenth century, under Edward the Elder, and his son, Athelstan, the House of Wessex would make several continental marriages, choosing to ally with both the kingdom of the West Franks and the East Franks, as well as with two powerful noblemen on the continent. This was perhaps sound policy on the part of Edward and Athelstan. The thought of a rival royal claim in England to the throne was not a palatable one, and the early years of King Edward the Elder's reign had been made difficult by the assertions of his cousin, Æthelwold, son of Alfred's older brother, Æthelred I, until he died in 902/3 at the Battle of the Holme. Sooner to marry these daughters and sisters far from England's shores. The two daughters of Alfred's who made political matches secured Mercia as a permanent ally and also Flanders. It seems the Wessex royal family were determined to continue the policy after his death.

Equally, it might have been an attempt to dispense with the vast quantity of royal daughters born to Edward and his three wives. If this was the case, these marriages had varying degrees of success, but certainly show that these royal daughters were valuable prizes for kings and dukes in the slowly disintegrating Carolingian Empire. It might also have been specifically because they were Alfred's granddaughters; equally, their mother, Lady Ælfflæd, may have been determined to secure advantageous marriages for her daughters, perhaps when she found herself being replaced by her husband. Foot comments that, 'Edward must take much credit for initiating the policy that Athelstan would continue and develop to excellent effect of locating husbands for these women across the political divides of contemporary Europe.'[49]

Ortenberg has also made the suggestion, a beguiling one, that with the crumbling of the Carolingian Empire of Charlemagne, the rival claimants to the kingdoms evolving in the wake of this were as keen to look for a powerful ally, as the Wessex royal family might have been, to provide daughters with marriages where the offspring would not add to the already cluttered and well-served number of potential claimants to the kingdom. Ortenberg goes further and suggests that in the figure of Athelstan, these rival families found the heir to the Carolingian inheritance, an emperor, and indeed, Athelstan is himself styled as emperor in some of his charters.

'While the civil wars and the Viking attacks on the Continent had spelled the end of unity for the Carolingian Empire, which had already disintegrated into separate kingdoms, military successes had enabled Athelstan to triumph at home.'[50] Indeed, 'by the early 930s Athelstan was thus related to every major aristocratic family vying for power in West Francia':

> he was the cousin of Arnulf of Flanders, the brother-in-law of the late Charles the Simple (III) and now uncle to the current Carolingian king, Louis IV, brother-in-law to Hugh the Great and possibly to Conrad of Burgundy and to the Duke of Aquitaine ... he was related to at least six different ways to Carolingian family.[51]

And in the same vein, it must also be noted that during the 940s, 'Louis married his Aunt Edith's [Eadgyth] sister-in-law, Gerberga; subsequently he became brother-in-law to his uncle by marriage, Hugh, when the latter remarried ... Hadwig.'[52]

Ortenberg has also highlighted that following the death of Athelstan, which must indeed have been unexpected, it was the family of Eadgyth's through her husband, Otto I, who became the main force in Europe:

> Louis's rescue from Hugh's imprisonment through his uncle King Edmund of England and Gerberga's request to her brother Otto to come to her husband's help show to what extent, after the death of Æthelstan [Athelstan], it was the Liudolfings [the family of Otto] who had become the main force in Europe.[53]

Through his daughters, Edward the Elder's family extended into both East and West Frankia. In time, his grandson, great-grandson and great-great-grandson wore the crown of West Frankia (descended from Queen Eadgifu – Louis IV, Lothar and Louis V), while a great-grandchild through Queen Eadgyth's line became the pope (Pope Gregory V (996–999)) and another became Holy Roman Emperor (Conrad II).

But none of Edward's daughters birthed a dynasty that ruled for centuries. This is their tragedy and the reason their story is so little known.

To Edward goes the initiative of marrying Eadgifu to Charles of West Frankia, and he is also credited with Eadhild's marriage to Hugh, Count, and later Duke, of the Franks. It is interesting to think what Edward would have done with the remainder of his daughters had he lived longer.

And so, to pick up the story of Countess Ælfthryth's sons following her death in 929.

In 929, Arnulf allied with Hugh the Great, the husband of his cousin, Eadhild, in what would merely be one of many interactions between the two men, not all of them without violence. On this occasion, they united against a common enemy.

In 933, we are told by the author of *Gesta Abbatum S. Bertini Sithiensium* that:

> when the same King Eadwine [Edwin], driven by some disturbance in his kingdom, embarked on a ship, wishing to cross to this side of the sea, a storm arose and the ship was wrecked and he was overwhelmed in the midst of the waves. And when his body was washed ashore, Count Adelolf [Adalulf] since he was his kinsman, received it with honour and bore it to the monastery of St-Bertin for burial.[54]

This must have been before Adalulf's death, if this is a true record of what happened. Certainly, Edwin, Athelstan's half-brother, perished in 933, but whether he was purposefully drowned following an uprising against Athelstan, or whether he merely sought sanctuary with his Flanders relatives, and died on the way, is unknown.

Adalulf also died in 933. He left at least two legitimate sons, believed to have been named Arnulf, and perhaps also Adalulf, and also an illegitimate son, Baldwin Balzo. On the death of Adalulf in 933, Arnulf assumed control of his brother's holdings 'regardless of the claims of his nephews'.[55] Adalulf was buried at St Bertin, if the story of Edwin is correct, in the same place as his English cousin.

The identity of Arnulf's first wife is unknown. With her he seems to have had two daughters, an unnamed daughter who married Isaac, Count of Cambrai. His second daughter was called Liutgarde. The third daughter, Hildegarde, was perhaps the daughter of Arnulf and his second wife, as the name Hildegarde was a family name of the Vermandois dynasty. Arnulf married Adela (910–960) the daughter of Herbert II, Count of Vermandois, and his wife, Adela, the daughter of Robert, king of the West Franks from 922 to 923, in 934.

This marriage pitched Arnulf against his extended family connections. After all it was Herbert II who had been involved in the death of Charles III, Eadgifu's husband, and who had kept Charles III a prisoner in Peronne in 923.

However, Arnulf arranged for Louis IV to arrive at Bolougne on his return to West Frankia in 936.[56] This must have been done either at the request of Hugh the Great, who was instrumental in bringing Louis back to West Frankia, or perhaps, on the request of Arnulf's cousin, Athelstan. However, it should be noted that three of the main driving forces in West Frankia at this time were Arnulf of Flanders, Hugh the Great and Herbert II of Vermandois.

The year 936 could have been the culmination of all of Athelstan's plans, which was only reinforced in 937 and the great victory at Brunanburh against the Dublin Norse, the kingdom of the Scots, and Strathclyde. His death in 939, unexpected as he was only in his forties, made his young half-brother king and might well have added to the destabilisation between East and West Frankia at the time. Without Athelstan to sort out the bickering, the bickering continued.

In 938, Otto I of East Frankia was facing a rebellion in Saxony and Lotharingia, which Louis IV encouraged. Otto struck back and won the support of Arnulf and other men, including Hugh the Great and Herbert II. Arnulf, according to Flodoard, after capturing Montreuil in 939, and although his hold on his enemy's land was only brief, seems to have sent his enemy's children and wife to Athelstan as hostages.[57] Louis sought aid from Athelstan and Athelstan's fleet was sent to assist Louis. However, the fleet ravaged the Flemish coastline, and it is possible that this brought an end, if not Athelstan's death, to any joint accords between Arnulf and his cousin, Athelstan.

'For the rest of his reign there is no more evidence of friendly relations between the English and Flemish courts. Flanders became a haven for Englishmen out of favour at home.'[58] The most famous exile being Dunstan, during the reign of King Eadwig (955–959). The friendship between Flanders and what had become the English kingdom, which had begun with the marriage of Judith to Alfred's father, and continued with the marriage of Ælfthryth to Baldwin II, thus came to an end in 939.

However, the relatives of the Wessex royal house were by now, deeply embroiled in matters in both East and West Frankia. One of the rebels, Duke Gilbert of Lotharingia, drowned in the Rhine, and Louis IV married his widow, Gerberga, who was the sister of Otto I, without the permission of her brother. In 940, Louis won back Count Arnulf's allegiance. This royal marriage was perhaps a means of offsetting the third union of Hugh the Great with Hadwig, another of Otto's sisters.

In 942, William Longsword, the son and successor of Rollo, the Viking raider given land in Normandy by Charles III, was murdered at the instigation of Arnulf.[59] Once more, Arnulf was at war, and he only reconciled with Herluin in 944. In 945, Louis IV was taken hostage by Hugh the Great, who kept him captive until July 946 and he was only released in exchange for his youngest son being held as a hostage, during which time Gerberga prevailed on her brother, and Edmund, her cousin in England, to bring about Louis's release. Otto I sent an army to West Frankia, under the command of Conrad the Pacific, king of Burgundy in response to Gerberga's request. On Louis's release, Hugh the Great resumed his war, and Louis and Arnulf attacked Montreuil but failed to take it. Arnulf seized Amiens in 949 with the support of Louis IV. In 950, Hugh the Great besieged Arnulf in his fortress in Amiens, but Arnulf prevailed, only to be attacked once more by Hugh the Great in the spring of 951.

But 'by late 952, Arnulf had secured his control of the major cities and their castles along the Roman roads in the north – Boulogne, Thérouanne, Casset, Tournai, Arras and Amiens – and thereby secured his counties of Boulogne, Ternois, Artois, Ostrevant and Flanders.'[60]

On the death of Louis IV in 956, his wife moved quickly to secure their son Lothar's inheritance. Hugh the Great was given the title Duke of Burgundy and Aquitaine, and this may be when Arnulf delegated Bolougne and Ternois to his son Baldwin:

> Flemish-Boulonnais fidelity to Lothar allowed Arnulf and his son to consolidate their hold on northern Ponthieu, Artois and Ostrevant, and to hold their own against Hugh the Great, Arnulf's long-standing adversary. In addition, Arnulf's sons in law, Thierry of Gent, and Isaac of Cambrai, had strong ties to the Ottonian court and in representatives in Lotharingia, Bruno of Cologne, who was the new king's maternal uncle.[61]

It seems though, that the premature death of Baldwin of Bolougne in 962 from smallpox, leaving a child, another Arnulf (II), of no more than 4, undid many of Arnulf's gains. Lothar, Louis IV's son and heir, gained back more direct control with the aid of Adalulf's sons. One of these sons seems to have been captured and killed by his uncle. Arnulf negotiated a settlement with Lothar, so that Flanders remained for his grandson, while Bolougne, Ternois, Montreuil, Northern Ponthieu and Amiens were returned to Lothar's control.

When Arnulf II died in 988, Hugh Capet married his son to Arnulf's widow, Susanna, and Flanders temporarily came under the control of the Capetians. Hugh Capet was the son of Hugh the Great (Eadhild's husband) and his third wife, Hadwig, the sister of Otto I of East Francia.

It is impossible to reconstruct an accurate timeline of events in 929/930, 936/937 and certainly not from 939/942. The causality of events can only be inferred – did Athelstan marry his sisters off to counter the death of King Charles III? Or had the marriages been arranged? Did the death of Eadhild turn Duke Hugh against Louis? And whatever the nobility of West Frankia was up to in 939–942, had the untimely death of Athelstan incited them to discard their young king?

The infighting and fighting seems to have been on a wholly new level compared to the more 'placid' account of events in England, where the problem of 'overmighty' subjects is either ignored in sources from the period or did not occur at all until the later eleventh century, other than potentially during the reign of Eadwig.

Perhaps, in ensuring these daughters married far from England's shores, Edward and Athelstan guaranteed the somewhat smoother succession of their sons, brothers and descendants.

Chapter 8

The First Wife and the Daughters of Æthelred II

Ælfgifu, daughter of Thored, Ealdorman of Northumbria
  m. Æthelred II, king of England (r.978–1013, and then 1013–1016)
    Athelstan d.1014
    Ecgberht d.*c.*1005
    Edmund, king of the English, 1016
    Eadred d.*c.*1012
    Eadwig d.1017
    Edgar d.*c.*1008
    Eadgyth m. Ealdorman Eadric Streona (Mercia)
    Ælfgifu m. Ealdorman Uhtred (Northumbria/Bamburgh)
      Ealdgyth[1] m. Maldred
        Gospatric
    Wulfhild m. Ulfcytel of East Anglia (never named as an ealdorman)
    Ælfthryth, abbess of Wherwell, during the reign of her half-brother, Edward the Confessor (r.1042–1066)

While the scope is to tell the story of the royal women of the House of Wessex during the tenth century, it would be remiss not to mention the daughters of Æthelred II, even if only briefly. Like his father before him, Æthelred II had more than one wife. His first wife[2] is as shadowy as his father's first wife, but she does seem to have presented him with a large number of daughters, as well as sons. These daughters were to make good marriages, although to English noblemen, unlike the many daughters of Edward the Elder.

Æthelred II ruled England. He was not just king of Wessex, or the Anglo-Saxons. But, in order to ensure the kingdom remained loyal to him, it appears he married the daughter of the ealdorman of Northumbria. The entry for 1010 in the *Anglo-Saxon Chronicle* records that, 'There was killed Athelstan, the king's son-in-law.'[3] It is not known who Athelstan was married to, but the same word in the original text could also mean brother-in-law and so might be referencing his first wife's brother.

It seems highly possible that Æthelred II's wife was never consecrated as queen, and that for much of the reign it was his mother, and not his wife, who fulfilled the obligations of being the queen of the English. It might be no coincidence that the death of Æthelred's mother, Elfrida, gave way to the far better-known queenship of Lady Emma, twice a queen of England, through her marriages to Æthelred II and Cnut.

In the matter of his marriage, Æthelred II did not step away from similar positions taken by his father, grandfather and great-grandfather. Where Æthelred is different is in what happened to his daughters.

Little is known of these daughters. There is no proven date of birth for them, and for many, it is unknown when they married or when they died. And everything that is known about them comes from later sources. None of the daughters are mentioned by name in the *Anglo-Saxon Chronicle*. A twelfth-century source gives the name of Ælfgifu and her marriage to Uhtred of Bamburgh.[4] 'His mother was Algitha the daughter of earl Uchtred [Uhtred], whom he had of Algiva, daughter of king Agelred [Æthelred]',[5] who succeeded her mother's father as ealdorman there.

Eadgyth, wife of Eadric of Mercia, first appears in the later source of John of Worcester. Wulfhild only appears in the Jomsviking saga in *Flateyjarbok*, which mentions her marriage to Ulfcytel, and then her subsequent marriage to Thorkell, known as the Tall, his successor as the ealdorman/earl in East Anglia.

The *Anglo-Saxon Chronicle* D and E for 1051 identifies a sister of Edward's as abbess at Wherwell, when discussing the setting aside of Queen Edith by her husband 'and committed her to his sister at Wherwell'.[6]

In the matter of affairs of the royal women of the eleventh century, it is Lady Emma and then Queen Edith, the wives of the kings, who were significant. But this falls outside the scope of this work.

Chapter 9

Women in Law

While the intention is to tell the lives of the royal women who were members of the House of Wessex, it is worth stepping aside to discuss some other women known from this period. We have already encountered the will of Wynflæd, the (probable) mother of Ælfgifu of Shaftesbury, and that of Ælfgifu, the wife of Eadwig. They are by no means the only women who are mentioned in the charters and existing wills of the period, showing that women were able to take legal action against their contemporaries.

The religious women of the 940s

There is a small collection of charters from this period, notable because the recipients of these charters are women, and are named as either nuns or religious women. Foot, with her discussion on the two types of religious women, perhaps casts new light on who these women were and why they had charters issued for them.

Under Edmund, there were seven of these charters issued from 940 to 944, to Æthelswith,[1] Æthelthryth,[2] Ælfflæd,[3] Sæthryth,[4] Wynnflæd,[5] Ælswith/Alfswith[6] and Alfgyth.[7] These were all charters that show land being given to these women, five of whom are named as nuns, while Ælfflæd and Alfswith are said to be religious women. These charters are all deemed as authentic.

S464, dated to 940 and surviving in one manuscript, reads, 'King Edmund to Æthelswith,[8] a nun; grant of 10 hides (mansae) at Oswaldingtune (near Ashford, Kent)'.[9]

S465, dated to 940 and surviving in one manuscript, reads, 'Edmund, king of the English and of the other peoples round about, to the nun Ætheldryth [Æthelthryth],[10] 5 mansae at *Polhœmatunœ* (Poolhampton in Overton), free of all but the three common dues'.[11]

S474 dated to 941, and surviving in three manuscripts, reads, 'Edmund, king of the English and of the other peoples round about, to the

109

religious woman Elfleda [Ælfflæd],[12] 15 mansae in two places; *Boclonde* [Buckland] and *Plussh* [Plush], free of all but the three common dues'.[13]

S482, dated to 942, 'Edmund, king of the English and the other places round about, to Sæthryth, a nun, 11 'mansae' in the place called *æt Wincanfelda* (Winkfield) and *æt Swinlea* (Swinly), free of all but the three common dues.' This survives in three copies, although two are in the same manuscript.[14]

S485 dated to 942 and surviving in two manuscripts, reads, 'Edmund, king of the English and of the other peoples round about, to the nun Wynflæd.[15] Restitution of 7 mansae granted by his predecessors, and addition of 8 mansae at Cheselburne [Cheselbourne], free of all but the three most common dues'.[16]

S487 dated to 943 and surviving in one manuscript reads, 'Edmund, king of the English and of the other peoples round about to the religious lady Alfswith [Ælfswith],[17] 15 mansae at *Clearan* [Clere], free of all but the three common dues. Any former charter is annulled.'[18]

S493 dated to 944 and surviving in one manuscript reads, 'Edmund, king of the English and of the other peoples round about, to the nun Alfgyth [Ælfgyth],[19] 2 mansae at Rollandune [Rollington in Bulbridge, near Wilton], free of all but the three common dues'.[20]

Under Eadred, there are six such charters, three of them seem to have been the king's to gift land to, and these women are all termed religious women or nuns.

S517a dated to 946 and surviving in one manuscript reads, 'King Eadred to Æthelgifu, a religious woman; grant of 4 hides (mansae) at Tolleshunt, Essex'.[21] S517b, also dated to 946 and surviving in one manuscript, 'King Eadred to Eawyn, a religious woman; grant of 19 hides (mansae) at Hockley, Essex'.[22]

The charter to a nun, Ælfwynn,[23] is actually an exchange of land, in S535, dated to 948 and surviving in one manuscript. 'King Eadred to Ælfwyn, a religious woman; grant of 6 hides (mansae), equated with 6 sulungs, at Wickhambreux, Kent, in return for 2 pounds of purest gold'.[24] This may well be Ælfwynn, the second Lady of the Mercians.

The nun, Ælfgyth, seems to have purchased the land from the king in charter S563. All apart from S563 are dated to 946 or 948, and so the early years of Eadred's reign. She may be the Ælfgyth of S493.

S534 dated to 948 and surviving in two manuscripts, reads, 'Eadred, king of the English and of the peoples round about, to the religious lady Althrith [Ælfthryth],[25] at the bequest of her father and in return for a payment of 60 mancusus. 8 mansae in *Purbicinga* [Purbeck], free of all but the three common dues'.[26]

S563 dated to 955 and surviving in two manuscripts, although one is now lost, reads, 'Eadred, king and chieftain of all Albion, to Ælfgith [Ælfgyth],[27] a nun of Wilton, for 120 gold shillings. 20 cassati at *Pengeard Mynster* (Pennard Minister), free of all but the three common dues'.[28]

What, then are we to make of these charters? Are these women perhaps extended members of the royal household? Or are these women either taking the veil or deciding to become lay women, perhaps when they're widowed? Are they calling on the king to confirm their land, which will fund their retirements in the nunneries? If this is a possibility, then it is equally likely that the grants to the royal religious sisters were perhaps doing the same.

On the death of their husbands, these women, if they were married, will have been left with their dower lands. Perhaps, in an attempt to stop others from claiming the land as theirs, the recourse to the king was necessary. And, in light of Foot's discussion about the terms *nunne*[29] and *mynecena*, are we to understand that these women, titled as a nun, were widowed women religious, perhaps not in a nunnery but instead widows who had determined not to remarry and perhaps continued to live a secluded life but in their own homes. Equally, while the women should have been protected by the church, perhaps at this time the religious protection offered by the church was not deemed a large enough deterrent to stop disputes. Which brings us to Wynflæd below.

The legal dispute between Wynflæd[30] and Leofwine

The details of this charter concern a land dispute.

Charter S1454,[31] dated from 990 to 992 and surviving in three manuscripts, records that Wynflæd initially presented her claims directly to the king accompanied by Archbishop Sigeric of Canterbury, Bishop Ordbriht of Selsey, ealdorman Ælfric of Winchester and the king's mother, Lady Elfrida as witnesses. When Leofwine was summoned to court by the king, he refused to appear, and 'possibly pointing to the laws of King Edgar decreeing that royal appeals cannot precede local judgment, Leofwine demanded that the king withhold his ruling and recognise the jurisdiction of the regional shire-court.'[32] Æthelred instructed the judges to resolve the matter in a way 'that ever seemed just to them'.[33] In response, Wynflæd then produced twenty-five witnesses, again including Lady Elfrida, and still the eventual resolution was a compromise because the judges predicted that 'thereafter there would be no friendship',[34] if they did not do so.

This, in and of itself, is interesting, but equally, in relation to the above charters of the religious women, I think is worthy of further exploration. It would seem that appealing to the king on matters of justice was not always a sure way of gaining victory. Perhaps the nuns and religious women felt that if their charters were granted by the king, as opposed to being witnessed by the king, then they would have more chance of being upheld should they find themselves being questioned over their rights to the lands in the charters.

This case reveals that calling upon the king to mediate, and having the support of so many figures, an archbishop, a bishop and ealdorman, as well as the king's mother, was not a means of immediately securing a ruling in favour of Wynflæd.

Wills

The will of Æthelgifu S1497

This will, dated between 990 and 1001, survives in four manuscripts and records the following:

> To St Albans; estates at *westwicum* [Westwick Hall], *gætesdene* (Great Gaddesden), oxen from Gaddesden and *acyrsce* [Oakhurst in Shenley], sheep from Langford (Bedfordshire), swine from Oakhurst, the reversion of *standune* [Standon], food-rents and beasts from *offanlege* [Offley], Standon, and *gædesdene* [Gaddesden], and reversion of Offley (except for some holdings) if Leofsige has no legitimate child.

> To Ælfnoth, for his lifetime, Langford [Bedfordshire].
> To (the church at) Hitchin (Hertfordshire) the reversion of Langford, sheep from the estate, and food-rents while Ælfnoth holds it.
> To (the church at) *bedaford* (Bedford) 50 sheep from Langford.
> To (the church at) *flittan* (Flitton) 30 sheep from Langford.
> To (the church at) æscewyllan (Ashwell); 20 sheep from Langford

To (the church at) *heanhlæwe* (Henlow) 10 sheep from Langford.

To the church of Edwin the priest (? at Standon) half a hide of land.

To Ælfwold: *mundane* (Great and Little Munden) for his life, the reversion of Standon for his life, half a 'haga' in London.

To the minister at *brahingum* (Braughing); the reversion of half the estate at Munden, food-rent while Ælfwold holds it, cattle from Standon.

To the minister at *welingum* (Welwyn); the reversion of half Munden, food-rents and cattle from there.

To (the church at) *heortfordinganyrig* (Hertingfordbury) 4 oxen from Munden.

To Leofsige, then to Ælfwold, then to St Albans: *standune* (Standon).

To Leofsige: *offanlege* (Great and Little Offley), swine-pasture at *twingum* (Tewin), *weodune* (Weedon Bec, Northants.).

To Ælfheah: half the 'haga' in London.

To Ælfgifu: a herd of swine at *gætesdene* (Gaddesden).

To Leofrun: *wadforda* (Watford, Northants., also spelt *watforda*) and *ðrope* (Thrupp, Northants.), slaves and stock from Weedon Bec (Northants).

150 sheep from *langaforda* (Langford).

To Leofwine *cliftune* (Clifton).

Byrhstan's sister is to be given to *standune* (Stondon) for Edwin.[35]

The following is translated elsewhere from the same will.

And to my kinswoman [mæga] [is to be given] a dish and a brooch and a wall-hanging and a seat-cover and all the best bedsteads she has available and her brightest kirtle; and to her kinsman [mæge] Wulfmær the smaller silver cup. And 5 mancuses are to be cut from her headband for Wihtsige, unless she should have done it before, and 5 for Leofwine, and Wulfmær's son, and 5 for Wulfmær, my sister's son, and 5 for Godwif and 5 for Ælfgifu, my sister's daughter. And my blue kirtle which is untrimmed at the bottom and her best head-dresses are to be given to Beorhtwine. And her 3 purple kirtles are to be given to Leoftæt and Ælfgifu and, Godwif, and Wulfwigu, is to be given some of her other, dun-coloured kirtles. And afterwards her household women are to divide what is left between them. And 3 wall-hangings, the better of such as are then there, and 2 seat-covers and 2 bedsteads are to be given to Leofsige. And Godwif and Ælfgifu are to divide the others between them.[36]

Æthelgifu, just like Wulfwaru below, was clearly a wealthy individual.

The Old English will of Wulfwaru,[37] S1538 (984–1016)

This document, surviving in one manuscript, is included in *English Historical Documents* Volume I, a fascinating compendium of many important sources for the period 500–1042. The compiler includes this particular will 'as a specimen of a woman's will to illustrate the type of evidence for social conditions that can be gathered from the will of a women of no historic importance. Nothing is known of Wulfwaru or her family elsewhere.'[38] I include it below in its entirety.

I, Wulfwaru, pray my dear lord King Ethelred, of his charity, that I may be entitled to make my will. I make known to you, Sire, here in this document, what I grant to St Peter's Monastery at Bath for my soul and for the souls of my ancestors from whom my property and my possessions came to me; namely then, that I grant to that holy place there an armlet which consists of 60 mancuses of gold, and a bowl of two and a half pounds, and two gold crucifixes, and a set of Mass-vestaments with everything that belongs to it, and the best dorsal that I have, and set of bed-clothing with tapestry and curtain and with everything that belongs to it. And I grant to the Abbot Ælfhere the estate at Freshford with the produce and the men and all the profits which is obtained there.

And I grant to my elder son Wulfmær the estate at Claverston, with produce and with men and with all profits; and the estate at Compton with produce and men and all profits; and I grant him half the estate at Butcombe with produce and men and all profits, and half of it I grant to my younger daughter Ælfwaru, with produce and men and all profits. And they are to share the principal residence between them as evenly as they can, so that each of them shall have a just portion of it.

And to my younger son Ælfwine I grant the estate at Leigh, with produce and men and all profits; and the estate at Holton, with produce and men and all profits; and the estate at *Hocgestun*, with produce and men and all the profits; and 30 mancuses of gold.

And I grant to my elder daughter, Gode,[39] the estate at Winford, with produce and men and all profits; and two cups of four pounds; and a band of 30 mancuses of gold and two brooches and a woman's attire complete. And to my youngest daughter, Ælfwaru,[40] I grant all the women's clothing which is left.

And to my son Wulfmær and my second son Ælfwine and my daughter Ælfwaru – to each of the three of them – I grant two cups of good value. And I grant to my son Wulfmær a hall-tapestry and a set of bed-clothes. To Ælfwine my second son I grant a tapestry for a chamber, together with a table-cover and with all the clothes which go with it.

And I grant to my retainers Ælmær, Ælfweard, Wulfric and Wulfstan, a band of 20 mancuses of gold. And I grant to all my household women, in common, a good chest well decorated.

And I desire that those who succeed to my property provide 20 freemen, 10 in the east and 10 in the west; and all together furnish a food-rent for Bath every year for ever as good as ever they can afford, at such season as it seems to all of them that they can accomplish it best and most fittingly. Whichever of them shall discharge this, may he have God's favour and mine; and whichever of them will not discharge it, may he have to account for it with the Most High, who is the true God, who created and made all creatures.

Given what has gone before, it is interesting that this will is directed to the king to ensure the wishes of the grantee are carried out. It is also fascinating to see a detailed account of all that Wulfwaru could lay claim to and that which she left to her sons and daughters. Equally, and as part of the overall narrative of the largely 'lost women' of the tenth century, royal or not, it is disappointing that a woman of such obvious wealth leaves no other mark in the written records.

The charters of King Edgar to his kinswomen

During King Edgar's reign, twelve of his surviving charters are issued to women, one to his second wife, Wulfthryth, S799 discussed elsewhere, addressed to her as an abbess, two to his wife, Elfrida, S742 and S725, and one to his grandmother, Eadgifu, S811, also discussed elsewhere. Of the other eight, one is to Æthelflæd,[41] one to Beorhtgifu,[42] one to Ælfswith and her husband,[43] one to Ælfflæd,[44] one to Abbess Heanflæd,[45] one to Quen, his matrona,[46] and the below two to Ælfgifu.[47]

'Edgar, king of the English and of the other races round about, to Ælfgifu, his kinswoman, 10 'cassatae' in the place called æt Lhincgelade [Linslade], free of all but the three common dues'.[48]

'Eadgar [Edgar], king of the English and of the other races round about, to Ælfgifu, his kinswoman. 10 cassati at *Niwanham* [Newnham Murren], free of all but the three common dues'.[49]

I can see no reference to this Ælfgifu being the wife of King Eadwig, Edgar's brother, but it seems possible. The same could be true for Æthelflæd, who might have been Edgar's father's widow, Æthelflæd of Damerham.

Eadflæd, a landed lady

In charter S937,[50] dated between 990 and 1006 and surviving in two manuscripts, but perhaps from 999, King Æthelred gifts land to St Mary's, Abingdon. This document includes an intriguing account of Lady Eadgifu's lands, which had been seized by Ealdorman Ælfric from a widow, Eadflæd.[51] It is possible that Ælfric was Eadflæd's brother by marriage. These lands were subsequently forfeited by him and restored to Eadflæd, who then bequeathed them to King Æthelred II. These lands were at Farnborough and Wormleighton, Warwickshire, and South Cerney, Gloucestershire. This Ælfric is mentioned in the *Anglo-Saxon Chronicle* for 985 (C) 'in this year Ealdorman Ælfric was driven out of the land'.[52] It seems that Ælfric did a lot more than just lay claim to lands that did not belong to him.

The abbesses of the later tenth century

While nothing else is known about either of these two women, I have included them, as their positions as abbesses would have made them powerful figures. 'The same year two abbesses in Dorset passed away; Herelufu[53] in

Shaftesbury and Wulfwynn in Wareham.'[54] (982, the *Anglo-Saxon Chronicle* (C).) The inclusion of this reference in the *Anglo-Saxon Chronicle* is intriguing, especially as it is sandwiched between an account of a Viking raid, and events in the Holy Roman Empire, and especially because it is about the only reference to the nunneries at this time in the Anglo-Saxon Chronicles.

The sister of Æthelflæd of Damerham wife of King Edmund, and her daughter, Ælfflæd and Leofflæd

Ælfflæd was the sister of Æthelflæd, and wife of Ealdorman Byrhtnoth. Her daughter was Leofflæd. Ælfflæd's will survives in S1486, in two manuscripts, just as her sister's does in S1494. Similar landed interests are obviously mentioned:

> A Will of Ælfflæd, including bequests of land at Dovercourt, Fulanpettæ [Beaumont], Alresford, Stanway, Byrton in Stanway [lost], Lexden, Essex; Elmsett and Buxhall, Suffolk, to the king; at Stoke, Suffolk; Hatfield [?] Peverel, Essex], Stratford St Mary, Freston, Wiston, Lavenham, Balsdon, Polstead, Withermarsh, Suffolk; Greenstead [near Colchester], Peldon, [West] Mersea, Totham, Colne and Tey, Essex, to Stoke [? Stoke-by-Nayland, Suffolk]; and at Monks Eleigh, Suffolk, to Christ Church, Canterbury; at Hadham, Herts., and at Tidwoldingtune [Heybridge near Maldon, Essex] to St Paul's, London; and at Baythorn, Essex, to Barking Abbey; at Woodham, Essex, to Ælfthryth, the king's mother, for life, with reversion to St Mary's, Barking; at Chelsworth and Cockfield, Suffolk, to St Edmund's Abbey; and at Nedging, Suffolk, to the same after the death of Crawe, her kinswoman; at Fingringhoe and Mersea, Essex, to the minster at Mersea; at Waldingfield, Suffolk, to St Gregory's, Sudbury, after the death of Crawe; at Rettendon, Essex; Soham, Ditton and Cheveley, Cambs., to Ely Abbey; at Lawling, Essex, to Ealdorman Æthelmær; and at Liston, Essex, to Æthelmær.[55]

Leofflæd's will also survives, in S1520, dated to between 1017 and 1035, so falling outside the tenth century, and both mother and daughter are mentioned in the *Liber Eliensis*.

Wives

Eadgifu, wife of Ælfsige
S561 dated to 953 and surviving in one manuscript reads as follows, 'Eadred, king and chieftain of all Albion, to his "minister" Ælfsige, and Ælfsige's wife, Eadgifu. 33 cassati at *Æcesburh* [Uffington Castle]'.[56]

Ælfswith, wife of Ealdorman Ælfheah
S747, dated to 967, survives in three manuscripts, although one of these is now lost. Ealdorman Ælfheah was the Ealdorman of Hampshire from *c.*959 to 972.

'Edgar, emperor of all Britain, to Alphea [Ælfheah], his faithful "comes", and his wife Elswite [Ælfswith], 20 cassati in the place called *at Mertone* [Merton], 5 cassati at Dilwihs [Dulwich], and another piece of salty land by the River Thames, free of all but the three common dues'.[57] This charter shows the king granting land to the ealdorman and his wife.

The wife of Ealdorman Æthelwine, Æthelflæd
Another Æthelflæd, bequeathed land to Ramsey. It is written:

> For while the father of Æthelflæd, Æthelwine's wife, was still alive and possessed a certain part of the countryside legally by hereditary right, he gave it to a man called Athelstan, an ealdorman, in mutual exchange for some other land which was more acceptable to him. Later, indeed, this same Æthelflæd, after her aforesaid father and that same Athelstan had been cheated of life by the fateful dice, made a claim concerning the above land and she took it back by judicial order into the jurisdiction of her own hereditary right. Then she granted the land she had regained to God and St Benedict of Ramsey with the burial of her body and the cost of her interment for the remission of her sins.[58]

The foster mother of Athelstan, Ælfswith, son of King Æthelred II, and the other women mentioned in his will
Athelstan predeceased his father, and his will survives as S1503, dated to 1014, in twelve different manuscripts. It contains a detailed dispersal of Athelstan's goods and also mentions four women, his foster mother,

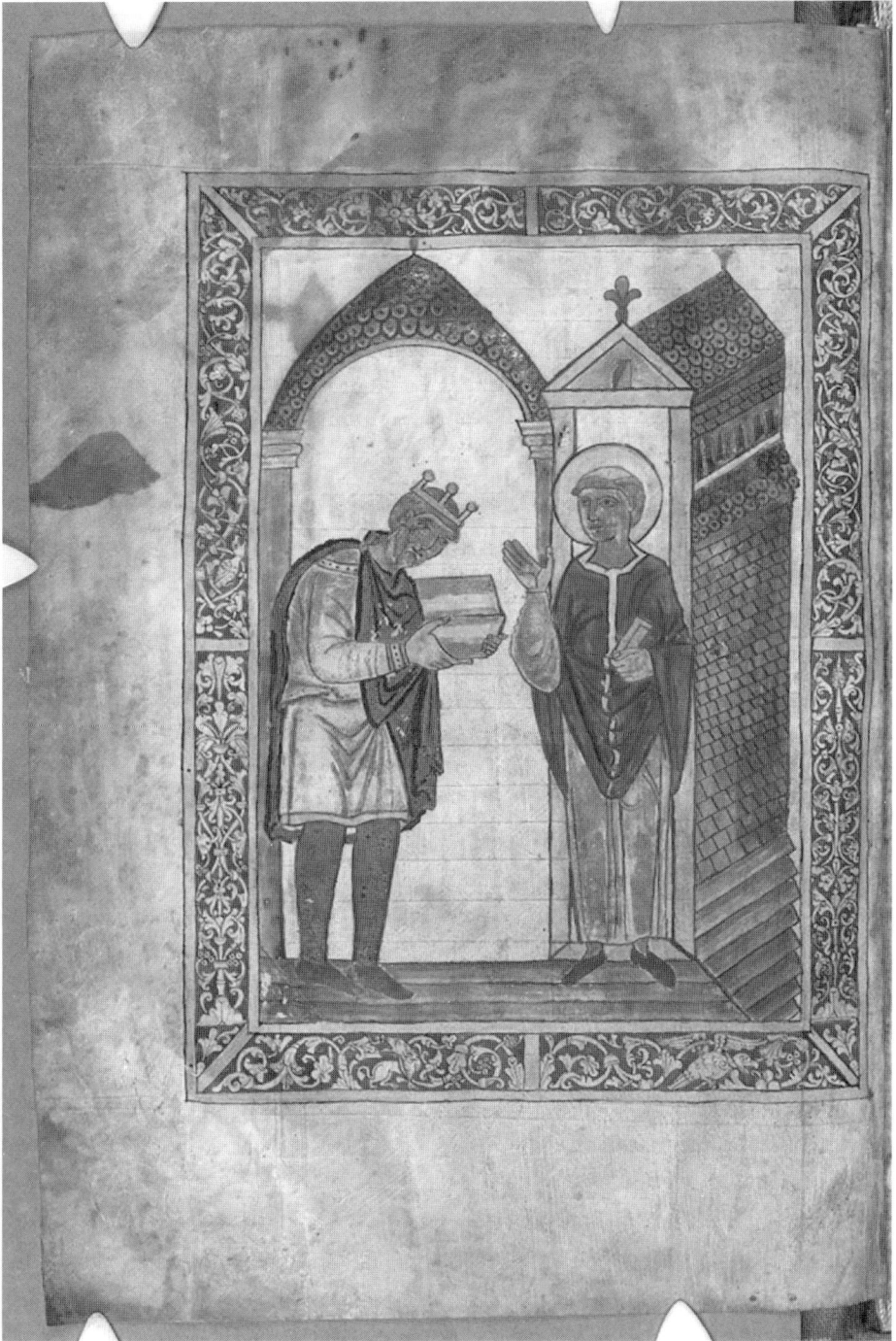

King Athelstan from the frontispiece of Bede's *Life of St Cuthbert*, showing King Æthelstan (924–39) presenting a copy of the book to the saint himself. (Full acknowledgement is made to The Parker Library, Corpus Christi College, Cambridge)

King Edgar from Edgar's refoundation charter of the New Minster, Winchester, 966. (© The British Library Board Cotton Vespasian A. VIII, f.2v)

Above: Coin of King
Athelstan, king
of England 924-
939. London mint.
Moneyer Biorneard.
(Public domain)

Right: Æthelflæd, the
lady of Mercia, as
depicted in the cartulary
of Abingdon Abbey.
(© The British Library
Board Cotton Claudius
B. VI, f.14)

man cƿeðe ꝼie mine mǣᵹcild oððe ꝥl
ꝺꝛan oððe ᵹinᵹꝛan mꝺ þo ꝼoꝛ ꝺemꝺe.
⁊ hy þa ealle to ꝛihte ᵹeꝛiehton ⁊ cƿǣꝺon
ꝥ hy nan ꝛihtꝛe ꝛiht ᵹe þencan ne mihtan.
ne on þam yꝼꝛe ᵹeꝛꝛite ᵹe hyꝛ an nuhit
eall aᵹan iſ þeꝛ on oð þine hanꝺ. þonne
þu hit be cƿeðe ⁊ ſylle ſƿa ᵹe ſibꝛe hanꝺa
ſƿa ꝼꝛemꝺꝛe ſƿaðeꝛ þe leoꝼꝛe ſy. ⁊ hi ealle
me þæſ hyꝛa ƿeðꝺ ſealꝺon ⁊ hyꝛa hanꝺ
ſetene ꝥ be hyꝛa liꝼe hit næniᵹ mann næꝼꝛe
ne on penꝺe on nane oðꝛe ƿiſan butan ſƿa
ſƿa ic hit ſylꝼ ᵹe cƿeðe æt þam nyhſtan
ꝺæᵹe.   Testamentum.

Ic ælꝼꝛeꝺ ƿeſt ſeaxena cinᵹe miꝺ ᵹoꝺeſ
ᵹyꝼe ⁊ miꝺ þiſſe ᵹe ꝛineſſe ᵹe cƿeðe huic
ymbe min yꝼꝛe ƿille æꝼteꝛ minum ꝺæᵹe.
æꝛeſt ic an eaꝺƿeaꝛꝺe minum yl ꝺꝛan
ſuna þeſ lanꝺeſ æt ſtꝛꝺæt neat on tꝛuconſcꝛpe.
⁊ heoꝛꝛiᵹ tuneſ. ⁊ þa boc lanꝺ ealle þe leoꝼ
heah hylt. ⁊ ꝥ lanꝺ æt caꝛuꝛmtune. ⁊ æt
cylꝼantune. ⁊ æt buꝛnhamme. ⁊ æt ƿeꝺmoꝛ.
⁊ ic eom pyꝛꝛꝺiᵹ to þam hiꝛum æt ceoꝺꝛe.
ꝥ hy hine ceoſan on þa ᵹe ꝛaꝺ þeꝛe æꝛ ᵹe
cƿeꝺen hæꝼꝺon miꝺ þam lanꝺe æt aꝛtune. ⁊
þam þe þæꝛ to hyꝛaꝺ. ⁊ ic him an þæſ lanꝺeſ
æt canꞇuꝛtune. ⁊ æt beꝺeꝛuꝛꝺan ⁊ æt ƿeꝼeſ
iſſe. ⁊ hyſſe buꝛnan. ⁊ æt ſuꝛtune. ⁊ æt

King Edward the Elder,
899-924, Miniature
of Edward the Elder.
(Public domain)

King Æthelred II, (979-1013/1013-
1016) Æthelred the Unready.
Illuminated manuscript, The
Chronicle of Abingdon, c.1220.
MS Cott. Claude B.VI folio
87, verso, The British Library.
(Public domain)

King Edmund (939-946) Obverse (front) of a silver penny of Edmund I. (Image courtesy of York Museums Trust: https://yorkmuseumstrust.org.uk/. Public Domain)

Æthelflæd, (c.866-918) the lady of Mercia, Statue of Æthelflæd, outside Tamworth Castle. (CC by SA 2.0 (http://tinyurl.com/4s6uk35t), Humphrey Bolton)

Tamworth Castle from the bridge. (© MJ Porter)

The Ruins of St Oswald's Priory, Gloucester, burial place of Lady Æthelflæd, and her husband, Lord Æthelred. (© MJ Porter)

his grandmother, Lady Elfrida, as well as Æthelwold's widow and Wynflæd:[59] 'And I desire that the money which Æthelwold's widow ought to pay me, which I contributed towards her income, i.e. twelve pounds by tale, be taken and entrusted to Bishop Ælfsie at the Old Minster for my soul.' And Wynflæd's son, Eadric, who is granted 'the sword on which the hand is marked'. Eadric is named as Wynflæd's son, with no mention of his father.

Athelstan's foster mother, named as Ælfswith[60] is granted 'because of her great deserts, the estate at Weston'. No more is known of Ælfswith, but as with his grandfather, Edgar, and probably his father, although we have no record of this, Athelstan was raised by a foster mother, perhaps with the oversight of his grandmother, as below.

Athelstan's will ends by stating that all that he has granted to the Church is 'for the soul of my dear father, King Ethelred, and for mine, and for the soul of Ælfthryth [Elfrida], my grandmother, who brought me up'.[61]

Why Athelstan does not mention his mother when explaining his actions, is worth questioning. We know that his mother disappears at some point before Æthelred II remarries. Did Athelstan have no memory of her, or was it not politic to mention his mother in a legal document which he wished his father to confirm?

Including these charters, bequests and legal documents adds a further almost forty known names of women who lived in the tenth century. This is more than are known for the royal women. It is frustrating that there is so little additional information, but the surviving information about them highlights that it was not just members of the House of Wessex who had recourse to legal problems or were able to grant land throughout the tenth century. The royal women were not extraordinary in being able to determine their effects with a will, or in taking legal action, or even in being recognised by the king.

Chapter 10

The Written Record

Many histories of the period will begin with a detailed accounting of the available sources. While this is an excellent place to start, it can also be a little dry. As such, I have resisted until a little further into the narrative.

Asser's Life of King Alfred

De rebus gestis Ælfredi regis (The Latin Life of King Alfred), was written by the king's biographer, Asser, in 893, and is the only contemporary account of a pre-conquest king. It survives in only manuscript, which was unfortunately lost in the Cotton Library fire of 1731. The version that survives is a sixteenth-century copy.[1]

The Anglo-Saxon Chronicle

The *Anglo-Saxon Chronicle* survives in a possible nine 'recensions' – the simplest way to explain this is to say that there is a 'base' document (now lost), and these versions all share some common elements of the base document, but that they were then, potentially, kept in regional centres and, potentially, reflect the bias there, as additions were then made to these regional copies. There was no attempt to ensure the same information was recorded in these regional copies, although some scribes, at points in time, did attempt work to bring some of the annals into agreement with other versions. But the history of this, one of our most valuable resources, is the subject of much current debate. Stafford in *After Alfred: Anglo-Saxon Chronicles and Chroniclers 900–1150* is telling the story of these manuscripts, and they are a part of the history of this period and particularly relevant for the royal women of the tenth century, although few of them are named within the text.

The *Winchester Manuscript* (known as version A and the Parker manuscript) is the oldest surviving manuscript of the *Chronicle*.

(Cambridge, Corpus Christi College MS173, ff. 1v–32r). It was sadly lost in a fire at the Cotton Library in 1731, although it had been copied in 1641, and this edition does survive as British Library MS Cotton Otho Bxi, 2 (G).

There are two versions of the *Abingdon Manuscripts*. The first was written by a single person in the second half of the tenth century, and ended in 977 (version B, British Library MSS Cotton Tiberius Aiii, f. 178 + Avi, ff. 1–34). This edition was used to make a compilation for the second of the two manuscripts, although details were added at this stage, in the middle of the eleventh century (version C, British Library MS Cotton Tiberius Bi, ff. 115v–64).

The *Worcester Manuscript* (version D British Library MS Cotton Tiberius Biv, ff. 3–86) was written in the middle of the eleventh century, probably at Worcester, as it contains some local entries for 1033 onwards. This seems to have been based on a lost Northern Recension as the diocese of Worcester and York were closely connected as they shared the same incumbent between 972 and 1016.

The *Peterborough Manuscript* (version E, Oxford, Bodleian Library MC Laud 636) was written from 1121 onwards, and is in one hand until that date, and probably copied from a *Kentish Chronicle*.

The *Canterbury Manuscript* (version F, British Library MS Cotton Domitian Aviii, ff. 30–70) was written at about 1100.

Version H is a twelfth-century single leaf dated to 1113–1114, British Library MS Cotton Domitian Aix, f. 9.

The interactions between these surviving versions are complex to explain, and it is often impossible to truly untangle which influenced the other. It is sobering to appreciate that all we know about the *Anglo-Saxon Chronicle* survives in only seven extant manuscripts, a fragment of an eighth, and a debatable ninth. Without them, our understanding of the period would be severely hampered, and yet, equally, the bias, and potential for propaganda, in the surviving sources must also be appreciated. These were a series of chronicles, potentially written by monks or nuns, in monasteries or nunneries. As far as is known, no female hand is present in the surviving sources, but it is of course, not possible to determine the identity of the scribe merely from their handwriting, although, it is possible to trace documents written in the same hand. The study of the manuscripts is not just the work of historians but also of language scholars. While I have used translations of the *Anglo-Saxon Chronicle* throughout this text, there is also something to be said for consulting the original, written, language.

And, those through whose hands these documents have passed in the intervening millennium have not done so without leaving a trace. To again turn to Stafford's work on the chronicles, and Joscelyn, Archbishop Parker's secretary, who studied all the available manuscripts:

> Thus he copied bits of Chronicle B into A, used Chronicle C to insert annal numbers into B, and used B to make additions to Chronicle D. Joscelyn also annotated A with readings from Chronicle E. He filled in what he saw as lacunae in C from D and supplied the lost material after folio 9 in D from other chronicles.[2]

Such a detailed account of the changes Joscelyn made is possible because of his penmanship. Where the original documents are now lost, it is impossible to determine what was added when and why.

That said, the events of the tenth century are mostly recorded in the earliest surviving manuscripts, perhaps at particular moments in time. Stafford determines that there was an original version of the chronicle, running to *c.*890 which has not survived. 'The various annals for the 890s already show divergences, but also contact, dialogue and "political" debate … It was produced in the West Saxon kingdom, and much of the content reflects its origin.'[3] Stafford suggests that the original document may have covered the period during the 870s when there was much war, and that 892 may have proven to be its first point of circulation, if not the date that it was written. This version of the *Anglo-Saxon Chronicle*, she names *Alfred's Chronicle*, and states that 'Alfred's Chronicle was thus a dynastic chronicle, but also a wider Christian, if not an Anglo-Saxon Christian one.'[4] It was 'from the start "political", not in the sense of propaganda more as a celebratory, legitimising text.'[5]

Chronicle A is the oldest surviving of the texts, produced in the decades around 900 and receiving additions on an intermittent basis until the twelfth century. But it was not the only chronicle at this time. A dates from the beginning of the century, and B dates from its end. This then, is where one of the first notable divides makes itself known in the surviving versions, the *Chronicles of Edward* and his sister, *The Annals of Æthelflæd*, which are seen in the B, C and D versions. However, 'these attempts at recording contemporary history had played themselves out by *c.*930.'[6] Stafford has a reasoning as to why this occurred. These version of the *Anglo-Saxon Chronicle*, whether they centred on Edward or Æthelflæd, 'spoke to the issue of succession to Alfred in Wessex and Mercia, and dried up when this was resolved with Athelstan'.[7] Stafford argues that Chronicle A was part of the argument surrounding Edward's succession to his father's kingdom, and thus reducing the legitimacy of his cousin Æthelwold to succeed, whereas *The Annals of Æthelflæd* used holy imagery to justify her rule, and she ruled through military might and God's will.

Chronicles B and C contained *The Annals of Æthelflæd* as a separate block, whereas D combined them with Edward's annals. C and D are both later manuscripts, dated to the middle of the eleventh century, and therefore may have benefited from either hindsight, or access to both versions.

Yet, as has been said above, the contemporary history-writing did not extend beyond the 930s, although the military triumphs of the 940s and 950s are written about, and B extends this to 977, because the regnal list that makes up part of the manuscript included the reign of Edward the Martyr. Stafford writes that, 'Chronicle B is evidence of someone's interest in vernacular chronicles in the last decades of the tenth century.'[8] And, 'it shows little or no sign of continuation of use before 1066'.[9] Stafford here is arguing for the existence of a manuscript tradition from which B may have been copied (and also C) in her attempts to determine the causality of the creation of the chronicle.

Stafford has gone further. She has determined that the block of entries in the A version:

> were added as part of a single, scribal stint, no earlier than the 950s. They are copied into A but are unlikely to have been authored for that chronicle.[10]

> There are grounds for seeing annals 972, 974 and 975 as a group and as one which underlies all surviving vernacular chronicles at this point [in B and C].[11]

> It should be noted that these annals, and especially the poems, elaborate a monastic or ecclesiastical account, what might even be called a panegyric, of Edgar. This was a retrospective portrayal made in the context of events after his death most likely during the troubled reign of his son, Edward, whose rule was challenged.[12]

> The combination of chronicle and regnal list suggests that Chronicle B was one made, during, if not specifically addressing, a current political crisis.[13]

However, Stafford also argues that Chronicle B and the mid-century annals of A have moved away from 'court chroniclers' and the audience has changed, and that it is something different that is fuelling the continual updating and writing of these entries.

This then, is a lot to understand. For the tenth century, it seems as though the entries written concerning Edward the Elder and Æthelflæd had a legitimising quality about them, those written about Athelstan, Edmund and Eadred more of a militaristic account of their successes against the enemy and the later entries, concerning Edgar, the retrospective account of a man who was perceived as a 'good' king before the chaos of the reigns of his martyred son, Edward, and also the later perceptions that Æthelred II was a weak king.

What then does this mean for the tenth-century women? Once more, it points to Æthelflæd, Lady of the Mercians, as being in a very different situation from any of the other women mentioned in the *Anglo-Saxon Chronicle*, of which there is only her daughter, and her two cousins, the unnamed sister of Athelstan and Eadgyth, again unnamed, and married to Otto. However, if Stafford's argument is followed, then the later chronicle tradition was not written for the same reason; it was no longer a legitimising text but something else entirely. The very fact that Ælfwynn, the unnamed sister of Athelstan, and Eadgyth, his cousin, are named is because they work towards legitimising Athelstan's kingship; the marriage of Eadgyth showing how far the Wessex royal family had come. Perhaps.

The argument becomes further complicated because although only A and B can be deemed as contemporary in their construction and current formats, the other surviving chronicles also add additional detail, perhaps from other lost recensions, and therefore, I have not relied exclusively on the A and B versions. But scholars should be aware that the information contained in the *Anglo-Saxon Chronicle* is complicated by continual additions and editing. It is not, regrettably, the 'history' of the Saxons that it might be perceived to be.

Flodoard's *Annals*

Flodoard's *Annals* were written by a contemporary, drawing on a long-established tradition of annal-keeping at the archdiocese of Reims. Yet, for all he lived through tumultuous times, 'Flodoard did not use his writing excessively to attack the prevailing political situation.'[14] Neither was this his only written work. He wrote extensively and was also the archivist at Reims. 'Flodoard was very close to a series of archbishops over the course of four decades and worked as a diplomat in the service of his church and of the west Frankish king.'[15]

> Flodoard's *Annals* are an annual recording of current events. Flodoard strove to begin each year's events on 25 December, Christmas (the first day of the new year in the calendar used in northern Europe), and continues throughout the year to record the salient happenings of the period in close chronological order.[16]

Flodoard is informative on events that befell the royal women in their marriages into the rival families in what had been the empire of Charlemagne. Flodoard informs of Louis IV's rebellion against Hugh[17] and how he recalled his mother, Eadgifu, to his side. He is a contemporary chronicler.

His annals survive in six manuscripts, of which three are most useful.[18]

The *Chronicon* of Æthelweard

The *Chronicon* of Æthelweard, which has proven so important to the discussion of the royal women of the tenth century, is available as a translation undertaken by A. Campbell and first published in 1962. Campbell informs that while this chronicle was clearly known by William of Malmesbury who uses it when 'dealing with royal marriages of the house of Wessex',[19] it seems that Æthelweard's work then went unstudied until the sixteenth century. Only two translations of the work were known to Campbell in 1962, undertaken in the mid-nineteenth century by J.A. Giles and J. Stevenson. It only survives in one manuscript, that of Cotton Otho A x. and this was badly damaged in the fire of 23 October 1731, although Henry Savile had previously printed a copy of the *Chronicon* in his *Rereum Anglicarum scriptores post Dedam praecipua* in 1596, although without giving the details of this source. Hence, Savile might have been working from a different manuscript tradition, but this is impossible to say with any accuracy. The fragments that survived the fire are from an eleventh-century 'first fair copy',[20] and thus, Campbell worked from these two surviving 'copies' to produce his translation.

The *Chronicon*, a Latin translation of the *Anglo-Saxon Chronicle*, was dedicated by Æthelweard to Matilda (949–1011 and abbess from 974), the abbess of Essen, and his relative via Eadgyth, her grandmother's, marriage to Otto I of East Frankia, and his descent from Æthelred I, the brother of Alfred, Eadgyth's grandfather. The identification of Æthelweard as the ealdorman originates from his use of the term 'consul' when describing himself, which has been translated to mean earl.

It is the introduction and Book 4 of the *Chronicon* that have been used throughout. Stafford, in her work on the *Anglo-Saxon Chronicle*, stated that 'Æthelweard is not only a later user of a vernacular chronicle writing in a new political context, but a recognised editor and abbreviator.'[21] This then is a word of caution. Æthelweard's copy of the *Anglo-Saxon Chronicle*, not only written in archaic Latin, already shows evidence of the available chronicle being edited to suit Æthelweard's purpose.

The Life of St Dunstan by B

The earlier *Vita S Dunstani* (BHL 2342) was composed by an author who gives only the first letter of his name – B – and who describes himself as a *uilis Saxonum indigena*, 'a worthless native of the Saxon race'. The work is dedicated to Ælfric, archbishop of Canterbury, the dates of whose archiepiscopacy – 21 April 995 to 16 November 1005 – provide the outer dating termini for its composition and presentation. These dates can be narrowed slightly by the fact that Wulfric, abbot of St Augustine's, Canterbury, sent a copy of B's work to Abbo of Fluery, with the request that he turn it into verse; since Abbo was martyred on 13 November 1004, the *Vita S Dunstani* must have been written before that date.[22] It is this source which mentions yet another Æthelflæd. 'More importantly, the lady Æthelflæd, whom B. describes as the niece – *neptis* – of King Æthelstan (10. 3), is said to be related to Dunstan *causa religionis simul etiam propinquitatis* (10. 2).'[23]

The Anonymous Life of St Oswald, now assigned to Byrhtferth of Ramsey

The author of this work was a monk of Ramsey Abbey writing between 995 and 1005 and identified as Byrhtferth:

This *vita* was written within a decade at most of Oswald's death (on 28 February 992). The outer limits of dating are fixed by the archiepiscopacy of Ælfric of Canterbury (995–1005), who is described as a living witness to a recent event at one point in the *vita*. But these outer limits may be narrowed somewhat by noting that Byrhtferth's text makes no mention (and has no knowledge) of the translation of Oswald's remains, which took place about ten years after his death, on 15 April 1002; and by noting also that Byrhtferth refers to Wulfstan's *Vita s. Æthelwoldi*, which was not completed until after the translation of St Æthelwold in September 996.[24]

Whitelock states, 'It has important information on political history, especially on the confusion after the death of Edgar and on the murder of Edward, being probably the oldest surviving account of this crime.'[25] However, some caution should be exercised. As Lapidge suggests, Byrhtferth 'clearly did not possess' a 'concern for historical accuracy',[26] in his account of the writing of the text. It survives in only one manuscript, British Museum Cotton Nero E1. On the murder of Edward the Martyr, the text informs:

> Certain of the chief men of this land wished to elect as king the king's elder son, Edward by name; some of the nobles wanted the younger, because he appeared to all gentler in speech and deeds. The elder, in fact, inspired in all not only fear but even terror, for [he scourged them] not only with words but truly with dire blows, and especially his own men dwelling with him. Meanwhile nine and five months had run out and the tenth moon was shining for mortals, after he had been elected; the zealous thegns of his brother rose up against him when he was hastening to come to talk with his beloved brother. Treacherous and evil, they sought the life of the innocent youth, whom, Christ predestined and pre-ordained to share a martyr's dignity. When a certain day was nearing evening, the illustrious and elected king came as we have said to the house where his much-loved brother dwelt with the queen, desiring the consolation of brotherly love; there came out to meet him, as was fitting, nobles and chief

men, who stayed with the queen, his mother. They formed among them a wicked plan, for they possessed minds so accursed and such dark diabolical blindness that they did not fear to lay hands on the Lord's anointed ... The thegns then holding him, one drew him on the right towards him as if he wished to give him a kiss, but another seized roughly his left hand and also wounded him. And he shouted, so far as he could: 'What are you doing-breaking my right arm?' And suddenly leapt from the horse and died.[27]

As such, it makes mention of the queen, Elfrida, although it does not specifically lay the blame for Edward's death at her feet, but rather those staying with her. It is intriguing, as it was written while Elfrida still lived, and, certainly, while her son was living. It does point to the murder of Edward being acknowledged by all.

Ælfric's Life of St Æthelwold

The preface of Ælfric's Life of St Æthelwold was written 1005/6.[28] It contains information on Lady Eadgifu and how she was instrumental in keeping Bishop Æthelwold in England. It is largely based on an earlier version of a Life of St Æthelwold, attributed to Wulfstan and which, while containing this story, does not mention Eadgifu by name, but rather lists her as the king's mother. It is interesting that her name is given when Ælfric's work is considered 'an abbreviation of Wulfstan's earlier *vita* of Æthelwold':[29]

> At length, when a time had passed after he [Æthelwold] had received monastic orders, he determined to go to lands across the sea, to train himself more perfectly in sacred books and monastic discipline but the venerable Queen Eadgifu, King Eadred's mother, prevented his attempts, advising the king not to let such a man depart from his kingdom. It then pleased King Eadred by his mother's persuasion to give to the venerable Æthelwold a certain place, Abingdon by name, in which a little monastery was situated in ancient days; but it was then waste and deserted, consisting of poor buildings and possessing only 40 hides.[30]

This life is 'preserved uniquely in Paris, BN lat.5362, ff. 74–81, a manuscript written *c.*1100 by a Norman scribe, either in England or possibly in Normandy'.[31]

The Life of St Dunstan by Osbern

This account was written by an English monk of Christ Church, Canterbury at some point during the later 1000s (from 1050 to 1090). It survives in around twenty copies.[32]

Charters/Wills

The charters and wills of the period have survived in an assortment of combined manuscripts and copies. Many of these have a particularly religious element to them – the great monasteries gathering together all the information they had as a means of 'proving' their ownership to the lands they claimed in later centuries. The dissolution of the monasteries has made this process more complex; equally, it perhaps also gave rise to a growth in the readership of these sources, and allowed them to be better known.

This need of the monasteries, however, also gives rise to the spurious and fabricated charters that have been mentioned, academic historians spending a huge amount of time and effort to determine the true nature of each charter. Not all of them always agree, which adds to some of the confusion. I find it strange that there is no chancellorship that held these manuscripts in one place, and preserved them for future generations, but no doubt, if such existed, it has long since had its assets distributed elsewhere.

Some of these charters survive in only one instance, others survive in over forty manuscripts. S739, a charter in which Lady Elfrida is named as queen survives in only one version, in Aberystwyth, National Library of Wales, Peniarth 390, fl. 1–184, f. 11v (s, xiii med.) written mostly by one scribe between c.1240 and 1264, containing thirty-eight charters, running from Lady Æthelflæd until King Edward the Confessor.[33] S731 survives in thirty-three manuscripts, each with its own unique history.[34]

As such, S739, surviving in a compilation written between *c.*1240 and 1264, will, more than likely, have suffered some corruption in places. We do not know what it was copied from and what the history of these documents was. Each surviving charter and will has its own complex history to consider.

The Life of St Edward the Martyr *c.*1070s now assigned to Goscelin of Saint-Bertin

Passio Sancti Eadwardi Regis et Martyris, an account of Edward's life, murder and miracles probably written in the 1070s by the Anglo-Norman hagiographer Goscelin. This survives in nine versions.

The Life of St Edith, *c.*1080, by Goscelin of Saint-Bertin

This saint's life falls from just outside the period of Saxon England, but its writer arrived in England in *c.*1058 so he would have lived through the upheaval of the events of 1066. Goscelin escorted his master, Hermann, who was to hold the sees of Sherbone and Ramsey, to England. The writing of his texts occurred after the death of Hermann.

That said:

> to read Goscelin is to enter a world where his historical facts are almost – but not entirely – subsumed within the saintly milieu that he created … He claims to have consulted existing vita and extant charters, and most important, went to great lengths to converse with those who had known the saints in question, or were knowledgeable of the history of their own nunneries … Much of Goscelin's information on Wulfthryth and Edith appears to have come directly from Wilton, where he was probably chaplain to the nuns in the 1060s.[35]

The Life of St Wulfhild, *c.*1087, by Goscelin of Saint-Bertin

From the Life of St Wulfhild we are told:

> Elfrida ordered that Wulfhild be stripped of her position and forced to leave the nunnery. According to the Life, when

Wulfhild prepared to leave, her nuns, 'accompanied the sweet mother as she left, like a funeral column of weeping daughters, as if wishing to accompany her on her exile'. The abbess, undaunted, declared that she would go to Barking's sister house at Hortin, but that she would return in twenty years time to rule as abbess over them once more.[36]

The Gesta Normannorum Ducum of William of Jumièges *c.*1060–1070

William of Jumièges falls into the category of writers both before and after the events of the Norman Conquest of 1066. It is believed that the first version of his work was completed by 1060 but added to after the events of the conquest. 'It seems reasonable to assume he [William] was born some time about the year 1000.'[37] The account survives in three manuscripts as written by William himself: C1, C2 and C4.[38] His work, known as Redaction C4, is the 'oldest surviving of the GND'.[39]

The Anglo-Norman Histories of the Twelfth Century

Following the Norman Conquest of 1066, and especially in the twelfth century, a number of 'new' 'histories' were written about the era of Saxon England. For some of the women discussed, there was a particular fascination, most notably because of events during the Anarchy, and the very real threat or belief, that England might have its first female monarch, in the form of Empress Matilda, and a desire to find a previous example who could fulfil the role of success, or failure, depending on what the historians were looking for. This is true of Lady Æthelflæd of the Mercians, a woman who ruled almost as a king, who according to Henry of Huntingdon's account 'some call her not only lady, or queen, but even king'.[40]

These pseudo-historians, William of Malmesbury, a Benedictine monk, writing his *Gesta Regum Anglorum*, in 1125–1127 and his *Gesta Pontificum Anglorum* by that date; Geoffrey Gaimar's *L'Estorie des Engles*, written in 1136; John of Worcester, a monk writing the *Chronicon ex chronicic*, completed by 1141; and Henry of Huntingdon, a secular cleric, writing *Historia Anglorum* 1129–1154, wrote for a reason. Some had a powerful patron, and none of them were above some form of bias in their work. They were writing for the new Anglo-Norman aristocracy, and as such were often writing in Latin, although Geoffrey Gaimar wrote in French. They based much of their writings on the *Anglo-Saxon Chronicle* and information available to them in their monasteries.

Æthelflæd of Mercia is mentioned by all of these writers. Likewise, Lady Elfrida, England's first crowned queen, was harshly treated in later sources, particularly in relation to her role or not in the murder of Edward the Martyr (see particularly William of Malmesbury's account following).

These authors all wrote for a reason, and manipulated the past for their own ends. There is nothing new to this, but when trying to unpick historical 'fact' from the many 'fictions' it is important to be aware of the motivations of our authors and the stories that they pass on. There is an entire body of literature on why the Anglo-Normans chose to portray events in Saxon England as they did. The way Æthelflæd of Mercia was portrayed is also an area of particular study.[41]

It is also important to appreciate the length of time that had elapsed between the writing of these pseudo-histories and the times they depict. While some will argue for the importance of lost sources and oral histories to make these later depictions relevant, this must be done with care. All the same, below is a collection of the information from these later sources, much of it repetition from the *Anglo-Saxon Chronicle*, but also showing the additions.

The initial intention was not to include this in the details of each of the women's lives, but much has now been included with the proviso that it is not contemporary to the events discussed, but speaks to the reputation the women gained within two to three centuries of their lives. Stafford has summed up the use of them succinctly, 'The freedom of their approach to their sources mean that they must be used with care.'[42] It is also important to understand that some versions of the *Anglo-Saxon Chronicle* were still being written and added to during the early years of the twelfth century.

William of Malmesbury's, *Gesta Regum Anglorum* (writing 1125–1127)

William of Malmesbury was born *c.*1095, not far from Malmesbury, Wiltshire. He was of mixed Norman and English parentage. He entered the monastery at Malmesbury and stayed there all his life. Both *Gesta Regum Anglorum* (The Deeds of the Kings of England) and *Gesta Pontificum Anglorum* (The Deeds of the Bishops of England) were completed by 1125.[43]

William of Malmesbury's *Gesta Regum Anglorum* retells much of the information already known from the *Anglo-Saxon Chronicle*, and adds to this information with some tales and scurrilous rumours. The work is dated to the second quarter of the twelfth century. William's work makes mention of Ealhswith, King Alfred's wife, although some of the names used are either incorrect or written in a different format to those we have encountered before. He also makes mention of Æthelflæd and her sisters,[44] referring to Æthelflæd, the Lady of Mercia's marriage[45] as well as her death.[46]

Interestingly, William also has a tale to tell of Edward the Elder's first wife, Athelstan's birth mother, how the girl had 'had a marvellous dream', which she shared with her companions who believed it and as rumours spread, she was taken in by a woman who had been the wet-nurse to Alfred's children. It just so happened that Edward then visited the woman, when 'He saw the girl, fell in love with her, and asked whether he might sleep with her. That one night left her with child, and bearing a son, who was Æthelstan [Athelstan].'[47] William also states that he understands 'The ground of this opposition [to Athelstan's rule], it is said, was Æthelstan's origin as the son of a concubine.'[48] And makes the claim that it was Alfred's wish that Athelstan be brought up in 'the court of his daughter Æthelflæd and Æthelred his son in law'.[49]

Ælfflæd, the second wife of King Edward and the Elder, and her daughters (it is to William that the confusion regarding the number of Edward's daughters us assigned), is also mentioned – in about as much detail as it has already been possible to determine[50] – as well as their marriages.[51] He includes details of Athelstan's peace with Sihtric,[52] and of Athelstan's sister's marriage to Sihtric.[53] As well as the details of Eadhild's marriage to Otto,[54] and the part that Adalulf of Flanders played in the marriage of Eadgyth and Hugh, naming Athelstan's aunt, Æthelswith.[55]

It is William of Malmesbury who tells the story of the marriage of Elfrida to King Edgar.[56]

To William also go to the tales of Edgar violating a nun and the story whereby he was tricked into spending the night with a noblewoman's daughter's slave as opposed to the woman herself. William names Æthelflæd:[57]

> also called Candida, daughter of the powerful ealdorman Ordmær, he begat Edward, and St Eadgyth by Wulfthryth, who was certainly not a nun at the time but as a girl of lay status had adopted the veil out of fear of the king, but later had it snatched away and was forced into royal marriage.

William also associates Edward the Martyr's murder with Ælfthryth/Elfrida, despite that fact that Edward treated his stepmother:

> with proper warmth of feeling … The woman however, with a stepmother's hatred and a viper's guile, in her anxiety that her son should also enjoy the title of king, laid plots against her stepson's life … On his arrival, his stepmother, with a woman's wiles, distracted his attention, and with a kiss of welcome offered him a drink. As he greedily drank it, she had him pierced with a dagger by one of her servants … Ælfthryth fell from her pride of royalty into a dire repentance, such that for many years at Wherwell she clad her delicately nurtured limbs in haircloth.[58]

William of Malmesbury's *Gesta Pontificum Anglorum*

The *Gesta Pontificum Anglorum* adds to the information from *Gesta Regum Anglorum*. This was written and then amended by William himself. The second version 'in which he excised some extensive passages of bitter invective written in his younger days' survives in one manuscript, copied soon after William's death (BL. Claud. A.V), and a thirteenth-century copy of version two, (BL. Reg. D.V). There is also a version surviving in William's own hand, and it is this version which has been translated into English.[59]

William is also aware that Æthelflæd, Lady of the Mercians was involved in translating Saint Oswald's relics from Bardney to Gloucester.[60]

William writes about Edward the Elder's young daughter and her early faith,[61] and later adds the details that she was buried at Pershore.[62]

William mentions Eadgifu's part in keeping Æthelwold in England,[63] and of Ælfgifu's role at Shaftesbury Abbey,[64] as well as Elfrida's involvement in the death of Edward the Martyr,[65] and the penance she undertook.[66] He is effusive about St Edith/Eadgyth,[67] and her sainthood,[68] and King Cnut visiting her tomb.[69]

William confirms that St Edith's feast day is still celebrated and adds details about her mother, Wulfthryth.[70]

Geoffrey Gaimar's *L'Estorie des Engles* (writing before 1147)

As stated in Hardy, R.D. and Martin, C.T. (trans. and ed.) *Lestorie des Engles Solum la Translacion Maistre Geffrei Gaimar:*

> He wrote the book at the request of Custance, wife of Ralf FitzGilbert, using for it manuscripts borrowed by their friend Walter Espec from Robert Earl of Gloucester. This nobleman was the natural son of Henry I – according to Gaimar. Gloucester died in 1147, and as it is clear from Gaimar's words that he wrote in his lifetime, this date is the latest limit of time for the composition of the work.[71]
>
> He was, no doubt, a Norman, the French in which he writes being his natural tongue.[72]

Gaimar, writing in verse, tells us of the meeting of Elfrida and Edgar and also of her involvement in the death of Edward the Martyr, 'that the queen had murdered him'.[73]

The Chronicle of John of Worcester 450–1066

'The Chronicle used to go under the name of Florence of Worcester.'[74] It was compiled at Worcester in the first half of the twelfth century. It survives in five copies and in a single leaf from a sixth.[75]

Having been written at Worcester, it would have been in the heart of Lady Æthelflæd of Mercia's kingdom. It tells that, 'Æthelflæd, Lady of the Mercians, built two towns, namely Chirbury and Weardyrig, after Christmas, and a third, Runcorn, before Christmas.'[76]

Further:

> While these things were taking place his sister Æthelflæd, Lady of the Mercians, distinguished by her prudence and justice, a woman of outstanding virtue, in the eighth year after that in which she began to rule on her own the kingdom of the Mercians with vigorous and just government, died on the nineteenth day before the calends of July, leaving Ælfwynn, her only daughter by Æthelred, the under-king, as heiress to her kingdom.[77]

Under 955, Henry tells of the accession of Eadwig, and the death of Louis, 'king of the West Franks, son of King Charles and of the daughter of the English King Edward the Elder'.

'Liudolf, also, son of the Emperor Otto and of another daughter of that same Edward, died and was buried in the choir of the monastery of St Alban at Mainz.'[78]

Under 958, John writes that, 'St Oda, archbishop of Canterbury, separated Eadwig, king of the West Saxons, and Ælfgifu, either because, as they say, she was Eadwig's relative, or because the king loved her adulterously as if she were his own wife.'[79]

Under 971, John writes, 'The ætheling Edmund, son of King Edgar, died and was buried honourably in the monastery of Romsey.'[80]

Henry of Huntingdon's *Historia Anglorum* (writing 1129–1154)

Henry makes reference to Æthelwold, Edward the Elder's cousin marrying without the consent of the king[81] and also references the death of Ealdorman Sigehelm (amongst others) in 902, the father of Lady Eadgifu, third wife to Edward the Elder:[82]

> In the following year [911], on the death of Æthelred, ealdorman of Mercia, King Edward took possession of London and Oxford, and all the land belonging to the Mercian province.[83]

> In the same year Æthelflæd, the lady of the Mercian, who was ruling the kingdom of Mercia under her sick father [*recte* husband], Æthelred, built the burh at Bremesbyrig.[84]
>
> In King Edward's eighteenth year, Æthelred lord of the Mercians, and father [*recte* husband] of Æthelflæd, who had been ill, died, and gave his land to his daughter [*recte* wife], because he had no son.

Henry then explains, in some detail, Æthelflæd's achievements on a year by year basis and then offers the following when recording her death:

> This lady is said to have been so powerful that in praise and exaltation of her wonderful gifts, some call her not only lady, or queen, but even king. And the view has been put forward that if fate had not snatched her away so swiftly, she would have surpassed all men in valour. In memory of such prowess I have forced the muse, granter of immortality, to say just a little.
>
> O mighty Æthelflæd! O virgin, the dread of men, conqueror of nature, worthy of a man's name! Nature made you a girl, so you would be more illustrious, your prowess made you acquire the name of man. For you alone it is right to change the name of your sex; you were a mighty queen and a king who won victories. Even Caesar's triumphs did not bring such great rewards. Virgin heroine, more illustrious than Caesar, farewell.[85]
>
> In the twenty-sixth [*recte* twenty-first, 920] year of your reign, king Edward, acting with regard to expediency rather than to justice, disinherited Ælfwynn, Æthelflæd's sister [*recte* daughter], who had succeeded her, of the lordship of the whole of Mercia.[86]

The *Liber Eliensis*, A History of the Isle of Ely from the seventh to the twelfth century

This was composed towards the end of the twelfth century, and is a cartulary-chronicle. 'A cartulary-chronicle is not a fully integrated piece of historiography but resembles a modern source book designed to present primary texts as the basis of a course for students on some historical theme.'[87]

It contains information on the two wives of King Edmund and Æthelflæd's sister as well as details of the possible father of King Edgar's first wife, also called Æthelflæd, plus an early reference to Elfrida, the third wife of King Edgar.

Elfrida had displayed her support of Bishop Æthelwold while still married to her first husband:

> A woman called Ælfthryth pleaded with King Edgar that he sell to the blessed Æthelwold ten hides at Stoke, which is near Ipswich, and two mills which are situated in the southern part. Her entreaties availed with him. For the bishop gave the king one hundred mancuses for that land and the mills, [and] he afterwards presented [the same land and mills] to St Æthelthryth.[88]

Chronicon Abbatie Ramesiensis

The *Chronicon* was compiled around 1170, with the addition of some later charters up to 1200. The author is unknown. It survives, as far as I can determine, in two manuscripts, Public Records Office, E 164/28 and Bodleian Library, Rawlinson MS. B. 333 a thirteenth-century manuscript.[89] It contains information about those who made bequests to the abbey and this includes the family of Athelstan Half-King as well as containing the information that Ælfwynn may have been King Edgar's foster mother.

Chapter 11

The Royal Women of the Long Tenth Century

To tell the story of the royal women who made England, the focus has so far been much on what is known about them as individuals from the surviving source material. Many of these women are little more than stray names, but some of them were undoubtedly unimaginably powerful, if not for the entirety of their lives. Now is the time to add the context of their lives to the known events of the tenth century.

The death of Alfred, and the rule of Edward the Elder (his unnamed first wife, Lady Ælfflæd, Lady Eadgifu, Lady Æthelflæd of Mercia and her daughter, Ælfwynn)

King Alfred died on 26 October 899. His oldest son's coronation occurred on 8 June 900 at Kingston upon Thames, or perhaps Winchester. There is some disagreement about this.[1]

There is also dispute about another important element of the coronation ceremony. Wessex's kings had, until either 899, or the coronation of Athelstan in 925, been consecrated with a helmet, not a crown. After all, these men were warrior kings. Foot has discussed this at length, assigning the development of coronation with a crown to the reign of Athelstan, not Edward. As such, if we follow this reasoning, Edward the Elder would have undergone his coronation wearing a helmet, although not a simple everyday helmet, perhaps one more akin to that discovered at Sutton Hoo or reconstructed in the wake of the find of the Staffordshire Horde.

At this time, Edward would have already been the father of two children, Athelstan, and his unnamed daughter who went on to marry Sihtric of York. The mother of the children is believed to have been his wife and named Ecgwynn, and later attempts to label her as the king's concubine might well have more to do with the efforts, in 924, to discredit Athelstan's claim to rule following the deaths of his father and brother. (Her obscurity may also, perhaps, have something to do with the churches stricture about marrying more than twice.) While much of the woman's identity is unknown, it is believed that she was most likely the daughter of one of the Wessex ealdormen. What happened to her is unknown. She may have died, perhaps in childbirth. She may have simply retired to a nunnery, as was the preferred method for the discarded women of the House of Wessex. As such, Edward was either already married to Lady Ælfflæd, his second wife, or would soon be after his father died. But there is another context to explore.

For all the coronation seems to have proceeded smoothly following the death of Edward's father, buried firstly at the Old Minister, Winchester, and then transferred to the New Minister, Winchester, on completion of the building work he had instigated, there were problems on the horizon for the newly proclaimed king. While the period of time between his father's death and his coronation may have been more to do with the logistics of the event, or the need to wait for a more auspicious holy day, the delay is still noteworthy, at nearly eight months. 'The fact that Edward succeeded his father Alfred, and that all succeeding Anglo-Saxon kings were his direct descendants, can make it seem that his accession was inevitable.'[2]

Alfred had been the fourth of four brothers to rule. He was to enjoy his kingdom for the longest period, but he had two nephews, arguably with a better claim to rule the House of Wessex than Edward, being the sons of the older brother, Æthelred. Æthelwold was the only one to still be living at the death of Alfred, but the discussion around the land bequeathed to Æthelwold through Alfred's will seems to have been raging for some time.

Alfred had not, for whatever reason, quite followed the letter of the agreement reached between him and his brother in 871 at Swinbeorg when distributing the lands following the death of Æthelred, and this persisted into Alfred's will. Æthelwold, therefore, had a grievance and one that was perhaps legitimate. It is possible that Æthelwold was not only the son of a king, but he might also have been the son of a queen. A surviving charter, S340, dated to 868 and surviving in one manuscript, from King Æthelred's reign names Wulfthryth,[3] Æthelred's wife as *regina*.[4] As such, Æthelwold might well have been the son of both a consecrated king and a consecrated queen, unlike Alfred's wife, who was never titled as queen. (The title assigned to Wulfthryth is most unusual in Wessex before the reign of King Edgar's wife in the 960s, and is the only known occurrence.)

It is in this context that Edward's second marriage should perhaps be assessed. Ælfflæd is believed to have been the daughter of a powerful ealdorman.[5] She, therefore, brought Edward much-needed support at a time when his kingship was threatened by his cousin. If his first wife had died, it would have been natural for the king to remarry. If she had been put aside, her children deemed illegitimate, then the same would have been the case. As such, Ælfflæd could have been a means of securing the kingship and the loyalty of a powerful family at a difficult time for the king. That the union was a success cannot be denied. Lady Ælfflæd had two sons who lived to adulthood, as well as at least six daughters. She was not well rewarded for her attention to her wifely duties, either dying or retiring to Wilton nunnery alongside her daughters.

Affairs in Mercia at this time were firmly in the hands of Lady Æthelflæd, following the death of her husband at some point around 911. Lady Æthelflæd and Lord Æthelred only produced one daughter but were a successful, in fact, very successful force in Mercia from *c.*886 onwards, until Æthelflæd's death in June 918. After the death of her husband in 911, it was Æthelflæd who continued their work, holding firm against the Viking raiders, and attacking into Wales. Æthelflæd's reputation saw her consistently mentioned in the *Anglo-Saxon Chronicle*, with the suggestion that one version of the *Chronicle* was actually being kept as a specifically Æthelflædian chronicle, recounting her successes against the Viking raiders:

> And the same year Æthelflæd built the stronghold at *Bremesbyrig.* (910-C)

> Here, on the eve of the Invention of the Holy Cross, Æthelflæd, Lady of the Mercians, came to *Scergeat* and built a stronghold there, and the same year that at Bridgnorth. (912-C)

> Here Æthelflæd built Tamworth and also Stafford stronghold. (913-D)

> Æthelflæd sent an army into Wales and broke down Breconmore and then took the wife of the king as of thirty-four. (916-C)

> Here before Lammas, God helping, Æthelflæd, Lady of the Mercians, took possession of the stronghold which is called Derby; together with all that belonged to it. (917-C)

While this perhaps makes it appear as though Æthelflæd was merely involved in building burhs, it would be difficult to think she did so without first winning back the land to then build the burhs.

Her death, reliably dated to June 918, quite likely caused a power vacuum in Mercia and, against the combined enemies of Wessex and Mercia, it was one which Edward the Elder might have needed to counter quickly.

Just before her death, Æthelflæd had taken control of Leicester and had reached an accord with York. (918-C). Her death, if unexpected, would have come at a time when Edward and Æthelflæd might have felt themselves on the brink of a final and, perhaps, defining success against the Viking raiders. After so many years of near-constant warfare, it must be supposed that Edward did not wish to lose the initiative.

Edward's third marriage, to Lady Eadgifu, should be considered in relation to the political situation at the time. Edward's rule was one of near-constant war against the Viking raiders, just like his sister's in Mercia. To look at the *Anglo-Saxon Chronicle* for the period is to read an almost unrelenting list of war and battle:

> Here Æthelwold came across the sea with all the fleet he could get and submission was made to him at Exeter.[6] (902-A)

> Then King Edward went after them as quickly as he could gather his army, and raided across all their land between the Dykes and the Wissey.[7] (903-A)

> Here King Edward, from necessity, confirmed peace both with the raiding-army from East Anglia, and with the Northumbrians.[8] (906-E)

> Here the Mercians and West Saxons fought against the raiding-army near Tettenhall on 6 August and had the victory.[9] (909-C)

> And the king gathered some hundred ships, and was then in Kent; and the ships went east along the south coast towards him ... Then the raiding-army imagined that the most part of his reinforcement was on these ships, and that they might go unfought wherever they wanted. Then when the king learned that they had gone on a raid, he sent his army both from

Wessex and from Mercia and then fought with them and put the raiding-army to flight, and killed many of it.[10] (910-D)

Here in this year after Easter the raiding-army rode out from Northampton and Leicester and broke the peace, and killed many men at Hook Norton and thereabouts.[11] (913-A)

The raiding-army from Northampton and from Leicester and north of there, broke the peace and went to Towcester and fought against the stronghold all day.[12] (917-A)

Edward's actions, on the death of his sister, amount to two things if the date of Edward's third marriage can be correctly dated to 918/919. Edward put his fertile and long-suffering wife aside, perhaps Lady Ælfflæd was no longer able to bear children, or perhaps she thought she had done enough, bearing eight children for her husband. Maybe she did die. For whatever reason, Edward dispensed with his second wife and promptly took a third wife and one strongly associated with the ancient kingdom of Kent and, also, the daughter of a man who had died fighting for him against Æthelwold at the Battle of the Holme in 902/3. [13]

Edward might have been shoring up his defences at the heartland of his Wessex kingdom, ready for what he must do next, and that was, secondly, to claim the kingship of Mercia, previously ruled by his sister, to make himself not just the king of the Anglo-Saxons, but the king of Wessex and Mercia.

If only there were some surviving charters from the later parts of his reign, it might be possible to see this evolution taking place. What are available, are the *Anglo-Saxon Chronicle* entries for the final years of Edward's rule:

From there he went to Nottingham and captured the stronghold.[14] (918-A)

In late harvest-time, King Edward went with an army to Thelwall, and ordered the stronghold to be made.[15] (919-A)

King Edward went to Nottingham with an army, and ordered a stronghold to be made opposite the other on the south side of the river.[16] (920-A)

Here King Edward built the stronghold at the mouth of the Clwyd.[17] (921-C)

And then the king of Scots and all the nation of the Scots chose him as father and lord; and [so also did] Rægnald [of York] and Eadwulf's [Bamburgh] sons and all those who live in Northumbria, both English and Danish and Norwegians and others; and also the king of the Strathclyde Britons and all Strathclyde Britons.[18] (920-A)

These entries reveal that Edward was quite possibly, rarely, if ever, in the kingdom of Wessex. He was prepared to take the fight to the enemy Norse. His death, occurring in 924 at Farndon, equally found him on the fringes of the extent of Mercia. He might have been putting down a Mercian revolt. Equally, he might have been fighting Wessex and Mercia's combined enemies. Whatever he died from, he died far from the heartland of Wessex.

It is possible that events fell in such a way that Edward was left with no choice but to remarry Lady Eadgifu of Kent, and to oust his niece, Lady Ælfwynn, from Mercia to ensure the hold of the House of Wessex on the kingdom remained. Ælfwynn might have been her mother's preferred successor, but Ælfwynn did not have the military reputation that her mother did (as far as we know). It might well be that while Edward's acts can be interpreted as rampant ambition, there might have been something else at play – the need to ensure his sister's Mercian legacy was maintained. This legacy was decades old, not just through Æthelflæd's marriage to Æthelred, Lord of Mercia, but also through their mother. Ealhswith had been a Mercian by birth. Her mother might have been a member of an ancient Mercian royal family. Her father was a Mercian ealdorman, and so was her brother.

It is, perhaps, in this context that the possibility that Ælfwynn, the second Lady of the Mercians, marrying Athelstan Half-King, as opposed to becoming a religious woman, could be explored. If this union occurred, the date of it is unknown. Athelstan Half-King was appointed as an ealdorman at some time before 932 and would have four sons, who were all powerful individuals (his oldest son would marry the future Queen Elfrida before her marriage to King Edgar). Athelstan Half-King was also one of four brothers, all of whom were ealdormen: Ælfstan in Mercia; Athelstan in East Anglia; Æthelwold in Kent; and Eadric in Wessex. Their father was an ealdorman, witnessing charters for Æthelred, Lord of Mercia and Edward.

It is his wife who is said to have been the foster mother of the young, orphaned Edgar, son of Edmund and Ælfgifu of Shaftesbury,[19] and so the son of her cousin. Athelstan was ealdorman of East Anglia, and his wife would therefore have been an important woman, whether or not she was the king's (Athelstan's) cousin. One fact that must go against this is that until the reign of Æthelred II, none of the king's daughters were married to an ealdorman, although the king often married an ealdorman's daughter. In this instance, it is quite probable that the marriage occurred before Athelstan Half-King was named as an ealdorman. He came from a powerful Mercian family, but perhaps here, Athelstan was continuing his father's policy of dynastic marriage, and utilising his cousin as a means of securing East Anglia. Perhaps, unlike his ambitious half-sisters, who all either married on the Continent, or became nuns, Athelstan trusted his cousin to continue her mother's work in extending the extent of the control of the Wessex royal house. After all, Athelstan's full sister had made a dynastic marriage with Sihtric of York. That is was ultimately unsuccessful does not mean that the policy was never tried again. None of the details about whether or not Ælfwynn married Athelstan Half-King, can be substantiated.

The sons of Edward the Elder (Ælfweard, Athelstan, Edwin, Edmund and Eadred) (Lady Eadgifu, Lady Ælfgifu of Shaftesbury, Lady Wynflæd, Lady Æthelflæd of Damerham)

Edward the Elder's death was unforeseen and, certainly, the death of Ælfweard only sixteen days later was very unexpected. If we are to believe what we are told in the *Anglo-Saxon Chronicle* entry for 924 in the D version, 'Athelstan was chosen as king by the Mercians', this perhaps points to a realisation on Edward's part that ruling both Wessex and Mercia was a task too huge for either of his sons. This does, to my mind at least, have the hallmark of a man who believed himself the only one capable of achieving such a feat. But, in practical terms, we are not told that Ælfweard was married. And it is known that Athelstan never married. Both of Edward's sons, therefore, did not have the support of a powerful family behind them. If Athelstan's mother was dead, and of course, we know nothing about her family, then he might not have been able to call on their assistance, no matter his military prowess. Equally, we know nothing of Ælfweard's military prowess, and we are never told whether he was married or not. Nor do we know if his mother, Lady Ælfflæd, retired to a nunnery, either forcibly or not, or had died by this time. If Ælfweard's full sister, the queen of West Frankia, had returned to Wessex with her son, then it is possible that she would have supported Ælfweard's claim for the kingship. Still, Athelstan's powerbase was Mercia, where his aunt, Æthelflæd, had raised him, if we believe the words of William of Malmesbury. It is unknown if Athelstan had spent any time in Wessex during his father's second marriage to Lady Ælfflæd, as all the surviving charters from that period are deemed spurious.

Put simply, neither Athelstan or Ælfweard had the capacity, at that time, to rule Mercia and Wessex combined confident that the heartland of Wessex would stay loyal to them if their attention was diverted elsewhere. Unlike his father, Edward seems to have been slow to ensure a smooth succession for his sons to rule after him. There is no mention of any sort of division, as had been agreed between Alfred and his brother, Æthelred in 871, and Edward's will has not survived, so his intentions are entirely unknown.

The fact that no mention is made in the surviving sources of Edwin as a successor to his dead brother, is intriguing. Perhaps Edwin was never in serious contention. Perhaps he was too young to rule. Perhaps there was an impediment to his rule.

Much has been made of the delay to Athelstan's coronation, which did not take place until 925 although his father, and half-brother died in the summer of 924. Yet, this delay might not be as extended as envisaged. Edward was not immediately consecrated on his father's death, and if Edward died in Farndon putting down a revolt of either the Mercians against his rule, or because of battle against the Viking raiders, then Athelstan might well have been with his father and been left with no choice but to continue his military aggressiveness. Events in Wessex, with the death of Ælfweard, might not have been his main area of priority. Especially as, while his mother might have been dead, and Lady Ælfflæd as well, the Wessex heartland was not without a strong ruler. Lady Eadgifu, Edward the Elder's third wife, probably younger than Athelstan, might well have fulfilled the projected role for Athelstan as she did for her husband when he was absent from Wessex.

Eadgifu, with her strong family connections in Kent, and her three children, two young sons, and a daughter who must already have been at the Nunnaminster, if the involvement of Edward the Elder in her placement there is to be believed, could have held Wessex secure while events played out to the north.

Yes, Edward the Elder might have been dead, his son Ælfweard as well, but the overriding concern must have been to secure the House of Wessex, on whoever's head the helmet or crown would rest.

Not for the first, or last, time, Lady Eadgifu must have played some part in securing the succession. Some might point to her lack of involvement in Athelstan's later affairs and her failure to appear as a witness to any of Athelstan's charters, but Athelstan's determination not to marry, and to accept her sons as his heirs, must have endowed her with influence, even if she does appear largely absent from his court. There is a suggestion she too might have become a religious woman on the death of her husband, but this cannot be said with any surety. That said, it has been commented that Athelstan, like his father, was very much a military man. Edward might have been involved in battle against the Viking raiders for much of his life, but it was Athelstan who pushed the boundaries even further, travelling far beyond anywhere a Wessex monarch has been recorded before (apart from a reference to his father's grandfather taking the submission of the Northumbrians in about 828).[20] Athelstan not only journeyed to the north, to York and Eamont in 927, and the location of Brunanburh in 937 but further still, into Scotland in 934, via Chester-le-Street. Athelstan himself might not often have been in the heartlands of Wessex. In fact, his decision to be buried at Malmesbury, on the border with Wessex and Mercia, points to someone who was not comfortable in the Wessex heartlands.

Foot has studied the movements of Athelstan and comments that while 'we do not know him to have issued charters or law-codes at many places in the former Mercian kingdom [it] does not necessarily mean that he did not spend much time in the midland counties'.[21]

Athelstan, like his father, was prepared to make war on his enemies, but even he seems at pains to have preferred peace. Athelstan wed his unnamed birth-sister to Sihtric of York. While the union broke down, it was a pretext for him to claim York after Sihtric's death. It is equally possible he wed his cousin, Ælfwynn, to a powerful noble family with roots in Mercia and East Anglia, and of course, three or four of his half-sisters made unions on the Continent. And when some of these unions were less than successful, Athelstan stepped in and aided until such time as his nephew, and wider network of foster children were able to reclaim their lost possessions.

It is possible, although impossible to say for sure, that the unions of Eadhild and Eadgyth, which occurred after the birth of Louis to Eadgifu and Charles III, and after Charles III had been deposed, were put in place with an expectation that, in time, their husbands would assist Louis to become king of West Frankia. While the tragedy is that none of Athelstan's half-sisters lived long enough to secure the success of their dynasties, Athelstan, following on from his father, might well have been pursuing the same policies. Who is to say that Alfred, when he arranged the union of his daughter to Baldwin II of Flanders, was not already envisaging a wider sphere of influence for the Wessex ruling family – after all, just like Charlemagne, he had an official biography written for him by Asser. Athelstan, and his father, may have simply been continuing this policy.

For those sisters who were not needed for this wider pursuit, the church provided another means of securing the Wessex ruling family. Shaftesbury, where Athelstan's aunt was abbess, became a centre of royal patronage, as did Wilton and the Nunnaminster. And who knows what was actually happening behind those cloister walls? Rather than thinking that these women were banished, perhaps they had their part to play in propagating the right for the Wessex ruling family to rule. After all, we do not know whose hands first penned the *Anglo-Saxon Chronicle*. And Stafford has made it clear that those quills might just have been wielded by female as well as male hands in monasteries and nunneries. And it is quite possible that these daughters of Christ still had worldly pursuits – why else would these women have needed gifts of land, witnessed by the king? They may not have been strictly 'locked up' behind the doors and walls of their nunneries as we might envisage it by the use of the word 'nun'.

But to return to Athelstan. Whatever his relationship with Lady Eadgifu, his father's third wife, what can be said with surety is that Athelstan's death in 939 propelled her to even greater influence in England.

When her husband died in 924, Lady Eadgifu's sons might have been no older than 4 and 2. As such, it is highly unlikely that they were given any consideration in the race to see who would become the next king. The same could not be said in 939, and indeed, there was potentially no hint of an alternative being suggested. Edmund is said to have fought at

Athelstan's side at Brunanburh. He might have still been a young man, but as the oldest of two surviving brothers, it was to him that the eyes of the Witan turned.

For all that, and despite the victory that Athelstan had enjoyed at Brunanburh, the kingdom of England was still far from assured. Edmund would spend much of his brief reign at war, in many ways redoing the work of Athelstan, halted by Athelstan's death. It has even been suggested that the famous naval expedition of 939, which ultimately eroded the friendship with relatives in Flanders, might have been supposed to be joined by Otto I, Athelstan's brother by marriage. We do not know what Athelstan's intentions were before his death. Certainly, his reign has the feel to it that great things could have been expected had he not died.

Yet, Athelstan's overwhelming victory at Brunanburh perhaps did much damage. Whereas at Eamont Athelstan had tried for a peace, the other rulers on the British Isles were not to be swayed, and events throughout his reign do seem to have burbled uncontrollably to all-out war. But, as with all battles, those left behind proved determined to undo the harm done to their family and kingdom.

It cannot be said for sure when the rebellion against Athelstan's claim to an imperium over Britain, and against his victory at Brunanburh,[22] began, whether it was before his death or whether it occurred as a consequence of it. What is sure is that Edmund faced almost immediate reverses in Mercia and further north. *The Anglo-Saxon Chronicle* records the following events:

> Here the Northumbrians belied their pledges, and chose
> Olaf from Ireland as their king.[23] (941-D)

> Here King Edmund, lord of the English,
> Guardian kinsmen, beloved instigator of deeds,
> Conquered Mercia, bounded by the Dore,
> Whitwell Gap and Humber river,
> Broad ocean-stream, five boroughs:
> Leicester and Lincoln,
> And Nottingham, likewise Stamford also
> And Derby. Earlier the Danes were under Northmen,
>   subjected by force
> In heathens' captive fetters,
> For a long time until they were ransomed again,

149

To the honour of Edward's son,
Protector of warriors, King Edmund.[24] (942-A & D)

Here Olaf broke down Tamworth and a great slaughter fell
on either side, and the Danes had the victory … Here King
Edmund besieged King Olaf and Archbishop Wulfstan in
Leicester, and he might have controlled them had they not
escaped from the stronghold in the night.[25] (943-D)

Here King Edmund brought all Northumbria into his
domain, and caused to flee away two kings, Olaf Sihtricson
and Rægnald Guthfrithson.[26] (944-A)

Here King Edmund raided across all the land of Cumbria
and ceded it to Malcolm, king of Scots on condition that he
would be his co-operator both on sea and land.[27] (945-A)

If Edmund spent so much of his time fighting in Mercia and further north,
who then was to protect his interests in the Wessex heartlands. Sadly,
we know very little about Edmund's first wife, Ælfgifu of Shaftesbury.
Certainly, she did her duty to the king, in producing two sons in very
short time. Equally, her mother, Wynflæd, may have been from a noble
family. But would either of these two women have been able to hold
firm to Wessex while Edmund was away? Or did this position once more
fall to Lady Eadgifu, his mother?

Admittedly, at this point, mention must be made of Edmund's brother,
Eadred. We have seen that he soon replaced his mother as the leading
witness to Edmund's charters, and perhaps the intention was that Eadred
should become the protector of the king's sons. But in this, the House of
Wessex was to suffer another set back, with Edmund's murder in 946.
If the entry for 945 is to be believed, the English king, as it is now right
to term him, was on the brink of success in the northern reaches of the
kingdom, having beaten back the Viking raiders at York, and indeed,
forged an alliance with the king of the Scots. By this time, Constantine of
the Scots had abdicated to become a monk (potentially not by choice), and
been replaced by Máel Coluim mac Domnail, also known as Malcolm I.
Malcolm was not a son of Constantine. That was not how the kings of the
Scots were determined. The line of succession strictly alternated between
two ruling families at this time. Constantine had replaced Máel Coluim's
father, and in turn, he was replaced by Máel Coluim himself.

Edmund's death threatened to undo all the military accomplishments the two English kings had so far achieved. And if Eadred, witnessing his brother's charters in second place, perhaps while their mother took a less directly involved approach now that Edmund had proved himself worthy of being Athelstan's successor, had been the person to whom the Wessex heartland had been left in Edmund's many absences, then who was to fulfil that role now it was Eadred who needed to fight England's battles in the north?

It would be remiss not to mention Edmund's second wife, Æthelflæd of Damerham, and yet it is difficult to find her while she was married to the king. The union might have only lasted a matter of months. There is no reference to her being queen, but it is possible she developed a close relationship with the king's two sons, even though they were very young.

Once more, attention must focus on Lady Eadgifu, Eadred's mother, and importantly, the grandmother of Eadwig and Edgar. Eadred had not yet married when Edmund was murdered in 946. While mention is made of the man who killed the king, named as a thief, nothing else is known of the motivations for the murder of the king. Was it pure happenstance or something more sinister? Could Edmund have been assassinated by England's enemies?

Whatever happened, the kingdom of England was once more in peril in 946. The entries concerning Eadred in the *Anglo-Saxon Chronicle* read just as much like a diary of military manoeuvres, as do those of his brothers, cousin and father:

> And then his brother the ætheling Eadred succeeded to the kingdom and reduced all the land of Northumbria to his control; and the Scots granted him oaths that they would do all that he wanted.[28] (946-A)

> Here King Eadred came to Tanshelf, and there Archbishop Wulfstan and all the councillors of Northumbria pledged themselves to the king, and within a short while they belied both pledge and oaths also.[29] (947-D)

> Here King Eadred raided across all of the lands of Northumbria, because they had taken Eric for their king … And then when the king was on his way home, the raiding-army [which] was within York overtook the king's army from behind at Castleford and a great slaughter was made there. Then the king became so angry that he wanted to invade again and completely do for the country. Then when

the council of the Northumbrians heard that, they abandoned Eric and compensated King Eadred for the act.[30] (948-D)

Here King Eadred ordered Wulfstan to be brought into Jedburgh, into the fort, because he was frequently accused to the king. And also in this year the king ordered a great slaughter to be made in the town of Thetford, in vengeance of the death of Abbot Eadhelm, whom they killed earlier.[31] (952-D)

Here the Northumbrians drove out Eric, and Eadred succeeded to the kingdom of Northumbria.[32] (954-E)

This Eric is believed to perhaps be Eric Bloodaxe, although there is some debate about whether the identification is correct.[33]

Eadred then was often to be at war with Northumbria, governed once more by the Dublin Norse.

Lady Eadgifu was no doubt instrumental in keeping the heartlands of Wessex secure throughout this period of Eadred's extended warfare. Eadwig and Edgar were still boys when their father died, and very young children at that. The court was probably not a good place to be raising such small children. The identity of the foster mothers is known.[34] If, as it is suggested, Ælfwynn is the daughter of Lady Æthelflæd, Lady of the Mercians, and the wife to Ealdorman Athelstan Half-King, then Edgar was placed in the care of a powerful family, perhaps as a means of growing his powerbase in later years. Even if this Ælfwynn is not the missing Ælfwynn, the family of Athelstan Half-King was still immensely powerful. Eadwig was also placed with an influential family, although less is known of this, other than it appears it may have been one of the ealdormen of Wessex, perhaps the family of the woman he went on to marry. There is the possibility that the woman's name was Ælfswith and that she was the recipient of land in charter S593, in which she is named as a faithful woman.[35] There is also a suggestion that Wynflæd, Eadwig and Edgar's maternal grandmother, remarried at this time into a family known to be powerful in Mercia. If this happened, then the boys were also members of another powerful ealdormanic family, which allowed Ealdorman Ælfhere to be named as *ex parentela regis* in S582 and his brother-in-law, Ælfric Cild, to be named as *adoptivus parens* in S597.[36]

What was potentially at play here was an attempt to garner support for two parentless children, one of whom was hoping to succeed to the kingship after his uncle, Eadred.

Lady Eadgifu's central role in this can be clearly gleaned from her position of importance in the surviving charter witness lists. Yet, it is unlikely that she was acting entirely alone. She could have relied on the support of Wynflæd, the boys' maternal grandmother, whether she remarried or not, and also on Æthelflæd of Damerham, the boys' stepmother. Is it possible, that at this time of military strife, the true power behind the Wessex royal family was not the militaristic approach of Eadred, and his predecessors, but rather three women (perhaps four or five, if the foster mothers are included in this tally), who laboured to ensure the kingdom remained whole until either, or both, of the young sons could inherit, including powerful ealdormanic families with roots in East Anglia, Mercia and also Wessex.

Here, a slight detour. Many will know that Alfred was often said to be unwell. There is also a belief that Eadred may also have been in ill-health. The children of Edward the Elder do not appear to have enjoyed long lives. Athelstan died at a young age, Edmund was murdered, and Edwin seems to have drowned. Already, by Eadred's death in 955, Eadgifu, Queen of the West Franks had perished, so too had Lady Eadhild, married to Hugh the Great, and Eadgyth, married to Otto I. It is unknown when the religious sisters died, although Eadburh, a nun from a young age, died in 952. The line was not long-lived, and neither was it overly fertile, until Æthelred II and his large family very much mirrored that of Edward the Elder's.

The sons of Edmund (Lady Eadgifu, Lady Æthelflæd of Damerham, Ælfgifu, Æthelflæd, Wulfthryth, Elfrida, Wynflæd)

At Eadred's death in 955, we are again told of a split between Mercia and Wessex in *the Anglo-Saxon Chronicle* D:

> Here King Eadred passed away, and he rests in the Old Minster. And Eadwig succeeded to the kingdom of Wessex, and his brother Edgar succeeded to the kingdom of Mercia.[37]

Does this split reflect the realities of the foster mothers of the two children? Or, does the D text err or record false information? The E text simply informs, 'Eadwig, son of Edmund, succeeded to the kingdom.'[38]

Both the B and C preserve the knowledge that while Eadwig succeeded to the kingdom in 957, 'Here the ætheling Edgar succeeded to the kingdom of Mercia.'[39]

This then is difficult to disentangle. Were Mercia and Wessex split once more, as perhaps would have been the intention had Ælfweard lived longer than sixteen days, when Athelstan was declared king by the Mercians, or was this a matter of Edgar being assigned an under-kingship in Mercia, as had happened in the past (famously Alfred's father was the under-king of Kent during his father's reign)? This would have been a means of both sons having some power following the early death of Eadred. And what did the women in their lives think of this arrangement?

Lady Eadgifu had now outlived all her children. She was probably in her fifties. None of her children had been long-lived, although it should be noted that Edmund's life was ended unnaturally by his murderer in 946.

Eadgifu had two grandsons, who, if the information we have is correct about their foster families, may have had very different experiences: Eadwig raised in the Wessex heartlands; Edgar raised by an ealdormanic family, with strong links to Mercia and East Anglia. And Lady Eadgifu, as a study of the charters during Eadred's reign shows, was a woman in a position of considerable power. Had she hoped, perhaps, to follow her daughter and retire from the tribulations of court life? Or was she forced out of it to shepherd in the reign of another king? Or was her grandson, Eadwig, attempting to oust her from an entrenched position that she had absolutely no intention of giving up?

Eadwig's elevation to the kingship, and his death, are mentioned in the *Anglo-Saxon Chronicle*. He ruled from his uncle's death on 23 November 955 until 1 October 959, just under four years. The *Anglo-Saxon Chronicle* offers no knowledge of military affairs during this period but is filled with details of holy men, Archbishop Wulfstan's death in 956-E, Abbot Dunstan's exile 956-A/957-D and then in 958-D the one event that Eadwig is most remembered for, his divorce from his wife, Lady Ælfgifu, carried out by Archbishop Oda 'because they were related'.[40] (958-D).

Lady Ælfgifu did not become the wife of the king in a vacuum. It is highly likely that two of her brothers, Æthelweard and Ælfweard, accompanied her in taking up a position at the king's court. And neither were her brothers the only 'new' men at court. Ælfhere of Mercia also became an ealdorman in 956 (and would remain one until 983). It is believed that his father,

Ealhhelm, was an ealdorman in Mercia during Edmund's reign but, prior to 955, neither Ælfhere nor two of his three brothers have any citations in court documents. One of the brothers, Ælfheah, had been the beneficiary of several charters (S531, S554 and S570).[41] It is into this family that Eadwig's maternal grandmother may have remarried.

Another new man, Byrhtnoth, became an ealdorman from 956 onwards (until his death at the Battle of Maldon in 991). Ealdorman Byrhtnoth married the sister of King Edmund's second wife, Æthelflæd of Damerham, Ælfflæd. And it is Ealdorman Byrhtnoth who became the ealdorman of Essex, replacing the wealthy father of Æthelflæd and Ælfflæd in the position, upon their father's death.

Why, then, would these 'new men' suddenly rise at the court? Why would Eadwig have to dispense with so much of his property in such a short space of time, as he seems to have done throughout 956 to 959? It appears as though he was trying to build a new faction for himself, one that ran counter to the one in power throughout the reigns of his father and his uncle. One that would assure his place as king and not that of his brother? Or perhaps, more importantly, not that of his grandmother. Much of this centred around his choice of wife, so much so that Archbishop Oda, loyal to Lady Eadgifu, ordered the two to be divorced in 958. It must have come as a relief for Eadwig when the archbishop died later in the year. But perhaps not for Lady Eadgifu, and another of her supporters, Bishop Dunstan, who was sent into exile. And not just any exile, but one where he might have turned to the family of King Alfred, and sought sanctuary in Flanders with Arnulf I of Flanders, the son of Alfred's daughter.

This then is somewhat difficult to account for. If Eadwig had made allies of the ealdorman of Mercia, why was it Edgar who was proclaimed as king there? Equally, if it was Lady Eadgifu who had been the steadying force throughout the reign of her two sons, why was it that Eadwig so violently turned against her when he became king? Did Lady Eadgifu represent all that was 'old' and Eadwig wished to distance himself from his overly powerful grandmother? Did he have all the arrogance of youth and determine that everything that had gone before was outdated? Did he chafe at the constraints that his grandmother might have placed upon him?

It is said that King Eadred's death in 955 was not unexpected. He had been ill for some time. And yet, Eadwig was little older than a boy, no more than 15 when he became king. This was the first time that such a young man had been declared king of Wessex, and he was certainly, the youngest king of England. Had Eadred's illness been so long that those unhappy with the current ruling elite had already begun to look to Eadwig as the chance for change, just as Hugh the Great with his nephew Louis, king of the West Franks, at no more than 16? Had powerful ealdormanic families determined to use Eadwig against Lady Eadgifu and those loyal to her, which included her other grandson, Edgar? Or, if not Edgar directly, then certainly his foster family? Was this split the result of factionalism that perhaps threatened to become violent?

Here, note must be taken of Ealdorman Athelstan Half-King who retired to Glastonbury in 957, having ensured his son could become ealdorman in his place. His son, Æthelwold, attests to two charters as a thegn in 957 before then ascending to the title of ealdorman. Was this a quick bit of political thinking on the part of Ealdorman Athelstan Half-King, desperate for his family to hold on to their possessions in the wake of such fierce resistance against the status quo? Is there even more to the ealdorman's retirement to Glastonbury than might be thought? Or were his actions merely those of a man grieving his wife and desperate to ensure her spiritual welfare as well as that of his family? Long a close adherent to the House of Wessex, did the death of Eadred, following the death of kings Edmund and Athelstan, both allies of Athelstan Half-King, make him aware of his mortality?

Lady Eadgifu later stated that she had been 'despoiled of all her property' and forced to retire also.[42] Perhaps then, there was a larger issue behind the dramatic events of 955–959. Eadwig issued eighty-seven charters during his reign. Seventy-one of these were to named individuals. Eadric, Æthelwold, Æthelgeard, Ælfric, Wulfric and Ælfheah are notable for being in receipt of at least three charters each, although it is possible that these charters were issued to individuals who shared a name, as opposed to the same identity. Fifty-seven of these charters were from the first two years of Eadwig's reign (555 and 556). Three of these fifty-seven charters may not be original.

This vast increase in surviving charters is telling. Lady Eadgifu is only a witness to one of these charters, S658, dated to 959, but deemed as spurious. So, if this spurious charter is ignored, Lady Eadgifu did not witness any of the huge number of charters that her oldest grandson issued during his brief reign. This is in stark contrast to the reigns of her two sons, and indeed, she witnesses four of Edgar's charters and has Edgar confirm the details for her land at Cooling, with charter S1211, during the seven years of his rule that she lived through (if she did die in 966, that is).

Having witnessed sixty-two of Eadwig's charters during 955, 956 and 957, Edgar then attests as king of Mercia in 958,[43] and Eadwig's name does not appear on these charters. Edgar is able to issue his own charters without recourse to an over-king, as Eadwig might have been perceived if Edgar was merely an under-king at this time.

This factionalism revolves around Eadwig's choice of a wife. Ignoring the more scurrilous works of later writers, it is the issue of who Lady Ælfgifu was that caused so many problems. Ælfgifu, is likely to have been the granddaughter of Æthelwold, cousin to King Edward the Elder, who was involved in the death of Lady Eadgifu's father at the Battle of the Holme in 902/3 when he rebelled against Edward the Elder's rule.

How then did Edgar become acclaimed as the king of Mercia? Was this the work of Lady Eadgifu and her powerful allies, one of whom was the bishop of Lichfield, working in partnership with the family of Ealdorman Athelstan Half-King? While unable to build a powerbase for Edgar in Wessex, did they go a step further and turn to Mercia, the former kingdom which was so loyal to Alfred's daughter and his grandson? Did Mercia once more aim to be the proving ground for the future king of England?

It is impossible to know. Eadwig's death, in 959, when he was perhaps no more than 19, brought an end to the split kingship of Mercia and Wessex. Edgar was quickly elected king of England, and Lady Eadgifu soon had her lands returned to her. Yet, the House of Wessex now had only a tenuous grasp on the future. Should Edgar die without an heir, there was no one to replace him. The 'spare' sons of Edward the Elder and Edmund had finally run out.

Edgar married quickly. The name of his first wife is unknown with surety, but the union was a success. Edward was born perhaps as early as 960. Certainly, to squeeze Edgar's three unions into the first five years of his rule, they need to have happened quickly.

Æthelflæd, if that was her name, is potentially only known from two sources, one which names her as Æthelflæd the White, and one which names her father and seems to make sense of the more tangled stories which confuse Æthelflæd and Elfrida. She attests to none of Edgar's surviving charters. Potentially, she died in childbirth. Maybe she retired to a nunnery, as Edgar's second wife would do. It is unfortunate that we know so little of her. Did Edgar perhaps marry her when he was king of Mercia and make a Mercian marriage to enforce his claims to rule there? Did he then need to remarry and take a more suitable Wessex wife, one who would be consecrated as queen and therefore produce sons who would be more acceptable as his heirs? Without more knowledge of who Edgar's first wife was, it is impossible to determine if, like his grandfather, Edgar's intention was to make a series of dynastic marriages that made ealdormanic families loyal to his rule during the years when he either did not yet have an heir or when he only had a very young son to rule after him. Equally, is the fog surrounding Edgar's first wife concerned with the stricture that people should not marry more than twice?

Certainly, it seems as though Edgar's second marriage was political, especially if the stories surrounding it are to be believed, that he wished to marry Wulfhild, but was content instead to marry her cousin, Wulfthryth, because he merely wanted a bride who was a member of the family. This family is believed to be Wessex based. It is possible that having spent time in Mercia, Edgar needed to shore up his support in Wessex. The family of Wulfhild and Wulfthryth, if related to the family of Æthelred I's wife, had a long pedigree. Jayakumar has examined information regarding the region and the family of Wulfthryth, named as the wife of Æthelred I (Alfred's brother). She has made connections between Wulfthryth and her brother, Wulfhere and traced their descent until about the middle of the 950s. As such, it has not been possible to directly connect the two Wulfthryths, but the name is unusual enough, and the location of the family consolidated enough that the relationship is indeed possible.[44]

This is rare at this time. Until the House of Leofwine (originally ealdorman of the Hwicce, a part of Mercia) from the end of the tenth century to just after 1066, no family other than the House of Wessex can be seen to have consistently held a position of power and influence for nearly 100 years (not even the family of Athelstan Half-King). In this, the House of Leofwine exceeded the House of Godwine, and indeed, the two families were united in marriage before the devastating events of 1066, when Harold Godwinesson was wed to Edith, daughter of Ælfgar, Leofwine's great-granddaughter, who had previously been wed to one of the Welsh kings, Gruffydd ap Llewelyn.[45]

Perhaps the unions of Edgar should be viewed in a slightly different light. Lady Eadgifu, for so long a stalwart of the Wessex ruling family, was perhaps nearing her sixties, if not already in her sixties. Since the death of her husband, she had not, as far as is known, remarried (it has been postulated that she might have remarried during Eadred's reign, but there is little proof of this). And, she had, other than during Eadwig's rule, remained a consistent member of the court for at least twenty years, if not over thirty, depending on what position she took during Athelstan's rule. She might have secured the kingdom of Kent for her husband and ensured the ancient kingdom was firmly embedded into the English kingdom, but she could not live forever. (Kent only became a part of Wessex during the 820s, when the Mercian overkingship of King Offa was fragmented during a time that could be termed civil war between the ruling families. King Ecgberht, Alfred's grandfather, was quick to take advantage of Mercia's weaknesses.)

If Lady Eadgifu were to die, where would Edgar look for his firmest support? To his foster family? Ealdorman Athelstan Half-King was dead by now, probably his wife as well. Edgar could be assured of support in East Anglia, but Athelstan Half-King's brothers were no longer ealdormen, and his brother had advanced many unknown men to the ealdordoms. (Ealdorman Ælfstan, Athelstan's brother, had only held the Mercian ealdordom for about four years, before his death in *c.*934. Ealdorman Æthelwold of Kent, no longer attested charters after 946 and Ealdorman Eadric of Wessex ceased to attest from 949, and so must be assumed to have been dead.) Only one of Edgar's foster brothers held an ealdordom, that of Æthelwold in East Anglia.

Eadwig had advanced Ealdorman Ælfhere to Mercia; Ealdorman Byrhtnoth in Essex; and Æthelweard, the brother of Eadwig's wife, while not yet an ealdorman, was also important at the royal court, as was his brother.

Did Edgar therefore need to assure himself of support in Wessex by marrying into a well-established family? If he did, the union with Wulfthryth did not last long. Elfrida, as we have seen, with her strong West Country roots, was the widow of Ealdorman Æthelwold. Perhaps it was this, more than anything else, that brought them together. Maybe, in their grief, they both wanted to be closer to one another. Or maybe not. Perhaps the union was as calculated as Edgar's union to Wulfthryth. Sadly, we will never know. The later rumours, of Elfrida's beauty and the murder of Ealdorman Æthelwold by Edgar, are more than likely just that, rumours, thought up by holy communities keen to have their revenge on both Edgar and Elfrida for their reforming movements throughout the 960s and 970s, until Edgar's death.

Elfrida might have been Edgar's third wife, but the union lasted until his death, despite the fact that only two children were born, and one of those children died in infancy. In such a situation, it would not be impossible for Edgar to have sought yet another wife. But he did not do so. Perhaps it was this that brought the older son, Edward, back into contention. It is possible that Elfrida was now in a position which had been denied to her predecessors. We know she was crowned queen. But it seems that her role included more than merely being the wife to the king and mother of his heirs.

Barrow has looked very closely at the chronology of the Benedictine Reform, which took place during Edgar's reign. She concludes that Ælfthryth/Elfrida was:

> hyperactive in the years 964–966, which saw her marriage to Edgar, her production of an heir and her assistance with the monastic takeover at New Minster. Ælfthryth belonged to a family which was interested in monasticism, she supported [Bishop] Æthelwold, and her reward, a very valuable one, was to be put in charge of all the nunneries (and thus of their assets, which … were considerable).[46]

The words from the *Regularis Concordia,* developed in the late 960s and early 970s to ensure the adoption of the Benedictine form of monasticism, state:

> And he [Edgar] saw to it wisely that his queen Ælfthryth [Elfrida], should be the protectress and fearless guardian of the monasteries; so that he himself helping the men and his consort helping the women there should be no cause for any breath of scandal.[47]

And further:

> No monk, nor indeed any man whatever his rank, should dare to enter and frequent the places set aside for nuns; and that those who have spiritual authority over nuns should use their powers not as worldly tyrants but in the interests of good discipline.[48]

There is an irony here, for Edgar was indeed held to account in later sources for doing just this. Were the later writings an excuse for scribes to draw attention to Edgar's duplicity, or were they meant, somehow, ironically? Were these rumours begun by those dispossessed of their livelihoods when the reforms took place? Put briefly, many of the complaints against the monastic order do seem to have been levied at the lay clerics, who might often have been married. The same complaints do not seem to have been levelled against the female monastics, but there was a belief that they perhaps meddled too greatly in worldly affairs.

In later life, after the death of Edgar, Elfrida was forced to justify some of her actions during this period, when she worked closely with Bishop Æthelwold. Charter S1242, dated from 995 to 1002, and surviving in one manuscript, reads:

> Ælfthryth [Elfrida] ... bear[s] witness that Archbishop Dunstan assigned Taunton to Bishop Æthelwold, in conformity with the bishop's charters. And King Edgar then relinquished it ... and moreover he put Ruishton under the bishop's control. And then Wulfgyrth rode to be at Combe and sought me. And I, then, because she was my kinswoman, and Ælfswith because he [i.e. Leofric] was her brother, obtained from Bishop Æthelwold that they [i.e. Wulfgyrth and Leofric] might enjoy the land for their lifetime, and after their death the land should go to Taunton ... And with great difficulty we two brought matter to this conclusion. Now I have been told that Bishop Æthelwold and I must have obtained the title-deed (*boc*) from Leofric by force. Now I, who am alive, am not aware of any force any more than he would be, if he were alive. For Leofric had a new title-deed (*boc*); when he gave it up he thereby manifested that he would engage no more in false dealings in the matter. Then Bishop Æthelwold told him that none of his successors could dispossess him. He then commanded two documents (*twa gewritu*) to be written, one he kept for himself, the other he gave to Leofric.[49]

Further:

> In 1002 Wherwell took the opportunity of Queen Ælfthryth's [Elfrida] death to clarify its relationship to her. It claimed that she had appropriated 60 hides at *Æthelingadene* for her own use, which were not to be restored and allocated to the

feeding and clothing of the nuns, and sought confirmation to the nunnery of the 70 hides at Wherwell which Ælfthryth [Elfrida] had possessed as long as she lived. Wherwell may not be typical. Its anxiety to face a new queen [Emma] armed with an unambiguous freedom may have led it to include all the lands on which Ælfthryth could possibly have a call.[50] (S904, dated to 1002, and surviving in eight manuscripts.)

Elfrida's role over the nunneries might well have brought her into conflict with Edgar's second wife, and equally the woman, Wulfhild, that Edgar sought to marry first before Wulfthryth. A study on Wilton has concluded that Wilton cannot be shown to have been reformed during Wulfthryth's time as abbess.[51] It also seems that Wulfhild was cast out of the nunnery at Barking for failing to live by the rule, and Elfrida is blamed for this. Wulfthryth then, did not agree with the reforming tendencies of Bishop Æthelwold and Elfrida, and perhaps, neither did Wulfhild.

There is equally the possibility that Edgar chose to remarry a reformer because his second wife had refused to become involved in this movement, undertaken most notably by Edgar's childhood tutor, Bishop Æthelwold. If a record in the *Liber Eliensis* is correct, Elfrida had displayed her support of Bishop Æthelwold while still married to her first husband:

> A woman called Ælfthryth pleaded with King Edgar that he sell to the blessed Æthelwold ten hides at Stoke, which is near Ipswich, and two mills which are situated in the southern part. Her entreaties availed with him. For the bishop gave the king one hundred mancuses for that land and the mills, [and] he afterwards presented [the same land and mills] to St Æthelthryth.[52]

The fervour for religious reform should not be dismissed as a passing phase, perhaps Edgar, his wife and Bishop Æthelwold, as well as Oswald, another reformer, were indeed swept along by the desire to bring about sweeping changes. Alternatively, it is possible that the sources simply mention the reform more than anything else. Maybe the changes were not quite as far-reaching as thought. However, what happened after Edgar's death does need considering.

The sons of Edgar the Peaceable (Elfrida)

If Edgar has earned himself the title 'the peaceable' in later sources, it certainly was not quite so peaceable following his unexpected death.

Edgar died a young man still, perhaps no older than 30 to 35. Much has been made of his second coronation perhaps taking place at the age of 30, in 973, in imitation of Christ taking up his holy vows.

Edgar left two sons, Edmund having died in 971 at a young age. Neither of his surviving children were particularly old, and they both had different mothers. Edward, the child of perhaps Æthelflæd, and Æthelred, the surviving child of Edgar and his queen, Elfrida, who had ruled at Edgar's side for about a decade. Edward was probably no more than 15 in 975, Æthelred perhaps as young as 8. While the kingdom of the English might well have endured years of peace (perhaps we should be wary of this 'peace'. There might be no mention of war, only reconciliation and alliances with the other kingdoms on the British Isles, but this could all have been part of the illusion, supplied by our chroniclers, writing at a later date, to contrast with the affairs of his son's reign) the same could not be said for the court.

The factionalism of the great monastic reform movement has much to do with those who lost land, and those who gained. As ever, religion was a mask for what was happening at a more basic level, it could just as easily be interpreted as a land grab. 'Attacks on church property were widespread. From York to Kent and Sussex, from the Severn valley to the Fens the death of Edgar was a signal to those who wished to recover property.'[53] Whether or not Edgar intended for his royal son, born to a consecrated mother and father to succeed after him, might have been irrelevant when faced with two opposing parties – one supporting the older Edward and one Æthelred. It has been suggested that the preferred heir would have been Edmund had he not predeceased his father.

Essentially, both sons could have been too young to rule England. Eadwig, their uncle, had hardly provided good and secure rule during his brief reign from 955 to 959, when no older than 15. But there was no other choice, unless note was made of the family of Ælfgifu, wife to Eadwig, and her collection of brothers, claiming descent from Æthelred I, Alfred's older brother. We have already met Æthelweard and his *Chronicon* on multiple occasions.

It seems that Edward was chosen to rule, with the support of one of the powerful factions, perhaps led by Ealdorman Æthelwine of the

East Angles, Elfrida's previous brother-in-law (perhaps there was no love lost between the two), and Edward's coronation was conducted by Archbishop Dunstan. Yet Elfrida believed her son should be king, no matter his young age. She too had support from Ealdorman Ælfhere of Mercia (an interesting twist as he had been an appointee of Eadwig during the last discord regarding the kingship). Perhaps this then, might have been a solution – a division of England once more. Yet 'questions of division or under-kingship were replaced by a straightforward struggle for the throne of the entire kingdom.'[54] This was a move away from what had gone before. Thinking back to Athelstan and Ælfweard, the one proclaimed king of Mercia and the other king of Wessex, and even of Eadwig and the division with his brother, Edgar, if indeed, it was more than just a matter of an administrative division.

And yet there might well be parallels unseen in the Athelstan/Ælfweard resolution, possibly in the Edmund/Eadred succession, if that was a crisis, and perhaps even in the Eadwig/Edgar one, only this time, it is known that young Edward was murdered. What we do not know, as with the murder of his grandfather, be it political or happenstance, is who killed Edward. The E text tells us of the date of Edward's murder and his burial place.[55]

The C text offers, 'Here on this year King Edward was martyred, and his brother, the young ætheling Æthelred, succeeded to the kingdom; and he was consecrated as king the same year.'[56]

The A text is simpler but still states that Edward was killed. It was therefore, an acknowledged truth, that Edward was killed, and in his place, Æthelred, at no more than perhaps 12 years of age, became king. This can only have been possible with strong support for Æthelred. Those backing Æthelred's claim must have been powerful enough to counter any other bid for the kingdom. It no doubt helped that few others could legitimately claim the kingship for themselves. Had they turned to any latent claim presented by Ealdorman Æthelweard, who by now was possibly a man in his late thirties or forties (his death is believed to have taken place in about 998 when he stops attesting Æthelred's charters), then his sons might not have been deemed acceptable to rule after him, having been born to a man not consecrated as king, and a woman who was certainly not regarded as a queen.

But did a lack of potential other claimants make it possible for such a young boy to become England's king, or was it those who supported him; those who, perhaps, and as later legend portrayed, had ordered the murder of his older brother, Edward the Martyr? Did Elfrida, England's first anointed queen, commit regicide in an attempt to win back the influence she unexpectedly lost on the death of her young husband?

There were certainly some who believed she had a hand in the murder of the young man.[57]

The involvement of Elfrida directly in the murder of her stepson is:

> derived ultimately from the *Passio Sancti Eadwardi Regis et Martyris*, an account of Edward's life, murder and miracles probably written in the 1070s by the Anglo-Norman hagiographer Goscelin and itself based partly on an earlier account of St Edward which may have been written at Shaftesbury in the early years of the eleventh century.[58]

Equally, the mid-eleventh century *Life of St Dunstan* by Osbern states that Edward was 'killed by a stepmother's deceit'.[59] Following the death of Æthelred, and his mother, her name, as well as his, were more easily assigned to the murder of Edward.

It is perplexing to consider the alleged involvement of Elfrida in the death of her stepson with the cult of Edward the Martyr that developed. Indeed, it has been noted that in the will of Athelstan, Æthelred's son who died in 1014, and who was raised by Elfrida, he makes a bequest to Shaftesbury to St Edward: 'And I give to the Holy Cross and St Edward at Shaftesbury the six pounds about which I have given directions to my brother Edmund.'[60]

Another near-contemporary source, The Sermon of the Wolf to the English, states that, 'Edward was betrayed and then killed, and afterwards burned and [Ethelred was driven out of his country].'[61] This dates from 1014, and therefore follows Æthelred's loss of the kingdom to King Swein of Denmark.

This is more than a strange thing to do if the family was keen to dismiss the concerns that Elfrida was involved in the king's murder. I also find it strange that, unlike with the murder of Thomas Becket, the argument has not been made that perhaps this was some sort of overheard conversation which was acted upon when there was no intention that it should be. Despite the reports that Edward the Martyr was not a pleasant individual, has it been considered that the murder was carried out because ALL believed they would benefit from a new king. Edward the Martyr, in the written details about him, does not have a good reputation, as the *Vita Oswaldi* states below:

> Certain of the chief men of this land wished to elect as king the king's elder son, Edward by name; some of the nobles wanted the younger because he appeared to all gentler in speech and deeds. The elder, in fact, inspired in all not only fear but even terror, for [he scrouged them] not only with words but truly with dire blows, and especially his own men dwelling with him.[62]

At such a distance in time, it is impossible to tell. Dismissing the later saints' lives and aspersions cast on Elfrida, by Adam of Bremen, Osbern of Canterbury, Florence of Worcester [John of Worcester], Henry of Huntingdon,[63] and Simeon of Durham, who wrote, Edward 'was miserably murdered by the treachery of his stepmother',[64] one thing is clear. Whatever had happened to pave the way for Æthelred to become king, it was accepted by the vast majority of the Witan and the holy men.

Sometimes, mention is made that Æthelred's coronation was delayed, taking place on 4 May 979, perhaps while negotiations took place, but this, as has been seen with Athelstan in particular, and possibly also Edward the Elder, was not unusual. Was it a delay because Æthelred was unacceptable, or merely one of politic? Or is it merely a confusion with the date, 979 for 978, or something else? Was Æthelred considered too young in 978 to undergo coronation? Was he ill? Sometimes, we forget the frailties of our forebears, too keen to see political intrigue everywhere.

There are two surviving charters from 979, deemed as authentic by Keynes in his detailed analysis of Æthelred's charters.[65] One is to Ealdorman Ælfhere, and one to Æthelwold, the bishop of Winchester, both supporters of the new king. S834, surviving in two manuscripts, has a long witness list, but amongst those, Elfrida is missing. S835, also surviving in two manuscripts, has a much shorter witness list, and Elfrida is recorded as one of those witnessing the charter, but only after the two archbishops and two bishops. This does not seem to have been an auspicious start for the king's mother. Unlike her predecessor, Lady Eadgifu, she does not witness these two charters directly beneath her son.

The same pattern repeats itself in 980. Of the two surviving charters, S836 and S837, Elfrida only witnesses S837, and then it is beneath the bishops.[66]

In 981, there is only one surviving charter, that of S838, surviving in two manuscripts, which Keynes determines as 'spurious as it stands'.[67] This charter, issued to Æthelred's uncle, Ordwulf, his mother's brother, in regards to Tavistock is unwitnessed by Elfrida, although it has a witness list of twenty-two other names. Ordwulf's association with Tavistock is mentioned in the *Anglo-Saxon Chronicle* under 997 (E) when the Viking raiders 'burned down Ordwulf's monastery at Tavistock'.[68]

This, then, is curious. While there are only five surviving charters, and one of them might well be a later forgery or certainly not authentic in its current format, Elfrida only witnesses half of the charters and not in a position of great strength. Instead, it seems to be the archbishops and bishops, alongside the ruling men, who are listed as witnesses.

During the remainder of her lifetime, Elfrida witnesses thirteen of Æthelred's charters, and is in receipt of one, while she acts as a witness in another legal document. In the same period, there are a total of seventy surviving charters. This does not point to Elfrida being a constant and consistent witness for her son's charters.[69] However, some caution is again needed, as Elfrida's charter witnessing is very much a matter of two halves, seven of these charters witnessed before 983, seven after 996, and with only two in the intervening thirteen years, one of which, S877, when she is the recipient of the charter, and this is then one of the same charters mentioned as under 996.

What then happened to Elfrida after 983 until 996, and why is she not an immediate witness for Æthelred's charters, as Lady Eadgifu was during the reign of Edmund and Eadred? Was she not, as has been suggested, instrumental in ensuring her son's position as England's king, but again found some use as the woman responsible for the upbringing of her oldest grandson, Athelstan? Perhaps Elfrida was keen to be absent from court, to hand over the running of the kingdom to the ambitious ealdormen, her former brother by marriage, and Ealdorman Ælfhere of Mercia, safe in the knowledge that the religious figures of Bishop Æthelwold and the archbishops would ensure the smooth running of the kingdom. Or was she sidelined, used as a scapegoat for the murder of Edward the Martyr?

These are questions that are impossible to answer, but certainly, it does not seem, on the available evidence, to be as simple as blackening her name as that of a murderess or as someone so ambitious that she fought her way to power and influence after the death of her stepson.

The grant of land in 988 and reiterated in 996 show that Elfrida was still in her son's thoughts. The fact that she was called as a witness in a legal case in the early 990s, again reveals she was deemed a woman of honour, able to bear witness in the legal case brought about by Wynflæd. 'Wynnflæd [Wynflæd] produced her witnesses at Woolmer before King Æthelred to bear witness that Ælfric gave her land at Hagbourne and Bradfield, Berks., in return for land at Datchet, Bucks.'[70]

And yet, it is certain that from 996, Elfrida was once more in the king's favour, and witnessing his charters. Where she had been for these years is unknown. It could be argued that the king's wife had supplanted her, and yet Ælfgifu, if that is her name, does not appear in any of the king's charters.

Ælfgifu's marriage to the king, while clearly successful, did not see her assigned any land in the charters that are available to us, and indeed, the end of the marriage may well have coincided not with her death, or her banishment to a nunnery, although that may have followed, but with the death of her father, Thored of Northumbria, or even his fall from grace with the king. Thored, mentioned in the *Anglo-Saxon Chronicle* for 992 was one of the men called upon to support the king against the Viking raiders and their renewed attacks in the early 990s. Into such a power vacuum, left by a dead wife or one banished for her ineffectual father, it might have been necessary to recall one of Æthelred's prime supporters, one who could be relied upon no matter what else was happening, that of his mother, Elfrida.

Here, perhaps, is to be seen Elfrida more closely mirroring her predecessor, Lady Eadgifu, in ensuring the continuing line of the House of Wessex by taking responsibility for the king's children, until her death in either 1001 or 1002. 'Elfrida was granted the estate of Dean in Sussex when she accepted the charge of her grandchildren. This has traditionally belonged to the æthelings in Anglo-Saxon England and she would have spent some time there with the children.'[71]

The years of the later tenth century, following the death of Edgar, but also perhaps during his lifetime, allow us to catch a glimpse of an ever-growing quantity of women who might have been present at the king's court. These women all had some connection to the House of

Wessex, if they were not directly a part of it. Amongst their number are: Æthelflæd of Damerham, and her sister and daughter Ælfflæd and Leoflæd; Ælfgifu, the wife of Eadwig; Æthelflæd, Edgar's first wife; Wulfthryth, his second wife and their daughter Edith; and Elfrida his third – as well as Eadgifu, the third wife of Edward the Elder, and possibly Wynflæd, Edgar's maternal grandmother. We also know the names of the thrice-married Ealdorman Æthelwine of East Anglia's wives, as well as the wife of Ealdorman Æthelweard. There is a real sense of a female presence at the royal court, perhaps even a court where the queen, in imitation of what we know would come in the future, had her own royal servants and allies. We hear mention of priests and seneschals, so why not ladies in waiting, ladies of the bedchamber? And equally, why not factions amongst the female members of the king's court. The suggestion of unease amongst the nunneries when Elfrida was named as their protector and attempted to instigate reforms, only to be rebuffed by Wulfthryth and the woman Edgar is supposed to have wanted to marry first, Wulfhild, may be the mere hint of deeper undercurrents.

And, of course, through all this discussion, Æthelred's wife, Ælfgifu, should not be forgotten. Like his great-grandfather before him, Æthelred was to father many daughters. What was the position of their mother in the court, and that of his daughters, who were married to English men of prominence, according to later sources? If there was a backwards step, and Ælfgifu was never consecrated or named as his queen, then what prompted this, only for Lady Emma to certainly be named as Æthelred's queen on their union in 1001/1002? Was it as simple as the fact that Elfrida yet lived, or was it as the pact in 856 which started the continental links between Flanders and Wessex, with the marriage of Æthelwulf to Judith, a part of the marriage treaty, which saw Emma anointed and consecrated as England's queen prior to her arrival in England?

This period sees interactions with the continental branch of the families seemingly fall away. Or does it? The *Anglo-Saxon Chronicle* entry for 982-C makes mention of Liudolf's son dying, the grandson of Eadgyth.[72] Indeed, this entry is quite long, and having discussed the Viking invasions in Dorset and Portland, the *Anglo-Saxon Chronicle* continues:

> And the same year Otto, emperor of the Romans, went to
> the land of the Greeks, and then met a great army of the

Saracens coming up from the sea [who] wanted to make a raid on the Christian people. And then the emperor fought against them, and there was great slaughter on either side, and the emperor had possession of the place of slaughter; and yet he was greatly harassed there before he turned back from there. And then, as he went home, his brother's son, who was called Otto, passed away, and he was the son of the ætheling Liudolf, and this Liudolf was son of Otto the Elder and King Edward's daughter.[73]

Perhaps, although there is little sight of it in the sources for the period, continental links were still important to the family. Although, here again, we must turn to Æthelweard's *Chronicon*, written for a relative of his, Matilda, Abbess of Essen. If the words of the *Chronicon* are to be believed, while the Wessex ruling family were aware of some of their living relatives, there were some for whom no one knew about their lives after their marriages. Æthelweard asks Matilda for assistance in finding some of the lost women. It is unfortunate that we do not know if the pair of them were able to resolve the loss of information.

The daughters of Æthelred II

While the intention has been to tell the story of the royal women of the tenth century, the death of Elfrida, and arrival of Lady Emma in 1001/1002, is a perfect place to bring the narrative to a conclusion; but what little is known of Æthelred's children is worthy of a brief exploration.

Æthelred II appears to have instigated a policy entirely at odds with that of his forebears. He did marry his daughters to the ealdormen of England throughout the early 1000s. We do not know how old any of his daughters were. They do not witness any of their father's charters, unlike Æthelred's sons, who by S904, dated to 1002 and surviving in eight manuscripts, were witnessing in force. Athelstan, Ecgberht, Eadmund [Edmund], Eadred, Eadwig and Eadgar; those names were certainly mindful of the House of Wessex's ancestry.

There is no mention of these sons marrying. Athelstan died in 1014, and yet, it might be supposed that he would have married long before his death. While his date of birth is unknown, he begins to attest charters from 993, alongside Eadred and after his grandmother, named as *mater regis* in S876, surviving in four manuscripts, and subsequent charters. As such, Athelstan must have been born by 993 at the very latest, and so he would have been at least 21 before his death.

However, by then, his father had remarried Emma of Normandy, and fathered another two sons, as well as a further daughter, Godgifu/ Gode. Perhaps Æthelred had determined that his heir would be Edward, the oldest of his sons born to Emma? We do know that Eadmund, or Edmund, married, and that he fathered two children, perhaps twins, before his death in 1016. We also know the identity of his wife, the widow of one of his allies, but this marriage union is more caught up in the political unease of the middle 1010s than anything else. Although, it is worth noting that she was a woman with strong roots in Mercia. Perhaps this was not by chance.

In stark contrast to his sons, it is believed that three of his daughters were married to ealdormen, or men almost deemed as ealdormen: Eadric of Mercia; Uhtred of Northumbria; and Oscytel of East Anglia. These unions may have taken place to secure the country against the growing threat of the Viking raider menace in the form of Swein and Cnut of Denmark. Alternatively, is it possible that Æthelred was attempting to develop a powerbase for himself, just as his father might have done? Æthelred's reign is so often overshadowed by the military triumphs of the Second Viking Age, that on occasion it is possible to lose sight of what might have been sound political strategy. Some might point to the union of his youngest daughter, Godgifu/Gode, with the Count of Vexin, Drogo, but this union was arranged by Godgifu/Gode's uncle when she was living in exile in Normandy.

The unions of Æthelred's daughters do seem to mirror the decisions of Kings Alfred and Athelstan. Alfred wed his daughter to Æthelred, Lord of Mercia. Athelstan arranged for his full sister to marry into the ruling family of York. (And if Ælfwynn, the wife of Ealdorman Athelstan Half-King was Athelstan's cousin, then again, perhaps another union arranged to bring East Anglia into closer control.) These marriages, which could be interpreted as 'external' unions to kingdoms not yet part of what would become England, might equally be seen as a way of ensuring the survival of Wessex. By the time Æthelred II came to rule, Wessex had become England, and it was an even bigger domain to control. Perhaps it is time to look at the unions Æthelred II made for his daughters, not as a weak king attempting to 'buy' the loyalty of his ealdormen, but as a man who knew the worth of his royal blood, and who wished to mirror the actions of his illustrious ancestors, those men who were most regaled for beating the attacks of the Viking raiders.

Maybe Æthelred II, in mimicry of the lives of his grandmother and mother, hoped to utilise his daughters, who were perhaps also raised by Lady Elfrida, to secure his dynasty for future generations. That the policy ultimately failed may have more to do with the fact that the Viking raiders' menace was so much more overwhelming than before. The attacks of the 1010s, which saw England conquered not once but twice, were headed not by Viking raider jarls keen to make money from the slave market but by the very king of Denmark and his son.

Chapter 12

Conclusion

The idea behind this work was to bring together as much contemporary information as possible about the royal women of the tenth century in one place, and to return their names to a narrative that has long forgotten them, so much so, that some of the women's names are not even known. As Foot comments, 'It appears ... that Edward the Elder had in fact just eight daughters in his large family.'[1] It feels more than bizarre that we are left desperately trying to reconcile accounts to even number the daughters of a king of the Anglo-Saxons. And still, there are descendants, especially on the Continent, that there is simply no knowledge about, and there was no knowledge of even within a few decades of their lifetime.

Along the way, it has been necessary to place these women in their context as members of the powerful family of the ruling Wessex royal family who came to rule what we know as 'England' by the middle part of the tenth century onwards. I make no bones that I have drawn on my imagination when considering what their part might have been in this, because without it, it is impossible to realise them as real people, who loved, hated and generally hoped to enjoy long and fulfilling lives, who were ambitious, perhaps sometimes ill, perhaps sometimes sad, and for some of these women, to endure long periods of widowhood, which they might have put to good use, but which might have forced them to endure years of loneliness rather than risk remarrying, and losing their position and influence.

It has also been necessary to consider the complex ideals that we should not see change where it might merely have been a natural extension of something that had gone before, but of which we have no knowledge. Was the position of 'queen' becoming more readily applied to these women, or was it just that some women, in particular, were accorded this title, perhaps not for their actions during the lives of their husbands, but rather, during the lives of their sons and grandsons, or was the title a prerequisite of the marriage negotiations? The information from the period, which we might think is contemporary, can often prove to not be. As such, although it was my intention to disregard later source material, I have chosen to include information that may date from up to three centuries later, but with the understanding that I acknowledge it speaks more of the reputation of these women than their lives.

It has been necessary to understand the complex and fragmentary source material, the bias and propaganda of saints' lives, later Norman pseudo-histories as well as the complex structure of the *Anglo-Saxon Chronicle*, as well as happenstance that accounts for the survival of some sources to the present day. It has also been necessary to detour to the Continent at a complex time in its history. And it is complex. I am a casual visitor to East and West Frankia, to Flanders and the county of Burgundy, and it feels as though I am wading in mud. Considering continental authors adds yet another layer of complexity to sources that are either written in Latin or Old English anyway. I am more than grateful to those who have gone before me and offered translations for these works, even while I acknowledge that relying on translations removes me from the original source as well. This is nowhere more marked than in Foot's examination of the meaning behind the word *nunne* in the source material. It has also been necessary to make mention of the Anglo-Norman histories written to explain some of what we think we know about these women.

I have included details of other women named in the sources. This has been for two reasons: to show that women who were not members of the House of Wessex could be wealthy, leave wills and take part in pursuing justice for themselves; they could be religious women, although this did not preclude them from being wealthy as well. And secondly because the brief knowledge we have of the House of Wessex royal women is not unusual. The survival of solitary wills hints at these 'lost' women and highlights just how much is unknown.

I cannot say that the task is complete, but hopefully, readers will now know more than that Lady Æthelflæd defeated the Viking raiders in Mercia, and that Lady Elfrida was responsible for regicide, as Anglo-Norman historians might wish us to believe. Readers will also, I hope, understand that dismissing the passage of time between events and their written record as merely the work of 'verbal history' is rife for misinterpretation and hindsight to have mashed the true history.

Lady Æthelflæd and Queen Elfrida were just two of many. Lady Æthelflæd may owe much of her renown to flowering interest in her, both during the Anarchy of the 1130s, and in current popular culture, as well as to a desire to return women to their place in the historical record, but without all these Wessex royal women, it is highly doubtful that the troubled period between the two Viking Ages would have resulted in the 'Peaceable' reign of King Edgar, or, as quoted at the beginning of this book, allowed one royal family to rule what would become England in an almost continuous line from 839 to 1013–1016, and then again from 1042 to 1066.

And to this end, I believe that more attention needs to be turned to Lady Eadgifu, third wife to King Edward the Elder, and to the stabilising force she played in the history of the period. She was the wife to a king, mother to two more (three if Athelstan, her stepson, is included), and the grandmother to two more (Eadwig and Edgar), as well as the great-grandmother to Edward the Martyr and Æthelred II, and then great-great-grandmother to Edmund Ironside, and Edward the Confessor. While it has been mentioned that Edward the Elder is the ancestor of all the Wessex royal kings to 1066, it would not have been possible without Eadgifu. She is, thus, more than a name on a charter and a name entirely missing from the *Anglo-Saxon Chronicle* in all of its recensions, unlike Lady Æthelflæd. And Lady Eadgifu is merely the most long-lived of all these women, for whom it is possible to assign a part in the very fabric of the tenth century.

Just think, if we knew only of the events of the wars that the late Queen Elizabeth II had lived through, what would we make of her reign, other than that she was a mother to four children, whose life we might try and tell through the fragmentary knowledge of their lives?

Biographical Details

Ælfflæd, (*c.*875–*c.*922) daughter of Ealdorman Æthelhelm,

m. King Edward the Elder (*c.*874–924, r. 899–17 July 924). She 'retired' to Wilton Nunnery when Edward remarried, or had perhaps already died.

> Ælfweard (d.924)
> Edwin (d.933)
> Æthelhild
> Eadgifu (d.951)
> Eadflæd
> Eadhild
> Eadgyth
> Ælfgifu

Ælfgifu, daughter of King Edward the Elder and Lady Ælfflæd
Married a certain 'Prince by the Alps'

Ælfgifu of Shaftesbury, d.*c.*944 daughter of unknown and Wynflæd

m. Edmund, King of England *c.*921–946 (r.939–946)

> Eadwig b.*c.*940–959 (r.955–959)
> Edgar b.*c.*942–975 (r.959–975)

Ælfgifu, d.*c.*966 to 975, daughter of unknown and Æthelgifu

m. King Eadwig (23 November 955 until 1 October 959), divorced in 958

Ælfgifu, daughter of Thored Ealdorman of Northumbria
m. Æthelred II, king of England *c.*968–1016 (r.978–1013/1014–1016)
Athelstan d.1014
Ecgberht d.*c.*1005
Edmund, king of the English, 1016
Eadred d.*c.*1012

Eadwig d.1017
Edgar d.*c*.1008
Eadgyth m. Ealdorman Eadric Streona (Mercia)
Ælfgifu m. Ealdorman Uhtred (Northumbria/Bamburgh)
Wulfhild m. Ulfcytel of East Anglia (never named as an ealdorman)
Ælfthryth, abbess of Wherwell in the reign of Edward the Confessor
(her stepbrother)

Ælfgifu, daughter of Æthelred II and Ælfgifu

m. Ealdorman Uhtred (Northumbria/Bamburgh)

Ælfthryth, (*c*.875–7 June 929) daughter of King Alfred and Lady
Ealhswith

m. Count Baldwin II of Flanders b. *c*.863–918

Arnulf (Count from 918 to 965)
Adalulf (Count from 918 to 933)
Ealhswith
Eormenthryth
Ælfthryth?

Ælfthryth/Elfrida, daughter of Ealdorman Ordgar

m. 1. Æthelwold, the ealdorman of the East Angles (d.962)

Ælfflæd step-daughter

m. 2. Edgar, king of the English b.*c*.942–975 (r.959–975)

Edmund *c*.966–d.971
Æthelred II *c*.968–d.1016

Ælfthryth, daughter of Æthelred II and Ælgifu

Abbess of Wherwell in the reign of Edward the Confessor (her
half-brother)

Ælfwynn, daughter of Æthelred of Mercia and Lady Æthelflæd
b.*c*.880/890–919/*c*.960
Either became a nun, or married Athelstan, Half-King of the East Angles

Æthelflæd, daughter of Alfred and Lady Ealhswith *c*.866–June 918

m. Æthelred of Mercia d. 911

    Ælfwynn

Æthelflæd (of Damerham), daughter of Ealdorman Ælfgar *c*.962–991

m. 1. Edmund, king of the English *c*.921–946 (r.939–946)

m. 2. Athelstan Rota

Æthelflæd (Eneda?), said to be the daughter of Ealdorman Ordmær

m. *c*.958 King Edgar b.*c*.942–975 (r.959–975)

    Edward b.*c*.960–978 r.975–978

Æthelgifu, (*c*.875–*c*.899), daughter of Alfred and Lady Ealhswith
Abbess of Shaftesbury

Æthelhild, daughter of Edward the Elder, and his second wife, Lady Ælfflæd
Lay sister at Wilton

Eadburh, daughter of Edward the Elder and Eadgifu
Nun at the Nunnaminster

Eadflæd, daughter of Edward the Elder and Ælfflæd
Nun at Wilton

Eadgifu, (*c*.902–964) daughter of Ealdorman Sigehelm of Kent, who died at the Battle of the Holme in 902

m. Edward the Elder (his third wife, her only husband)

    Eadburh *c*.919–952
    Edmund *c*.920/1–26 May 946
    Eadred *c*.923–23 November 955
    Eadgifu?

Eadgifu, daughter of King Edward the Elder and Lady Ælfflæd b.*c*.900–951

m.1. Charles III of West Frankia (879–929) king of West Frankia (898–922)

Louis b.921/922–954 (king of West Frankia 936–954)

m.2. Herbert 'the Elder' *c.*910–980/4

Eadgyth, d.946 daughter of Edward the Elder, and his second wife, Lady Ælfflæd

m. Otto I of East Frankia in 929 or 930, son of Henry the Fowler

    Liudolf, Duke of Bavaria m. Ida
           Matilda, Abbess of Essen
           Otto
    Liudgar m. Conrad the Red, Duke of Lotharingia
           Otto

Eadgyth, daughter of Æthelred II and Ælfgifu

m. Ealdorman Eadric Streona (Mercia)

Eadhild, daughter of King Edward the Elder and Lady Ælfflæd

b.*c.*902–937

m. Hugh, the Great, *dux Francorum c.*895–956

    No surviving children

Ealhswith, *c.*850-d.902 daughter of Ealdorman Æthelred Mucel and Eadburh

m. 864 Alfred of Wessex (before he became king)

    Æthelflæd, Lady of the Mercians
    Edward the Elder, king of the Anglo-Saxons
    Æthelgifu, the abbess of Shaftesbury
    Ælfthryth, Countess of Flanders
    Æthelweard, a nobleman

Ecgwynn?

m. King Edward the Elder *c.*874–17 July 924 (r.899–924), son of King Alfred and his wife, Lady Ealhswith.

    Athelstan
    Unknown daughter/Edith

Edith/unknown daughter, daughter of Edward the Elder, and his unnamed/Ecgwynn first wife

m. Sihtric, king of York in 925, repudiated by 927

Edith/Eadgyth daughter of King Edgar, and his second wife, Wulfthryth *c.*962–*c.*984 (date is given as 16 September 983 in her *Vitae*)

Wulfhild, daughter of Æthelred II and Ælfgifu

m. Ulfcytel of East Anglia (never named as an ealdorman)

Wulfthryth, d.*c.*1000

m. Edgar, king of the English in *c.*961 b.*c.*942–975 (r.959–975)

    Eadgyth/Edith *c.*961/2–984

Appendix I

Charters attested by Eadgifu

Charter Number	King	Year	Named Woman
S465	Edmund	940	Æthelthryth
S470	Edmund	940	
S475	Edmund	941	
S477	Edmund	941	SPURIOUS
S481	Edmund	942	
S483	Edmund	942	
S485	Edmund	942	Wynflæd
S487	Edmund	943	Ælfswith
S488	Edmund	943	
S489	Edmund	943	Eadgifu (mother)
S493	Edmund	944	Ælfgyth
S494	Edmund	944	
S495	Edmund	944	
S496	Edmund	942x944	
S497	Edmund	944	
S499	Edmund	944	SPURIOUS
S501	Edmund	944	
S505	Edmund	944	
S506	Edmund	945	
S512	Edmund	943	
S514	Edmund	942x946	

Charter Number	King	Year	Named Woman
S517	Eadred	945	
S519	Eadred	946	
S521	Eadred	947	SPURIOUS
S521a	Eadred	947	
S523	Eadred	947	
S525	Eadred	947	
S526	Eadred	947	
S527	Eadred	947	
S528	Eadred	947	
S529	Eadred	947	
S531	Eadred	948	
S532	Eadred	948	
S533	Eadred	948	
S535	Eadred	948	Ælfwynn
S536	Eadred	948	SPURIOUS
S540	Eadred	948	SPURIOUS
S542	Eadred	947	
S544	Eadred	949	
S545	Eadred	949	
S546	Eadred	949	
S551	Eadred	949	
S552	Eadred	949	
S552a	Eadred	950	
S553	Eadred	950	
S554	Eadred	951	
S558	Eadred	951	
S559	Eadred	953x955	

Charter Number	King	Year	Named Woman
S562	Eadred	953	Eadgifu (mother)
S565	Eadred	955	
S566	Eadred	955	
S567	Eadred	955	SPURIOUS
S569	Eadred	955	
S578	Eadred	946x951	
S658	Eadwig	959	
S673	Edgar	959	
S745	Edgar	966	
S746	Edgar	966	
S811	Edgar	959x963	Eadgifu (grandmother)

Appendix II

Charters attested by Elfrida

Charter Number	King	Year	Named Royal Woman
S671	Edgar	973	
S725	Edgar	964	Elfrida
S731	Edgar	963	
S739	Edgar	966	
S742	Edgar	966	Elfrida
S745	Edgar	966	
S746	Edgar	966	
S766	Edgar	968	
S767	Edgar	968	
S771	Edgar	969	
S779	Edgar	970	Spurious
S786	Edgar	972	
S788	Edgar	972	Spurious
S789	Edgar	972	
S794	Edgar	974	
S795	Edgar	974	
S800	Edgar	975	
S801	Edgar	974	
S805	Edgar	972	
S806	Edgar	968	
S807	Edgar	963x970	
S835	Æthelred	979	
S840	Æthelred	982	
S841	Æthelred	982	
S842	Æthelred	982	

Charter Number	King	Year	Named Royal Woman
S843	Æthelred	983	
S845	Æthelred	983	
S849	Æthelred	983	
S876	Æthelred	993	
S877	Æthelred	989	Elfrida
S878	Æthelred	996	
S879	Æthelred	996	spurious
S888	Æthelred	996	
S891	Æthelred	997	
S896	Æthelred	999	
S904	Æthelred	1002	
S1454	Æthelred	990x992	Wynflæd
S1242	Æthelred	995x1002	Elfrida

Appendix III

The House of Wessex in the Tenth Century

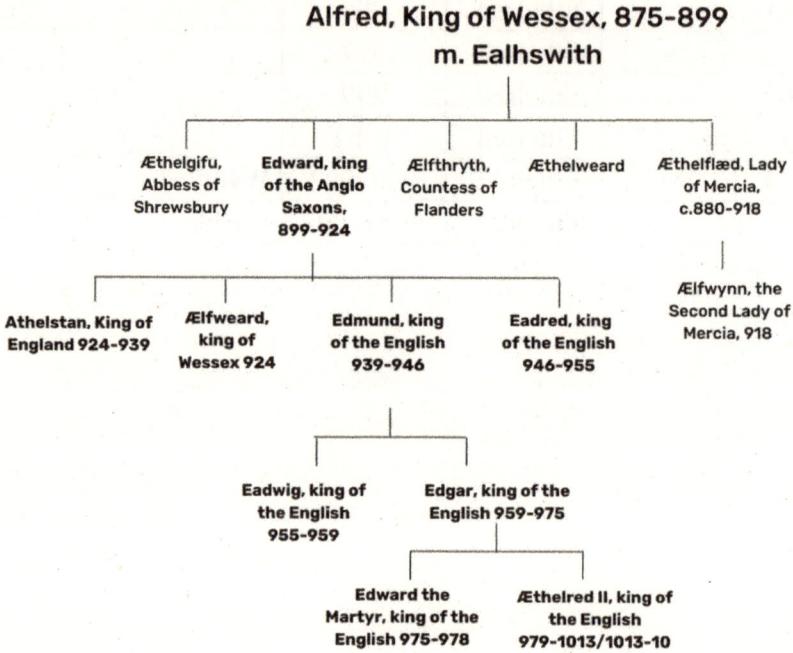

Alfred, King of Wessex, 875-899
m. Ealhswith

- **Æthelgifu,** Abbess of Shrewsbury
- **Edward, king of the Anglo Saxons, 899-924**
  - **Athelstan, King of England 924-939**
  - **Ælfweard, king of Wessex 924**
  - **Edmund, king of the English 939-946**
    - **Eadwig, king of the English 955-959**
    - **Edgar, king of the English 959-975**
      - **Edward the Martyr, king of the English 975-978**
      - **Æthelred II, king of the English 979-1013/1013-10**
  - **Eadred, king of the English 946-955**
- **Ælfthryth,** Countess of Flanders
- **Æthelweard**
- **Æthelflæd, Lady of Mercia, c.880-918**
  - **Ælfwynn, the Second Lady of Mercia, 918**

Appendix IV

The Marriages of Edward the Elder, King of the Anglo-Saxons 899–924

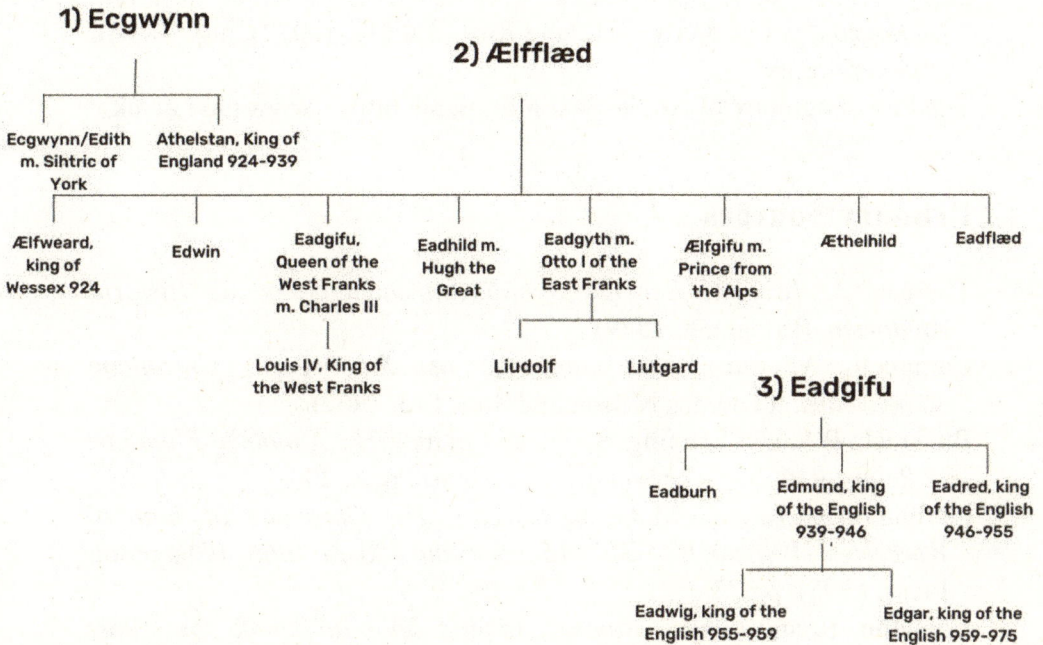

1) Ecgwynn

- Ecgwynn/Edith m. Sihtric of York
- Athelstan, King of England 924-939

2) Ælfflæd

- Ælfweard, king of Wessex 924
- Edwin
- Eadgifu, Queen of the West Franks m. Charles III
  - Louis IV, King of the West Franks
- Eadhild m. Hugh the Great
- Eadgyth m. Otto I of the East Franks
  - Liudolf
  - Liutgard
- Ælfgifu m. Prince from the Alps
- Æthelhild
- Eadflæd

3) Eadgifu

- Eadburh
- Edmund, king of the English 939-946
  - Eadwig, king of the English 955-959
  - Edgar, king of the English 959-975
- Eadred, king of the English 946-955

Bibliography

Online Resources

Sawyer, P.H. (ed.), *Anglo-Saxon Charters: An Annotated List and Bibliography*, rev. Kelly, S. E. and Rushforth, R., (2022), http://www.esawyer.org.uk/

The Prosopography of Anglo-Saxon England, https://www.pase.ac.uk

Primary Sources

Thomas, A. (trans.), *Henrici archidiaconi huntendunessis Historia Anglorum*, (Longman, 1879)

Campbell, A. (ed.), *The Chronicle of Æthelweard: Chronicon Æthelweardi*, (Thomas Nelson and Sons Ltd, 1962)

Bachrach, B.S. and Fanning, S. (ed. and trans.), *The Annals of Flodoard of Reims, 916–966*, (University of Toronto Press, 2004)

Darlington, R.R. and McGurk, P. (ed.), *The Chronicle of John of Worcester: Volume II – The Annals from 450 to 1066*, (Clarendon Press, 1995), p.373

Edington, S. and Others, *Ramsey Abbey's Book of Benefactors: Part One – The Abbey's Foundation,* (Hakedes, 1998)

Edington, S. and Others, *Ramsey Abbey's Book of Benefactors: Part Two – The Early Years,* (Hakedes, 2001)

Fairweather, J. (trans.), *Liber Eliensis: A History of the Isle of Ely from the Seventh Century to the Twelfth*, (Boydell Press, 2005)

Gaimar, G., and edited by T.D. Hardy and Martin, C.T. (eds.), *Lestorie des Engles*, (1889)

Greenway, D. (ed. and trans.), *Historia Anglorum*, The History of the English People: Henry of Huntingdon, (Clarendon Press, 1996)

Keynes, S. and Lapidge, M., *Asser's Life of King Alfred and Other Contemporary Sources,* (Penguin, 1983)

Lapidge, M. and Winterbottom, M. (ed. and trans.), *Wulfstan of Winchester: The Life of St Æthelwold,* (Clarendon Press, 1991)

Picard, A., *Les Annals De Flodoard*, (1905), https://openlibrary.org/books/OL13495473M/Les_annales_de_Flodoard

Mynors, R.A.B. (ed. and trans.), completed by Thomson, R.M. and Winterbottom, M., *William of Malmesbury: Gesta Regum Anglorum – The History of the English Kings,* (Clarendon Press, 1998)

Priest, D. (trans.), *William of Malmesbury: Gesta Pontificum Anglorum – The Deeds of the Bishops of England,* (Boydell Press, 2002)

South, T.J. (ed.), *Historia de Sancto Cuthberto*, (D.S. Brewer, 2002)

Stevenson, J. (trans.), *Simeon of Durham: A History of the Kings of England* (Llanerch Press, Facsimile reprint, 1987)

Stevenson, J. (ed. and trans.), *The Historical Works of Symeon of Durham*, (Llanerch Press, Facsimile reprint, 1993)

Swanton, M. (ed. and trans.), *The Anglo-Saxon Chronicles*, (Orion Publishing Group, 2000)

Thorpe, L. (trans.), *The History of the Kings of Britain: Geoffrey of Monmouth*, (Penguin, 1966)

Van Houts, E.M.C. (trans.), *The Gesta Normannorum Ducum of William of Jumièges, Orderic Vitalic, and Robert of Torigni,* (Clarenden Press, Oxford, 1992)

Winterbottom, M. and Lapidge, M. (eds.), *The Early Lives of St Dunstan*, (in Latin and English), (Oxford University Press, 2011)

Secondary Sources

Adams, M., *Ælfred's Britain*, (Head of Zeus, 2017)

Bailey. M., 'Ælfwynn, Second Lady of the Mercians', *Edward the Elder, 899–924* Higham, N.J. and Hill, D.H. (ed.), (Routledge, 2001)

Baker, N. and Holt, R., 'The City of Worcester in the Tenth Century', in *St Oswald of Worcester: Life and Influence*, Brooks, N. and Cubitt, C. (ed.), (Leicester University Press, 1996)

Barrow, J., The Chronology of Benedictine 'Reform' in *Edgar, King of the English 959–975*, (Boydell Press, 2008)

Brooks, N. and Cubitt, C. (ed.), *St Oswald of Worcester: Life and Influence*, (Leicester University Press, 1996)

Coatsworth, E., 'The Embroideries from the Tomb of St Cuthbert', in *Edward the Elder, 899–924* Higham, N.J. and Hill, D.H. (ed.), (Routledge, 2001)

Downham, C., *Viking Kings of Britain and Ireland: The Dynasty of Ivarr to AD 1014*,(Dnuedin, 2007)

Dumville, D.N., *Wessex and England from Alfred to Edgar*, (Boydell Press, 1992)

Finberg, H.P.R., *The Early Charters of the West Midlands*, (Leicester, 1972)

Finberg, H.P.R., *The Early Charters of Wessex*, (Leicester University Press, 1964)

Firth, M. and Schilling, C., 'The Lonely Afterlives of Early English Queens', in *Nephilologus*, September 2022, https://doi.org/10.1007/s11061–022–09739–4

Foot, S., *Athelstan*, (Yale University Press, 2011)

Foot, S., 'Dynastic Strategies: The West Saxon Royal Family in Europe', in *England and the Continent in the Tenth Century: Studies in Honour of Wilhelm Levison (1876–1947)*, (Brepols, 2012)

Foot, S., *Veiled Women: Volume 1 – The Disappearance of Nuns from Anglo-Saxon England,* (Routledge, 2000)

Gelling, M., *The Early Charters of the Thames Valley*, (Leicester University Press, 1979)

Hart, C.R., *The Early Charters of Northern England and the North Midlands*, (Leicester University Press, 1975)

Higham, N., 'Edward the Elder's Reputation: An Introduction' in *Edward the Elder, 899–924* Higham, N.J. and Hill, D.H. (ed.), (Routledge, 2001)

Hollis, S. (ed.), 'St Edith and the Wilton Community', in *Writing the Wilton Women*, (Turnhout, 2004)

Jayakumar, S. 'Eadwig and Edgar', in *Edgar, King of the English, 959–975*, Scragg, D. (ed.), (Boydell Press, 2008)

Jayakumar, Shashi, and Jayakumar, Sashi, 'Foundlings, Ealdormen, and Holy Women: Reflections on Some Aristocratic Families in Ninth- and Early Tenth-Century Wiltshire', *Medieval Prosopography*, Vol. 24, 2003, pp.103–43, *JSTOR*, http://www.jstor.org/stable/4494 6420 accessed 22 August 2022

Key, M.J., *Edward the Elder*, (Amberley, 2019)

Keynes, S., *The Diplomas of Æthelred 'the Unready' 978–1016*, (Cambridge University Press, 1980)

Keynes, S., 'Edward, king of the Anglo-Saxons', in *Edward the Elder, 899–924*, Higham, N.J. and Hill, D.H. (ed.), (Routledge, 2001)

Keynes, S., 'Edgar, rex admirabilis' in Scragg, D. (ed.), *Edgar, King of the English, 959–975*, (Boydell Press, 2008)

Lapidge, M., 'Byrhtferth and Oswald' in Brooks, N. and Cubitt, C. (ed.), *St Oswald of Worcester: Life and Influence*, (Leicester University Press, 1996)

Lavelle, R., Rolfey, S. and Weikert, K., *Early Medieval Winchester*, (Oxbow Books, 2021)

Livingston, M. and Cornwell, B., *Never Greater Slaughter: Brunanburh and the Birth of England*, (Osprey Publishing, 2021)

McKitterick, R., *The Frankish Kingdoms Under the Carolingians, 751–987*, (Longman, 1983)

Meijns, B., 'The Policy of Relic Translations of Baldwin II of Flanders (879–918), Edward of Wessex (899–924) and Æthelflæd of Mercia (d.924): A Key to Anglo-Flemish Relations?' in *England and the Continent in the Tenth-Century*, Rollason, D., Leyser, C. and Williams, H. (ed.), (Brepols, 2010)

Morris, M., *The Anglo-Saxons: A History of the Beginning of England*, (Penguin Random House, 2021)

Norton, E., *Elfrida: The First Crowned Queen*, (Amberley, 2013)

Ortenberg, V., 'The King From Overseas: Why did Athelstan Matter in Tenth Century Continental Affairs', in *England and the Continent in the Tenth Century: Studies in Honour of Wilhelm Levison (1876–1947)*, (Brepols, 2012)

Parker, E., *Winters in the World: A Journey Through the Anglo-Saxon Year*, (Reaktion Books, 2022)

Rabin, A., *Crime and Punishment in Anglo-Saxon England*, (Cambridge, 2020)

Rumble, A.R., 'The Laity and the Monastic Reform in the Reign of Edgar' in Scragg, D. (ed.), *Edgar, King of the English, 959–975*, (Boydell Press, 2008)

Sharp, S., 'The West Saxon Tradition of Dynastic Marriage: With Special Reference to Edward the Elder', in *Edward the Elder, 899–924*, Higham, N.J. and Hill, D.H. (ed.), (Routledge, 2001)

Scragg, D. (ed.), *Edgar, King of the English, 959–975*, (Boydell Press, 2008)

Stafford, P., *Queens, Concubines and Dowagers: The King's Wife in the Early Middle Ages*, (Batsford Academic and Educational Ltd, 1983)

Stafford, P., *Queen Emma and Queen Edith*, (Blackwell Publisher, 1997)

Stafford, P., *Unification and Conquest*, (Oxford University Press, 2002)

Stafford, P., Fathers and Daughters: The Case of Æthelred II in *Writing, Kingship and Power in Anglo-Saxon England*, (Cambridge University Press, 2018)

Stafford, P., *After Alfred: Anglo-Saxon Chronicles and Chroniclers 900–1150*, (Oxford University Press, 2020)

Story, J., *Carolingian Connections: Anglo-Saxon England and Carolingian Francia, c.750–870*, (Ashgate, 2003)

Tanner, H., *Families, Friends and Allies: Bolougne and Politics in Northern France and England c.879–1160*, (Brill, 2004)

Thacker, A., 'Dynastic Monasteries and Family Cults', in *Edward the Elder, 899–924*, Higham, N.J. and Hill, D.H. (ed.), (Routledge, 2001)

Whitelock, D., *English Historical Documents*: *c.500–1042 – Volume 1*, First Edition, (Eyre & Spottiswoode, 1955)

Winkler, E.A., 'Æthelflæd and Other Rulers in English History' in *English Historical Review* Vol. CXXXVII, No.587, (2022)

Woolf, A., 'View from the West: An Irish Perspective on West Saxon Dynastic Practise', in *Edward the Elder, 899–924*, Higham, N.J. and Hill, D.H. (ed.), (Routledge, 2001)

Wragg, S., *Early English Queens, 650–850: Speculum Reginae*, (Routledge, 2022)

Yorke, B., 'Æthelwold and the Politics of the Tenth Century' in *Æthelwold and the Politics of the Tenth Century* Yorke, B. (ed.), (Boydell Press, 1988)

Yorke, B., 'Edward as Ætheling', in *Edward the Elder, 899–924*, Higham, N.J. and Hill, D.H. (ed.), (Routledge, 2001)

Yorke, B., 'The Women in Edgar's Life', in *Edgar, King of the English, 959–975*, Scragg, D. (ed.), (Boydell Press, 2008)

Endnotes

Introduction

1. Wragg, S., *Early English Queens, 650–850: Speculum Reginae*, (Routledge, 2022), p.9
2. Stafford, P., 'Fathers and Daughters: The Case of Æthelred II', in *Writing, Kingship and Power in Anglo-Saxon England*, (Cambridge University Press, 2018), p.142
3. Wragg, S., *Early English Queens, 650–850: Speculum Reginae*, (Routledge, 2022), p.3
4. Foot, S., 'Dynastic Strategies: The West Saxon Royal Family in Europe', in *England and the Continent in the Tenth Century: Studies in Honour of Wilhelm Levison (1876–1947)*, (Brepols, 2012)
5. https://www.corpus.cam.ac.uk/articles/parkers-anglo-saxon-kingdoms-aethelstan-bede-ms-183-and-old-english-bede-ms-41
6. https://en.wikipedia.org/wiki/New_Minster_Charter#/media/File:Edgar_from_Winchester_Charter.jpg

Chapter 1: The Long Tenth Century and its Kings

1. I would sooner just name them as raiders, but Vikings is the most common term, and so, a compromise – Viking was a job description – to go Viking
2. There are several different charter numbering systems that have been used over the years. The S series – the Sawyer catalogue – is now most often used, and all should be available on Sawyer, P.H. (ed.), Anglo-Saxon Charters: An Annotated List and Bibliography, rev. Kelly, S.E. and Rushforth, R., (2022), http://www.esawyer.org.uk/, but not all with translations from the original Latin or Old English.

3. S399, S400, S403, S405, S407, S412 S413, S418a, S418, S419, S422, S423, and also on coins, which proclaimed him *rex totius Britanniae,* Stafford, P., *After Alfred: Anglo-Saxon Chronicles and Chroniclers 900–1150*, p.94

4. S391 PASE and Sawyer, P.H. (ed.), Anglo-Saxon Charters: An Annotated List and Bibliography, rev. Kelly, S.E. and Rushforth, R., (2022), http://www.esawyer.org.uk/

5. Yorke, B., 'The Women in Edgar's Life', in *Edgar, King of the English, 959–975*, Scragg, D. (ed.), (Boydell Press, 2008), p.147

6. Swanton, M. (ed. and trans.), *The Anglo-Saxon Chronicles*, (Orion Publishing Group, 2000), p.91, A, D and E text, p.91

7. Ibid., pp.91–2

8. Swanton, M. (ed. and trans.), *The Anglo-Saxon Chronicles*, (Orion Publishing Group, 2000), A text, p104, C text, p.105, D, E and F text, p.105

9. Higham, N., 'Edward the Elder's Reputation: an introduction' in *Edward the Elder, 899–924*, Higham, N.J. and Hill, D.H. (ed.), (Routledge, 2001), p.1

10. Swanton, M. (ed. and trans.), *The Anglo-Saxon Chronicles*, (Orion Publishing Group, 2000), D text, p.105

11. Mynors, R.A.B. (ed. and trans.), completed by Thomson, R.M. and Winterbottom, M., *William of Malmesbury: Gesta Regum Anglorum – The History of the English Kings,* (Clarendon Press, 1998), p.211, Book II.133

12. Please see Livingston, M. and Cornwell, B., *Never Greater Slaughter: Brunanburh and the Birth of England,* (Osprey Publishing, 2021), for further information on the archaeological attempts to uncover where the battle of Brunanburh took place

13. Swanton, M. (ed. and trans.), *The Anglo-Saxon Chronicles*, (Orion Publishing Group, 2000), p.110

14. Ibid., p.109

15. Ibid., p.112

16. Ibid., p.113

17. Ibid.

18. Ibid. B and C text, p.113

19. Ibid.

20. Ibid., D text, p.113

21. Ibid., B and C text, p.113

22. Ibid., D text, p.121

23. Ibid., D and E text, p.121
24. Ibid., C text, p.122
25. Ibid., A text, p.122
26. Ibid., E text, p.123

Chapter 2: The Royal Women

1. Twenty-two if Eadgyth (12) is correct (see below). It should also be noted that not all instances of a name appearing are assigned to the same person – as such Wynnflæd (3) is probably the same person as Wynnflæd (4) but the identification is not quite conclusive. Some of these royal women also don't appear on PASE.
2. PASE Eahlswith (1)
3. PASE Æthelflæd (4)
4. PASE Ælfwynn (2)
5. PASE Æthelgifu (4)
6. PASE Ælfthryth (5)
7. Not mentioned on PASE
8. Possibly Eadgyth (12) or Anon (584)
9. PASE Ælfflæd (10)
10. Not mentioned in PASE
11. PASE Eadgifu (3)
12. PASE Eadflæd (4)
13. PASE Eadhild (1)
14. PASE Eadgyth (2)
15. Not mentioned on PASE
16. PASE Eadgifu (4)
17. PASE Eadburgh (8)
18. PASE Ælfgifu (3)
19. PASE Wynnflæd (4)
20. PASE Æthelflæd (14)
21. PASE Ælfgifu (2)
22. Possibly not mentioned in PASE
23. PASE Wulfthryth (6)
24. PASE Ælfthryth (8)
25. PASE Eadgyth (4)
26. PASE Ælfgifu (17)
27. PASE Ælfgifu (25)

28. Not listed on PASE
29. Not listed on PASE
30. Not listed on PASE
31. PASE Gode (2)
32. PASE Ælfwaru (2)
33. PASE Ælfflæd (13)
34. PASE Leofflæd (5)
35. PASE Æthelflæd (15), Ælfgifu's brother's wife and PASE Æthelflæd (29)
36. PASE Ælfswith (7)
37. PASE Wulfwaru (3)
38. PASE Gode (1)
39. PASE Alfwaru (4)
40. PASE Wynnflæd (5)
41. PASE Æthelgyth (1)
42. Foot, S., *Athelstan*, (Yale University Press, 2011), pp.259–65
43. Stafford, P., *Queen Emma and Queen Edith*, (Blackwell Publisher, 1997), p.139

Chapter 3: The Mercian Royal Women

1. PASE Ealhswith (1)
2. Keynes, S. and Lapidge, M., *Asser's Life of King Alfred and Other Contemporary Sources,* (Penguin, 1983), p.77
3. S190, S192, S197, S198, S202, S204, S206, S207, S208, S210, S212 and S1140 dated from 836 to 866. There are a number of Mucel's attesting at this time.
4. Yorke, B., 'Edward as Ætheling', in *Edward the Elder, 899–924*, Higham, N.J. and Hill, D.H. (ed.), (Routledge, 2001), pp.26–7
5. Sawyer, P.H. (ed.), Anglo-Saxon Charters: An annotated List and Bibliography, rev. Kelly, S.E. and Rushforth, R., (2022), http://www.esawyer.org.uk/ S340
6. Ibid., interestingly, this is promulgated by Æthelswith, queen of Mercia
7. Ibid., http://www.esawyer.org.uk/ S337
8. Ibid., http://www.esawyer.org.uk/ S349
9. PASE Æthelswith (1)
10. Swanton, M. (ed. and trans.), *The Anglo-Saxon Chronicles*, (Orion Publishing Group, 2000), p.72

11. https://www.bl.uk/collection-items/assers-life-of-king-alfred. For a full account of the history of the manuscripts please see Keynes, S. and Lapidge, M., *Asser's Life of King Alfred and Other Contemporary Sources,* (Penguin, 1983)

12. Mynors, R.A.B. (ed. and trans.), completed by Thomson, R.M. and Winterbottom, M., *William of Malmesbury: Gesta Regum Anglorum – The History of the English Kings,* (Clarendon Press, 1998), p.189

13. Sawyer, P.H. (ed.), Anglo-Saxon Charters: An Annotated List and Bibliography, rev. Kelly, S.E. and Rushforth, R., (2022), http://www.esawyer.org.uk/ S363

14. See the section on Elfrida below

15. Wragg, S., *Early English Queens, 650–850: Speculum Reginae,* (Routledge, 2022), p.14

16. Sawyer, P.H. (ed.), Anglo-Saxon charters: An Annotated List and Bibliography, rev. Kelly, S.E. and Rushforth, R., (2022), http://www.esawyer.org.uk/ S1201. She also witnesses S206, S207, S208, S209, S210, S211, S212, S214 and S222.

17. Keynes, S. and Lapidge, M., *Asser's Life of King Alfred and Other Contemporary Sources,* (Penguin, 1983)

    And S1507, (Sawyer, P.H. (ed.), Anglo-Saxon Charters: An Annotated List and Bibliography, rev. Kelly, S.E. and Rushforth, R., (2022), http://www.esawyer.org.uk/), which survives in three manuscripts

18. S219, S220, S1441, S1442 Sawyer, P.H. (ed.), Anglo-Saxon Charters: An Annotated List and Bibliography, rev. Kelly, S.E. and Rushforth, R., (2022), http://www.esawyer.org.uk/

19. Swanton, M. ed. and trans. *The Anglo-Saxon Chronicles*, (Orion Publishing Group, 2000), p.92

20. Ibid., p.93

21. The New Minister, *Liber Vitae.*

22. Swanton, M. (ed. and trans.), *The Anglo-Saxon Chronicles*, (Orion Publishing Group, 2000), p.94

23. Ibid., p.93

24. PASE Æthelflæd (4)

25. Swanton, M. (ed. and trans.), *The Anglo-Saxon Chronicles*, (Orion Publishing Group, 2000), AD 918

26. S217, surviving in two manuscripts

27. Keynes, S. and Lapidge, M., *Asser's Life of King Alfred and Other Contemporary Sources,* (Penguin, 1983), p.175

28. Ibid., p.176
29. Whitelock, D., *English Historical Documents*: *c.500–1042 – Volume 1*, First Edition, (Eyre & Spottiswoode, 1955), p.498 (99)
30. Sawyer, P.H. (ed.), Anglo-Saxon Charters: An Annotated List and Bibliography, rev. Kelly, S.E. and Rushforth, R., (2022), http://www.esawyer.org.uk/ S217, surviving in two manuscripts
31. Ibid., http://www.esawyer.org.uk/ S896
32. Ibid., http://www.esawyer.org.uk/ S221
33. Ibid., http://www.esawyer.org.uk/ S367
34. C.R. Hart believes this is the father of Athelstan Half-King, and so Æthelgyth would have been his mother. See Ælfwynn below and also throughout later sections of the book for Athelstan Half-King, especially under Eadwig and Edgar.
35. Sawyer, P.H. (ed.), Anglo-Saxon Charters: An Annotated List and Bibliography, rev. Kelly, S.E. and Rushforth, R., (2022), http://www.esawyer.org.uk/ S367a
36. Ibid., http://www.esawyer.org.uk/ S367a
37. Ibid., http://www.esawyer.org.uk/ S371
38. Keynes, S., 'Edward, king of the Anglo-Saxons', in *Edward the Elder, 899–924* Higham, N.J. and Hill, D.H. (ed.), (Routledge, 2001), pp.53–4
39. Not that I would ever truly wish to argue with Simon Keynes about this.
40. PASE and the Sawyer, P.H. (ed.), Anglo-Saxon Charters: An Annotated List and Bibliography, rev. Kelly, S.E. and Rushforth, R., (2022), http://www.esawyer.org.uk/, S1280
41. Baker, N. and Holt, R. 'The city of Worcester in the tenth century', in *St Oswald of Worcester: Life and Influence* Brooks, N. and Cubitt, C. (ed.), (Leicester University Press, 1996), pp.134–5
42. Sawyer, P.H. (ed.), Anglo-Saxon Charters: An Annotated List and Bibliography, rev. Kelly, S.E. and Rushforth, R., (2022), http://www.esawyer.org.uk/ S1446
43. PASE and the Sawyer, P.H. (ed.), Anglo-Saxon Charters: An Annotated List and Bibliography, rev. Kelly, S.E., Rushforth, R., (2022), http://www.esawyer.org.uk/ S1446
44. Sawyer, P.H. (ed.), Anglo-Saxon Charters: An Annotated List and Bibliography, rev. Kelly, S.E., Rushforth, R., (2022), http://www.esawyer.org.uk/ S1282
45. Hart, C.R., *The Early Charters of Northern England and the North Midlands*, (Leicester University Press, 1975), p.102 (100)

46. PASE and the Sawyer, P.H. (ed.), Anglo-Saxon Charters: An Annotated List and Bibliography, rev. Kelly, S.E. and Rushforth, R., (2022), http://www.esawyer.org.uk/ S225

47. Stafford, P. *After Alfred: Anglo-Saxon Chronicles and Chroniclers 900–1150*, (Oxford University Press, 2020), p.78

48. Swanton, M. (ed. and trans.), *The Anglo-Saxon Chronicles*, (Orion Publishing Group, 2000), p.95

49. Ibid., p.94

50. Ibid., p.96

51. Ibid., p.96

52. Ibid., p.97

53. Ibid., p.100

54. Ibid., p.101

55. Ibid., p.103

56. Ibid., p.105

57. Campbell, A. (ed.), *The Chronicle of Æthelweard: Chronicon Æthelweardi, (Thomas Nelson and Sons Ltd, 1962)*, pp.53–4

58. See Stafford, P., *After Alfred: Anglo-Saxon Chronicles and Chroniclers 900–1150*, (Oxford University Press, 2020), for a full discussion of the Æthelflæd and Edward Chronicles

59. Mynors, R.A.B. (ed. and trans.), completed by Thomson, R.M. and Winterbottom, M., *William of Malmesbury: Gesta Regum Anglorum – The History of the English Kings,* (Clarendon Press, 1998), p.187

60. Ibid., p.199

61. Darlington, R.R. and McGurk, P. (ed.), *The Chronicle of John of Worcester – Volume II: The Annals from 450 to 1066*, (Clarendon Press, 1995), p.373 [916]

62. Ibid., pp.379–80 [919]

63. PASE Ælfwynn (2)

64. Sawyer, P.H. (ed.), Anglo-Saxon Charters: An Annotated List and Bibliography, rev. Kelly, S.E. and Rushforth, R., (2022), http://www.esawyer.org.uk/ S367

65. Ibid., http://www.esawyer.org.uk/ S1280. See above for the full details under Æthelflæd

66. Baker, N. and Holt, R. 'The city of Worcester in the Tenth Century', in *St Oswald of Worcester: Life and Influence* Brooks, N. and Cubitt, C. (ed.), (Leicester University Press, 1996)

67. Bailey. M., 'Ælfwynn, Second Lady of the Mercians', *Edward the Elder, 899–924* Higham, N.J. and Hill, D.H. (ed.), (Routledge,

2001). This does list Ælfwynn as a bishop, but it is believed to be a mistake in the copying of the text.

68. Sawyer, P.H. (ed.), Anglo-Saxon Charters: An Annotated List and Bibliography, rev. Kelly, S.E. and Rushforth, R., (2022), http://www.esawyer.org.uk/ S371

69. Swanton, M. (ed. and trans.), *The Anglo-Saxon Chronicles*, (Orion Publishing Group, 2000), p.105

70. Sawyer, P.H. (ed.), Anglo-Saxon Charters: An Annotated List and Bibliography, rev. Kelly, S.E. and Rushforth, R., (2022), http://www.esawyer.org.uk/ S535

71. Bailey. M. 'Ælfwynn, Second Lady of the Mercians', *Edward the Elder, 899–924*, Higham, N.J. and Hill, D.H. (ed.), (Routledge, 2001), p.125

72. Bailey. M., 'Ælfwynn, Second Lady of the Mercians', *Edward the Elder, 899–924*, Higham, N.J. and Hill, D.H. (ed.), (Routledge, 2001). This Athelstan who was the son of the Æthelfrith dux who had to have 3 of his charters reissued in 903.

73. Jayakumar, S., 'Eadwig and Edgar', in *Edgar, King of the English, 959–975*, D. Scragg (ed.), (Boydell Press, 2014), p.94

74. Edington, S. and Others, *Ramsey Abbey's Book of Benefactors – Part One: The Abbey's Foundation*, (Hakedes, 1998), pp.9–10

75. Jayakumar, S. 'Eadwig and Edgar', in *Edgar, King of the English, 959–975*, D. Scragg (ed.), (Boydell Press, 2014), p.94

76. Edith may be Anonymous (594) or Eadgyth (12) on PASE, in which case her death was *c.*937

77. Swanton, M. (ed. and trans.), *The Anglo-Saxon Chronicles*, (Orion Publishing Group, 2000), p.105

78. Ibid., p.105

79. Thacker, A., 'Dynastic Monasteries and Family Cults', in *Edward the Elder, 899–924*, Higham, N.J. and Hill, D.H., (ed.), (Routledge, 2001), p.257

80. Thacker, A., 'Dynastic Monasteries and Family Cults', in *Edward the Elder, 899–924*, Higham, N.J. and Hill, D.H., (ed.), (Routledge, 2001), p.258

Chapter 4: The Wives of Edward the Elder

1. Ecgwynn's name is not mentioned in pre-conquest sources, and, as such, she does not appear in the online resource PASE

2. Yorke, B. 'Edward as Ætheling', in *Edward the Elder, 899–924* Higham, N.J. and Hill, D.H. (ed.), (Routledge, 2001), p.33

3. Ibid., p.33, B. Yorke suggests that although Dunstan claimed a kinswoman of his, Æthelflæda, was of royal stock and related to King Athelstan, as Dunstan is not said to be related to any other member of the royal family, that this connection may be through Athelstan's mother. Yorke, B. (ed.), 'Æthelwold and the Politics of the Tenth Century', in *Æthelwold and the Politics of the Tenth Century*, (Boydell Press, 1988), pp.66–7

4. Mynors, R.A.B. (ed. and trans.), completed by Thomson, R.M. and Winterbottom, M., *William of Malmesbury: Gesta Regum Anglorum – The History of the English Kings,* (Clarendon Press, 1998), p199. Yorke, B., 'Edward as Ætheling', in *Edward the Elder, 899–924,* Higham, N.J. and Hill, D.H. (ed.), (Routledge, 2001), p.33

5. Sharp, S., 'The West Saxon Tradition of Dynastic Marriage: With Special Reference to Edward the Elder', in *Edward the Elder, 899–924*, Higham, N.J. and Hill, D.H. (ed.), (Routledge, 2001), p.81

6. Yorke, B., 'Edward as Ætheling', in *Edward the Elder, 899–924,* Higham, N.J. and Hill, D.H. (ed.), (Routledge, 2001), p.33

7. Ibid., p.33

8. Dumville, D.N., *Wessex and England from Alfred to Edgar*, (Boydell Press, 1992), p.146

9. Foot, S., *Athelstan*, (Yale University Press, 2011), p.37 Mynors, R.A.B. (ed. and trans.), completed by Thomson, R.M. and Winterbottom, M., *William of Malmesbury: Gesta Regum Anglorum – The History of the English Kings,* (Clarendon Press, 1998), p.199

10. Yorke, B., 'Edward as Ætheling', in *Edward the Elder, 899–924,* Higham, N.J. and Hill, D.H. (ed.), (Routledge, 2001), p.33

11. PASE Ælfflæd (10)

12. Sharp, S., 'The West Saxon Tradition of Dynastic Marriage: With Special Reference to Edward the Elder', in *Edward the Elder, 899–924*, Higham, N.J. and Hill, D.H. (ed.), (Routledge, 2001), p.82

13. Foot, S., *Athelstan*, (Yale University Press, 2011), Figure 2

14. Sawyer, P.H. (ed.), Anglo-Saxon Charters: An Annotated List and Bibliography, rev. Kelly, S.E. and Rushforth, R., (2022), http://www.esawyer.org.uk/ S363

15. Foot, S., *Athelstan* (Yale University Press, 2011), p.37, n.25

16. Campbell, A. (ed.), *The Chronicle of Æthelweard: Chronicon Æthelweardi*, (Thomas Nelson and Sons Ltd, 1962), p.51

17. Sawyer, P.H. (ed.), Anglo-Saxon Charters: An Annotated List and Bibliography, rev. Kelly, S.E. and Rushforth, R., (2022), http://www.esawyer.org.uk/ S365, S366, S371, S375, S376, S377, S378, S379, S381, S382, S383

18. Ibid., http://www.esawyer.org.uk/ S365, S375, S376, S377, S378, S381, S382, S383

19. Ibid., http://www.esawyer.org.uk/ S365, S366, S371

20. Ibid., http://www.esawyer.org.uk/ S365

21. Foot, S., *Athelstan*, (Yale University Press, 2011), p.57

22. Sharp, S., 'The West Saxon Tradition of Dynastic Marriage: With Special Reference to Edward the Elder', in *Edward the Elder, 899–924*, Higham, N.J. and Hill, D.H. (ed.), (Routledge, 2001), p.82

23. Foot, S., *Athelstan*, (Yale University Press, 2011), p.122–3

24. Coatsworth, E., 'The Embroideries from the Tomb of St Cuthbert', in *Edward the Elder, 899–924*, Higham, N.J. and Hill, D.H. (ed.), (Routledge, 2001), for a full and detailed analysis of these items. Bishop Frithestan did not support King Athelstan.

25. South, T.J. (ed.), *Historia de Sancto Cuthberto*, (D.S. Brewer, 2002), ch.26, pp.64–5

26. S365 Sawyer, P.H. (ed.), Anglo-Saxon Charters: An Annotated List and Bibliography, rev. Kelly, S.E. and Rushforth, R., (2022), http://www.esawyer.org.uk/

27. Swanton, M. (ed. and trans.), *The Anglo-Saxon Chronicles*, (Orion Publishing Group, 2000), p.105

28. Ibid., p.107

29. Ibid., p.105

30. Mynors, R.A.B. (ed. and trans.), completed by Thomson, R.M. and Winterbottom, M., *William of Malmesbury: Gesta Regum Anglorum – The History of the English Kings,* (Clarendon Press, 1998), p.199–201

31. Ibid., p.203

32. Ibid., p.207

33. Ibid., p.213

34. Ibid., p.217

35. Eadgifu (4) on PASE

36. Yorke, B., 'Edward as Ætheling', in *Edward the Elder, 899–924*, Higham, N.J. and Hill, D.H. (ed.), (Routledge, 2001), p.32

37. Swanton, M. (ed. and trans.), *The Anglo-Saxon Chronicles*, (Orion Publishing Group, 2000, pp.92–4

38. See S481 and S485 (942), S487, S488 and S491 (943), as well as S489, which was a charter in her favour

39. Swanton, M. (ed. and trans.), *The Anglo-Saxon Chronicles*, (Orion Publishing Group, 2000), A 941

40. Jayakumar, Shashi, and Jayakumar, Sashi, 'Foundlings, Ealdormen, and Holy Women: Reflections on Some Aristocratic Families in Ninth- and Early Tenth-Century Wiltshire'. *Medieval Prosopography*, Vol. 24, 2003, pp.103–43. *JSTOR*, http://www.jstor.org/stable/44946420 accessed 22 August 2022, p127

41. Thacker, A., 'Dynastic Monasteries and Family Cults', in *Edward the Elder, 899–924*, Higham, N.J. and Hill, D.H. (ed.), (Routledge, 2001), p.258

42. According to Ralph de Diceto, twelfth-century dean of St Paul's Cathedral, London, Edward 902, Edmund 940, Eadred 946 and Eadwig 950 also underwent coronation at Kingston-upon-Thames. Swanton, M. (ed. and trans.), *The Anglo-Saxon Chronicles*, (Orion Publishing Group, 2000), p.104, n.10

43. Firth, M. and Schilling, C., 'The Lonely Afterlives of Early English Queens', in *Nephilologus* September 2022, https://doi.org/10.1007/s11061-022-09739-4, p.7

44. Ibid.

45. Yorke, B., 'The Women in Edgar's Life', in *Edgar, King of the English, 959–975*, Scragg, D. (ed.), (Boydell Press, 2008), p.146

46. Swanton, M. (ed. and trans.), *The Anglo-Saxon Chronicles*, (Orion Publishing Group, 2000), ASC A (933) D, E and F (934)

47. The location of the Battle of Brunanburh is still contested, although there is now some consensus that it occurred on The Wirral.

48. Swanton, M. (ed. and trans.), *The Anglo-Saxon Chronicles*, (Orion Publishing Group, 2000), p.106

49. These entries concern Athelstan (A-937), Edmund (A-942) and Edmund's son, King Edgar (A-973 and 975).

50. Stafford discusses these entries in *After Alfred: Anglo-Saxon Chronicles and Chroniclers 900–1150*, p.95–6, assigning them as a possible Mercian composition, dated to the 940s and 950s.

51. PASE for details (Athelstan (18) Charter witnessing)

52. PASE for details (Edward (2) Charter witnessing)

53. PASE for details (Edmund (14) Charter witnessing)

54. Sawyer, P.H. (ed.), Anglo-Saxon Charters: An Annotated List and Bibliography, rev. Kelly, S.E. and Rushforth, R., (2022), http://www.

esawyer.org.uk/ S499 and S477 are said to be spurious, or forgeries. Of these two, Eadgifu attests S477 after the king and in S499 after the king, and then Eadred.

55. Sawyer, P.H. (ed.), Anglo-Saxon Charters: An Annotated List and Bibliography, rev. Kelly, S.E. and Rushforth, R., (2022), http://www.esawyer.org.uk/ S489

56. Ibid., (2022), http://www.esawyer.org.uk/ S465 S470, S475, S481, S483, S485, S487, S488, S489, S493, S494, S495, S496, S497, S501, S505, S506, S512, S514

57. Ibid., http://www.esawyer.org.uk/ S465, S470, S475, S483, S485, S487, S488, S491, S493, S496, S512

58. Ibid., http://www.esawyer.org.uk/ S494, S495, S497, S 506, S514

59. Ibid., http://www.esawyer.org.uk/ S505

60. Swanton, M. (ed. and trans.), *The Anglo-Saxon Chronicles*, (Orion Publishing Group, 2000), D (946) E (948 corrected to 946), A mentions his death, but not that he was murdered

61. Sawyer, P.H. (ed.), Anglo-Saxon Charters: An Annotated List and Bibliography, rev. Kelly, S.E. and Rushforth, R., (2022), http://www.esawyer.org.uk/ S517, S519, S521, S522a, S523, S525, S526, S527, S528, S529, S531, S532, S533, S535, S536, S540, S542, S544, S545, S546, S551, S552, S552a, S553, S554, S558, S559, S562, S565, S566, S567, S569, S578

62. Ibid., http://www.esawyer.org.uk/ S536, S521, S540, S567

63. Ibid., http://www.esawyer.org.uk/, S517, S519, S522a, S525, S526, S527, S528, S529, S531, S532, S533, S535, S536, S540, S542, S545, S551, S552, S553, S554, S558, S578

64. Ibid., http://www.esawyer.org.uk/ S565

65. Ibid., http://www.esawyer.org.uk/ S570 dated to 953/955

66. Bailey. M., 'Ælfwynn, Second Lady of the Mercians', *Edward the Elder, 899–924* Higham, N.J. and Hill, D.H. (ed.), (Routledge, 2001), p.125

67. Whitelock, D., *English Historical Documents: c.500–1042 – Volume 1*, First Edition, (Eyre & Spottiswoode, 1955), p.512 'Old English Will of King Eadred (951–955)'

68. Keynes, S. and Lapidge, M., *Asser's Life of King Alfred and Other Contemporary Sources*, (Penguin, 1983)

69. Sawyer, P.H. (ed.), Anglo-Saxon Charters: An Annotated List and Bibliography, rev. Kelly, S.E. and Rushforth, R., (2022), http://www.esawyer.org.uk/ S675, S676, S677, S677a, S678

70. Campbell, A. (ed.), *The Chronicle of Æthelweard: Chronicon Æthelweardi*, (Thomas Nelson and Sons Ltd, 1962), p.38

71. Jayakumar, S., 'Eadwig and Edgar', in *Edgar, King of the English, 959–975*, Scragg, D. (ed.), (Boydell Press, 2008), pp.89–90

72. Sawyer, P.H. (ed.), Anglo-Saxon Charters: An Annotated List and Bibliography, rev. Kelly, S.E. and Rushforth, R., (2022), http://www.esawyer.org.uk/ S1211

73. Firth, M. and Schilling, C., 'The Lonely Afterlives of Early English Queens', in *Nephilologus* September 2022, https://doi.org/10.1007/s11061-022-09739-4, pp.8–9

74. PASE S811

75. PASE S745

76. Mynors, R.A.B. (ed. and trans.), completed by Thomson, R.M. and Winterbottom, M., *William of Malmesbury: Gesta Regum Anglorum – The History of the English Kings,* (Clarendon Press, 1998), pp.199–201

77. Foot, S., *Athelstan* (Yale University Press, 2011), Figure 2

78. Priest, D. (trans.), *William of Malmesbury: Gesta Pontificum Anglorum – The Deeds of the Bishops of England,* (Boydell Press, 2002), p.109

79. Whitelock, D., *English Historical Documents*: *c.500–1042 – Volume 1*, First Edition, (Eyre & Spottiswoode, 1955), p.833

Chapter 5: The Religious

1. PASE Æthelgifu (4)

2. Yorke, B. 'Edward as Ætheling', in *Edward the Elder, 899–924* Higham, N.J. and Hill, D.H. (ed.), (Routledge, 2001), p.25

3. Keynes, S. and Lapidge, M., *Asser's Life of King Alfred and Other Contemporary Sources, (*Penguin, 1983), p.90

4. Ibid., p.105

5. Ibid., p.175

6. Ibid., p.177

7. I can find no reference to Æthelhild on PASE

8. Mynors, R.A.B. (ed. and trans.), completed by Thomson, R.M. and Winterbottom, M., *William of Malmesbury: Gesta Regum Anglorum – The History of the English Kings,* (Clarendon Press, 1998), pp.199–201

9. PASE Eadflæd (4)
10. Mynors, R.A.B. (ed. and trans.), completed by Thomson, R.M. and Winterbottom, M., *William of Malmesbury: Gesta Regum Anglorum – The History of the English Kings,* (Clarendon Press, 1998), pp.199–201
11. Believed to be Eadburgh (8) on PASE
12. Foot, S., *Athelstan,* (Yale University Press, 2011), p.45 Priest, D. (trans.), *William of Malmesbury: Gesta Pontificum Anglorum – The Deeds of the Bishops of England,* (Boydell Press, 2002)
13. Priest, D. (trans.), *William of Malmesbury: Gesta Pontificum Anglorum – The Deeds of the Bishops of England,* (Boydell Press, 2002), pp.115–16
14. Ibid., p.202
15. Sawyer, P.H. (ed.), Anglo-Saxon Charters: An Annotated List and Bibliography, rev. Kelly, S.E., Rushforth, R., (2022), http://www.esawyer.org.uk/ S446
16. PASE Eadgyth (4)
17. Priest, D. (trans.), *William of Malmesbury: Gesta Pontificum Anglorum – The Deeds of the Bishops of England,* (Boydell Press, 2002), p.126
18. Ibid., p.126
19. Ibid., p.127
20. Ibid., p.127

Chapter 6: English Wives

1. PASE Ælfgifu (3) and her mother is Wynnflæd (4) and also Wynnflæd (2) if the will of S485 is also hers
2. Sawyer, P.H. (ed.), Anglo-Saxon Charters: An Annotated List and Bibliography, rev. Kelly, S.E. and Rushforth, R., (2022), http://www.esawyer.org.uk/ S514
3. Campbell, A. (ed.), *The Chronicle of Æthelweard: Chronicon Æthelweardi,* (Thomas Nelson and Sons Ltd, 1962), p.54
4. Foot, S., *Veiled Women: Volume 1 – The Disappearance of Nuns from Anglo-Saxon England,* (Routledge, 2000), pp. 205–206, Sawyer, P.H. (ed.), Anglo-Saxon Charters: An Annotated List and Bibliography, rev. Kelly, S.E. and Rushforth, R., (2022), http://www.esawyer.org.uk/ S485

5. For a full discussion of the terminology of the religious women of the tenth century, see Foot, S., *Veiled Women: Volume 1 – The Disappearance of Nuns from Anglo-Saxon England,* (Routledge, 2000)

6. Foot, S., *Veiled Women: Volume 1 – The Disappearance of Nuns from Anglo-Saxon England,* (Routledge, 2000), pp.206–207

7. Ibid., p207

8. Ibid., p.208

9. Yorke, B., 'The Women in Edgar's Life', in *Edgar, King of the English, 959–975,* Scragg, D. (ed.), (Boydell Press, 2008), p.145, but Lapidge, M. (ed.), 'Lantfred of Winchester', in *The Cult of St Swithun,* (Oxford University Press, 2003)

10. Swanton, M. (ed. and trans.), *The Anglo-Saxon Chronicles,* (Orion Publishing Group, 2000), p.113

11. Fairweather, J. (trans.), *Liber Eliensis: A History of the Isle of Ely from the Seventh Century to the Twelfth,* (Boydell Press, 2005), Book 1.42, p.76

12. Ibid., Book 1.50, p.83

13. Priest, D. (trans.), *William of Malmesbury: Gesta Pontificum Anglorum – The Deeds of the Bishops of England,* (Boydell Press, 2002), p.124

14. Æthelflæd (14) on PASE. Her sister is believed to be Leofflæd (5), and her niece, Ælfflæd (13)

15. Swanton, M. (ed. and trans.), *The Anglo-Saxon Chronicles,* (Orion Publishing Group, 2000), D text, p.112

16. S513 PASE

17. S1483 PASE

18. Sawyer, P.H. (ed.), Anglo-Saxon Charters: An Annotated List and Bibliography, rev. Kelly, S.E. and Rushforth, R., (2022), http://www.esawyer.org.uk/ S493

19. Fairweather, J. (trans.), *Liber Eliensis: A History of the Isle of Ely from the Seventh Century to the Twelfth,* (Boydell Press, 2005), Book II:64, p.163

20. S1795 PASE

21. S1494 PASE

22. Ælfgifu (2) on PASE. Her mother is either Æthelgifu (7) or (9)

23. Swanton, M. (ed. and trans.), *The Anglo-Saxon Chronicles,* (Orion Publishing Group, 2000), p.113

24. Ibid., p.113

25. Ibid.
26. Campbell, A. (ed.), *The Chronicle of Æthelweard: Chronicon Æthelweardi*, (Thomas Nelson and Sons Ltd, 1962), p.2
27. Jayakumar, S., 'Eadwig and Edgar', in *Edgar, King of the English, 959–975*, Scragg, D. (ed.), (Boydell Press, 2008), p.88, but Campbell, A. (ed.), *The Chronicle of Æthelweard: Chronicon Æthelweardi*, (Thomas Nelson and Sons Ltd, 1962), p.31
28. Campbell, A. (ed.), *The Chronicle of Æthelweard: Chronicon Æthelweardi*, (Thomas Nelson and Sons Ltd, 1962), p.55
29. Jayakumar, S. 'Eadwig and Edgar', in *Edgar, King of the English, 959–975*, Scragg, D. (ed.), (Boydell Press, 2008), p.87, n28
30. Winterbottom, M. and Lapidge, M. (eds.), *The Early Lives of St Dunstan* (in Latin and English), (Oxford University Press, 2011), pp.67–9. Also found in translation in Whitelock, D., *English Historical Documents: c.500–1042 – Volume 1*, First Edition, (Eyre & Spottiswoode, 1955), p.829
31. The association of this will to Ælfgifu the wife of King Eadwig has not been proven beyond all doubt. As such, the will is assigned to Ælfgifu (4) on PASE, although it seems likely that she is also Ælfgifu (2).
32. PASE Æthelflæd (15)
33. Sawyer, P.H. (ed.), Anglo-Saxon Charters: An Annotated List and Bibliography, rev. Kelly, S.E. and Rushforth, R., (2022). http://www.esawyer.org.uk/ S1484 dated 966x975
34. I can find no reference for Æthelflæd on PASE
35. See Norton, E., *Elfrida: The First Crowned Queen*, (Amberley, 2013), p.46, for a discussion of this.
36. OASE Ordmær (2). Mentioned in the *Liber Eliensis*
37. Fairweather, J. (trans.), *Liber Eliensis, A History of the Isle of Ely from the Seventh Century to the Twelfth*, (Boydell Press, 2005), Book II, 7, p.103
38. Mynors, R.A.B. (ed. and trans.), completed by Thomson, R.M. and Winterbottom, M., *William of Malmesbury: Gesta Regum Anglorum – The History of the English Kings*, (Clarendon Press, 1998), *p.261*
39. See section on Æthelflæd of Damerham above.
40. PASE Wynnflæd (1), who may also be Wynnflæd (4) and possibly, also Wynnflæd (3).
41. Sawyer, P.H. (ed.), Anglo-Saxon Charters: An Annotated List and Bibliography, rev. Kelly, S.E. and Rushforth, R., (2022), http://www.esawyer.org.uk/ S1539

42. PASE Wulfthryth (6). Her daughter, Eadgyth (4)

43. Keynes, S., 'Edgar, rex admirabilis' in Scragg, D. (ed.), *Edgar, King of the English, 959–975*, (Boydell Press, 2008), p.4

44. Ibid., p.4

45. Ibid., p.5

46. Yorke, B., 'The Women in Edgar's Life', in *Edgar, King of the English, 959–975* Scragg, D. (ed.), (Boydell Press, 2008), p.152

47. I am indebted to Barbara Yorke's discussion of the saints' lives in regard to Edgar's wives

48. Sawyer, P.H. (ed.), Anglo-Saxon Charters: An Annotated List and Bibliography, rev. Kelly, S.E. and Rushforth, R., (2022), http://www.esawyer.org.uk/ S766

49. Ibid., http://www.esawyer.org.uk/ S799

50. Yorke, B., 'The Women in Edgar's Life', in *Edgar, King of the English, 959–975* Scragg, D. (ed.), (Boydell Press, 2008), p.149

51. Ælfthryth (9) on PASE

52. PASE S586, S651, S658, S660

53. Swanton, M. (ed. and trans.), *The Anglo-Saxon Chronicles*, (Orion Publishing Group, 2000), D, p.119

54. Yorke, B., 'The Women in Edgar's Life', in *Edgar, King of the English, 959–975*, Scragg, D. (ed.), (Boydell Press, 2008), p.145

55. Mynors, R.A.B. (ed. and trans.), completed by Thomson, R.M. and Winterbottom, M., *William of Malmesbury: Gesta Regum Anglorum – The History of the English Kings,* (Clarendon Press, 1998), pp.257–9

56. Hardy, R.D. and Martin, C.T. (trans. and ed.), *Lestorie des Engles Solum la Translacion Maistre Geffrei Gaimar*, (Cambridge University Press, 2012), pp.125–6

57. Barrow, J., The Chronology of Benedictine 'Reform' in *Edgar, King of the English 959–975*, (Boydell Press, 2008), p.217

58. Dated to 964 are S725 and S731, S725 is a charter to Elfrida.

59. Stafford, P., *Queen Emma and Queen Edith*, (Blackwell Publisher, 1997), pp.61–3

60. Sawyer, P.H. (ed.), Anglo-Saxon Charters: An Annotated List and Bibliography, rev. Kelly, S.E. and Rushforth, R., (2022), http://www.esawyer.org.uk/ S745

61. Yorke, B., 'The Women in Edgar's Life', in *Edgar, King of the English, 959–975*, Scragg, D. (ed.), (Boydell Press, 2008), p.147

62. Elfrida witnesses 21 of Edgar's charters, these are S671, S725, S731, S739, S742, S745, S746, S767, S771, S779, S786, S788, S789, S794, S795, S800, S801, S805, S807 and S806. During the period of their marriage, 90 surviving charters that Edgar issued are known.

63. Norton, E. *Elfrida: The First Crowned Queen*, (Amberley, 2013), p.2 *'clito legitimus prefati regis filius.'* Yorke, B., 'The Women in Edgar's Life', in *Edgar, King of the English, 959–975* Scragg, D. (ed.), (Boydell Press, 2008), p.148

64. Norton, E. *Elfrida: The First Crowned Queen*, (Amberley, 2013), p.2, *'eodem rege clito procreates.'* Yorke, B., 'The Women in Edgar's Life', in *Edgar, King of the English, 959–975* Scragg, D. (ed.), (Boydell Press, 2008), p.148

65. Yorke, B., 'The Women in Edgar's Life', in *Edgar, King of the English, 959–975*, Scragg, D. (ed.), (Boydell Press, 2008), p.148

66. Swanton, M. (ed. and trans.), *The Anglo-Saxon Chronicles*, (Orion Publishing Group, 2000), p.118, the E text has a similar entry but for 970

67. Ibid., p.118

68. Yorke, B., 'The Women in Edgar's Life', in *Edgar, King of the English, 959–975*, Scragg, D. (ed.), (Boydell Press, 2008), p.148

69. Norton, Elfrida p88

70. Swanton, M. (ed. and trans.), *The Anglo-Saxon Chronicles*, (Orion Publishing Group, 2000), pp.118–120

71. PASE S835, S840, S841, S842, S843, S845, S849, S876, S877, S878, S888, S891, S896, S904, S1454

72. PASE S671, S725, S731, S739, S742, S745, S746, S766, S767, S771, S779, S786, S788, S789, S794, S795, S800, S801, S805, S807, S806

73. Whitelock, D., *English Historical Documents*: *c.500–1042 – Volume 1*, First Edition, (Eyre & Spottiswoode, 1955), pp.841–3. It is believed that this annoymous work was written at Ramsey from 995 to 1005, and is now assigned to Byrthferth and so in the lifetime of Æthelred, and indeed, his mother.

74. Priest, D. (trans.), *William of Malmesbury: Gesta Pontificum Anglorum – The Deeds of the Bishops of England,* (Boydell Press, 2002), p.125

75. Ibid., p.135

76. Swanton, M. (ed. and trans.), *The Anglo-Saxon Chronicles*, (Orion Publishing Group, 2000), p.122

77. Whitelock, D., *English Historical Documents*: *c.500–1042 – Volume 1*, First Edition, (Eyre & Spottiswoode, 1955), p.531. Grant by King Ethelred to his mother, of Brabourne and other estates in Kent, which had been forfeited by a certain Wulfbald for many crimes (996).

78. Finberg, H.P.R., *The Early Charters of the West Midlands*, (Leicester, 1972), p.61 (149)

79. Foot, S., *Veiled Women: Volume 1 – The Disappearance of Nuns from Anglo-Saxon England*, (Routledge, 2000), p.194

80. Ibid.

Chapter 7: The Continental Connection

1. PASE Ælfthryth (5). Her daughter is Ealhswith (2)

2. Keynes, S. and Lapidge, M., *Asser's Life of King Alfred and Other Contemporary Sources, (*Penguin, 1983), p.90

3. Yorke, B., 'Edward as Ætheling', in *Edward the Elder, 899–924*, Higham, N.J. and Hill, D.H. (ed.), (Routledge, 2001), p.25

4. Ibid., p.27

5. Ibid., p.28

6. Campbell, 1962:2/ Yorke, B., 'Edward as Ætheling', in *Edward the Elder, 899–924*, Higham, N.J. and Hill, D.H. (ed.), (Routledge, 2001), p.28

7. McKitterick, R., *The Frankish Kingdoms Under the Carolingians, 751–987*, (Longman, 1983), pp.248–9

8. Tanner, H., *Families, Friends and Allies: Boulougne and Politics in Northern France and England c.879–1160*, (Brill, 2004), p.23

9. Ibid., p.27

10. Sawyer, P.H. (ed.), Anglo-Saxon Charters: An Annotated List and Bibliography, rev. Kelly, S.E. and Rushforth, R., (2022), http://www.esawyer.org.uk/ 1205b

11. Keynes, S. and Lapidge, M., *Asser's Life of King Alfred and Other Contemporary Sources,* (Penguin, 1983), p.175

12. Sawyer, P.H. (ed.), Anglo-Saxon Charters: An Annotated List and Bibliography, rev. Kelly, S.E. and Rushforth, R., (2022), http://www.esawyer.org.uk/ 1205b

13. Campbell, A. (ed.), *The Chronicle of Æthelweard: Chronicon Æthelweardi*, (Thomas Nelson and Sons Ltd, 1962), p.2

14. Tanner, H., *Families, Friends and Allies, Boulougne and Politics in Northern France and England c.879–1160*, (Brill, 2004), p.56

15. Mynors, R.A.B. (ed. and trans.), completed by Thomson, R.M. and Winterbottom, M., *Gesta Regvm Anglorvm, The History of the English Kings, William of Malmesbury*, (Clarendon Press, 1998), p.219

16. PASE Eadgifu (3)

17. Campbell, A. (ed.), *The Chronicle of Æthelweard: Chronicon Æthelweardi*, (Thomas Nelson and Sons Ltd, 1962), Prologue, p.2

18. Details taken from McKitterick, R., *The Frankish Kingdoms Under the Carolingians, 751–987*, (Longman, 1983), p.365, Genealogical table

19. The matter of marriages, and concubinage is gathering increasing levels of interest. It is becoming apparent that the need for legitimate marriages was a matter laid down by the Church as a means to garner legitimacy. Before this, unions of concubinage may have held as firmly as church recognised marriages.

20. Foot, S., *Athelstan* (Yale University Press, 2011), p.46

21. Bachrach, B.S. and Fanning, S. (ed. and trans.), *The Annals of Flodoard of Reims, 916–966*, (University of Toronto Press, 2004), 20A

22. William of Jumieges in his *Gesta Normannorum Ducum*, III.4 (PASE)

23. Bachrach, B.S. and Fanning, S. (ed. and trans.), *The Annals of Flodoard of Reims, 916–966* (University of Toronto Press, 2004), 18A (936). Foot, S., *Athelstan*, (Yale University Press, 2011), p.168

24. McKitterick, R., *The Frankish Kingdoms Under the Carolingians, 751–987*, (Longman, 1983), p.315

25. Van Houts, E.M.C. (trans.), *The Gesta Normannorum Ducum of William of Jumièges, Orderic Vitalic, and Robert of Torigni*, (Clarendon Press, Oxford, 1992), Book III.4, pp.82–3

26. Bachrach, B.S. and Fanning, S. (ed. and trans.), *The Annals of Flodoard of Reims, 916–966*, (University of Toronto Press, 2004), 33G

27. PASE Greater Domesday Book 353 (Lincolnshire 18:25)

28. Eadhild (1) PASE

29. Foot, S., *Athelstan*, (Yale University Press, 2011), p.47. Bachrach, B.S. and Fanning, S. (ed. and trans.), *The Annals of Flodoard of Reims, 916–966* (University of Toronto Press, 2004), 926

30. Campbell, A. (ed.), *The Chronicle of Æthelweard: Chronicon Æthelweardi*, (Thomas Nelson and Sons Ltd, 1962), Prologue, p.2

31. Bachrach, B.S. and Fanning, S. (ed. and trans.), *The Annals of Flodoard of Reims, 916–966*, (University of Toronto Press, 2004), 8E

32. Foot, S., *Athelstan* (Yale University Press, 2011), p.47. Mynors, R.A.B. (ed. and trans.), completed by Thomson, R.M. and Winterbottom, M., *William of Malmesbury: Gesta Regum Anglorum –The History of the English Kings*, (Clarendon Press, 1998), ii, 135, pp.218–19

33. McKitterick, R., *The Frankish Kingdoms Under the Carolingians, 751–987*, (Longman, 1983), p.314

34. Foot, S., *Athelstan*, (Yale University Press, 2011), p.47

35. McKitterick, R., *The Frankish Kingdoms Under the Carolingians, 751–987*, (Longman, 1983), p.314

36. PASE Eadgyth (2)

37. Swanton, M. (ed. and trans.), *The Anglo-Saxon Chronicles*, (Orion Publishing Group, 2000), p105. And Foot, S., *Athelstan*, (Yale University Press, 2011), p.49, n.69

38. Foot, S., *Athelstan*, (Yale University Press, 2011), p.48

39. Ibid.

40. Campbell, A. (ed.), *The Chronicle of Æthelweard: Chronicon Æthelweardi*, (Thomas Nelson and Sons Ltd, 1962), Prologue, p.2

41. Foot, S., *Athelstan*, (Yale University Press, 2011), p.49, but Hrotsvitha, *Gesta Ottonis*, lines 79–82 and 95–8, Berchin (ed.), 278–9

42. Swanton, M. (ed. and trans.), *The Anglo-Saxon Chronicles*, (Orion Publishing Group, 2000), C, p.124

43. This sister may appear as Anonymous 921 on PASE

44. Campbell, A. (ed.), *The Chronicle of Æthelweard: Chronicon Æthelweardi*, (Thomas Nelson and Sons Ltd, 1962), Prologue, p.2

45. Mynors, R.A.B. (ed. and trans.), completed by Thomson, R.M. and Winterbottom, M., *William of Malmesbury: Gesta Regum Anglorum – The History of the English Kings*, (Clarendon Press, 1998), pp.199–201

46. Foot, S., *Athelstan*, (Yale University Press, 2011), p.51

47. Please see Foot, S., *Athelstan*, (Yale University Press, 2011), p.51, for this fascinating discussion in its entirety

48. Foot, S., 'Dynastic Strategies: The West Saxon Royal Family in Europe', in *England and the Continent in the Tenth Century: Studies in Honour of Wilhelm Levison (1876–1947)*, (Brepols, 2012), p.250

49. Foot, S., *Athelstan*, (Yale University Press, 2011), pp.45–6

50. Ortenberg, V., 'The King From Overseas: Why did Athelstan matter in Tenth Century Continental Affairs', in *England and the Continent in the Tenth Century: Studies in Honour of Wilhelm Levison (1876–1947)*, (Brepols, 2012), p.222. Note that Ortenberg does not believe that William of Malmesbury miscounted the daughters born to King Edward the Elder.

51. Ibid., p.221

52. Foot, S., 'Dynastic Strategies: The West Saxon Royal Family in Europe', in *England and the Continent in the Tenth Century: Studies in Honour of Wilhelm Levison (1876–1947)*, (Brepols, 2012), pp.250–51

53. Ortenberg, V., 'The King from Overseas: Why did Athelstan matter in Tenth Century Continental Affairs', in *England and the Continent in the Tenth Century: Studies in Honour of Wilhelm Levison (1876–1947)*, (Brepols, 2012), pp.230–31

54. Foot, S., *Athelstan*, (Yale University Press, 2011) p.42, but Folcuin, *Gesta Abbatum S. Bertini Sithiensium*, ch.107, (Holder-Egger, O. (ed.))

55. McKitterick, R., *The Frankish Kingdoms Under the Carolingians, 751–987*, (Longman, 1983), p.251

56. Foot, S., *Athelstan*, (Yale University Press, 2011), p.169, but Flodoard, 936 (18A)

57. Ibid., p.53 but Flodoard, 939 (21B)

58. McKitterick, R., *The Frankish Kingdoms Under the Carolingians, 751–987*, (Longman, 1983), p.251

59. Ibid., p.238

60. Tanner, H., *Families, Friends and Allies, Boulougne and Politics in Northern France and England c.879–1160*, (Brill, 2004), p.38

61. Ibid., p38

Chapter 8: The First Wife and the Daughters of Æthelred II

1. PASE Ealdgyth (4)

2. PASE Ælfgifu (17). One of her daughters, Ælfgifu (25) is listed.

3. Swanton, M. (ed. and trans.), *The Anglo-Saxon Chronicles*, (Orion Publishing Group, 2000), p.140 E, also in C, D and F

4. Stevenson, J. (ed. and trans.), *The Historical Works of Symeon of Durham*, (Llanarch Press, Facsimile reprint, 1993), p.558

5. Stevenson, J. (trans.), *Simeon of Durham: A History of the Kings of England* (Facsimile reprint, 1987, Llanerch Press), p.144
6. Swanton, M. (ed. and trans.), *The Anglo-Saxon Chronicles*, (Orion Publishing Group, 2000), p.176

Chapter 9: Women in Law

1. Sawyer, P.H. (ed.), Anglo-Saxon Charters: An Annotated List and Bibliography, rev. Kelly, S.E. and Rushforth, R., (2022), http://www.esawyer.org.uk/ S464
2. Ibid., http://www.esawyer.org.uk/ S465, Finberg, H.P.R., *The Early Charters of Wessex*, (Leicester University Press, 1964), p.41, (59)
3. Sawyer, P.H. (ed.), Anglo-Saxon Charters: An Annotated List and Bibliography, rev. Kelly, S.E. and Rushforth, R., (2022), http://www.esawyer.org.uk/ S474
4. Ibid., http://www.esawyer.org.uk/ S482
5. Ibid., http://www.esawyer.org.uk/ S485
6. Ibid., http://www.esawyer.org.uk/ S487
7. Ibid., http://www.esawyer.org.uk/ S493
8. PASE Æthelswith [4]
9. Sawyer, P.H. (ed.), Anglo-Saxon Charters: An Annotated List and Bibliography, rev. Kelly, S.E. and Rushforth, R., (2022), http://www.esawyer.org.uk/ S464
10. PASE Æthelthryth [8]
11. Sawyer, P.H. (ed.), Anglo-Saxon Charters: An Annotated List and Bibliography, rev. Kelly, S.E. and Rushforth, R., (2022), http://www.esawyer.org.uk/ S465, Finberg, H.P.R., *The Early Charters of Wessex*, (Leicester University Press, 1964), p.41, (59)
12. PASE Ælfflæd [12]
13. Sawyer, P.H. (ed.), Anglo-Saxon Charters: An Annotated List and Bibliography, rev. Kelly, S.E. and Rushforth, R., (2022), http://www.esawyer.org.uk/ S474, Finberg, H.P.R., *The Early Charters of Wessex*, (Leicester University Press, 1964), p.168 (584)
14. Gelling, M., *The Early Charters of the Thames Valley*, p.35
15. PASE Wynnflæd [2])
16. Sawyer, P.H. (ed.), Anglo-Saxon Charters: An Annotated List and Bibliography, rev. Kelly, S.E. and Rushforth, R., (2022), http://

www.esawyer.org.uk/ S485, Finberg, H.P.R., *The Early Charters of Wessex*, (Leicester University Press, 1964), p.168, (585)]

17. PASE Ælfswith [4]
18. Sawyer, P.H. (ed.), Anglo-Saxon Charters: An Annotated List and Bibliography, rev. Kelly, S.E. and Rushforth, R., (2022), http://www.esawyer.org.uk/ S487, Finberg, H.P.R., *The Early Charters of Wessex*, (Leicester University Press, 1964), p.42, (62)]
19. PASE Ælfgyth [3])
20. Sawyer, P.H. (ed.), Anglo-Saxon Charters: An Annotated List and Bibliography, rev. Kelly, S.E. and Rushforth, R., (2022), http://www.esawyer.org.uk/ S493, Finberg, H.P.R., *The Early Charters of Wessex*, (Leicester University Press, 1964), p.88, (263) a
21. Electronic Sawyer S517ab
22. Electronic Sawyer S517bd
23. PASE Ælfwynn [3]. This could be Ælfwynn, Second Lady of the Mercians but she is given a separated entry on PASE as the identification is not assured
24. Sawyer, P.H. (ed.), Anglo-Saxon Charters: An Annotated List and Bibliography, rev. Kelly, S.E. and Rushforth, R., (2022), http://www.esawyer.org.uk/ S535]
25. PASE Ælfthryth [6])
26. Sawyer, P.H. (ed.), Anglo-Saxon Charters: An Annotated List and Bibliography, rev. Kelly, S.E. and Rushforth, R., (2022), http://www.esawyer.org.uk/ S534, Finberg, H.P.R., *The Early Charters of Wessex*, (Leicester University Press, 1964), p.170, (593)]
27. PASE Ælfgyth [5])
28. Sawyer, P.H. (ed.), Anglo-Saxon Charters: An Annotated List and Bibliography, rev. Kelly, S.E. and Rushforth, R., (2022), http://www.esawyer.org.uk/ S563, Finberg, H.P.R., *The Early Charters of Wessex*, (Leicester University Press, 1964), pp.137–8, (469) 0
29. 'The Old English noun *nunne* is obviously a loan-word from the late Latin *nonna*, which signified firstly a venerable, aged woman or grandmother, and only secondarily 'a nun'. Foot, S., *Veiled Women: Volume 1 – The Disappearance of Nuns from Anglo-Saxon England*, (Routledge, 2000), p.160
30. PASE Wynnflæd (5) 4
31. Sawyer, P.H. (ed.), Anglo-Saxon Charters: An Annotated List and Bibliography, rev. Kelly, S.E. and Rushforth, R., (2022), http://www.esawyer.org.uk/ S1454

32. Rabin, A., *Crime and Punishment in Anglo-Saxon England*, (Cambridge, 2020), p.1
33. Ibid.
34. Ibid.
35. Gelling, M., *The Early Charters of the Thames Valley*, (Leicester University Press, 1979) pp.18–19 and pp.86–87
36. PASE S1497
37. PASE Wulfwaru [3])
38. Whitelock, D., *English Historical Documents*: *c.500–1042 – Volume 1*, First Edition, (Eyre & Spottiswoode, 1955), p.524, (116)]
39. PASE Gode [1]]
40. PASE Ælfwaru [4]
41. Sawyer, P.H. (ed.), Anglo-Saxon Charters: An Annotated List and Bibliography, rev. Kelly, S.E. and Rushforth, R., (2022), http://www.esawyer.org.uk/ S7032
42. Ibid., http://www.esawyer.org.uk/ S762
43. Ibid., http://www.esawyer.org.uk/ S775
44. Ibid., http://www.esawyer.org.uk/ S784
45. Ibid., http://www.esawyer.org.uk/ S9041
46. Ibid., http://www.esawyer.org.uk/, S681
47. Ibid., http://www.esawyer.org.uk/ S737 and S738
48. Ibid., http://www.esawyer.org.uk/ S737, surviving in one manuscript. Gelling, M., *The Early Charters of the Thames Valley*, (Leicester University Press, 1979), p.75, (150)
49. Ibid., http://www.esawyer.org.uk/,S738, surviving in two manuscripts, Gelling, M., *The Early Charters of the Thames Valley*, (Leicester University Press, 1979), p.132, (277)
50. Ibid., http://www.esawyer.org.uk/ S937 and Whitelock, D., *English Historical Documents*: *c.500–1042 – Volume 1,* First Edition, (Eyre & Spottiswoode, 1955), p.537–9
51. PASE Eadflæd [2]
52. Whitelock, D., *English Historical Documents*: *c.500–1042 – Volume 1*, First Edition, (Eyre & Spottiswoode, 1955), 985, C, D and E, p.212
53. PASE Herelufu [1] and Wulfwynn [4]
54. Swanton, M. (ed. and trans.), *The Anglo-Saxon Chronicles*, (Orion Publishing Group, 2000), p.124
55. PASE and Sawyer, P.H. (ed.), Anglo-Saxon Charters: An Annotated List and Bibliography, rev. Kelly, S.E. and Rushforth, R., (2022), http://www.esawyer.org.uk/ S1486

56. Sawyer, P.H. (ed.), Anglo-Saxon Charters: An Annotated List and Bibliography, rev. Kelly, S.E. and Rushforth, R., (2022), http://www.esawyer.org.uk/ S561, Gelling, p.42, (62)

57. Gelling, M., *The Early Charters of the Thames Valley*, (Leicester University Press, 1979), p.159 (332) Sawyer, P.H. (ed.), Anglo-Saxon Charters: An Annotated List and Bibliography, rev. Kelly, S.E. and Rushforth, R., (2022), http://www.esawyer.org.uk/ S747

58. Edington, S.B. and Others (trans.), *Ramsey Abbey's Book of Benefactors – Part Two: The Early Years* (Hakedes, 2001), p.9, (28)

59. PASE Wynnflæd [6]

60. Ibid.

61. Whitelock, D., *English Historical Documents: c.500–1042 – Volume 1*, First Edition, (Eyre & Spottiswoode, 1955), p.550 (130)/S1503, Sawyer, P.H. (ed.), Anglo-Saxon Charters: An Annotated List and Bibliography, rev. Kelly, S.E. and Rushforth, R., (2022), http://www.esawyer.org.uk/

Chapter 10: The Written Record

1. https://www.bl.uk/collection-items/assers-life-of-king-alfred. For a full account of the history of the manuscripts, please see Keynes, S. and Lapidge, M., *Asser's Life of King Alfred and Other Contemporary Sources,* (Penguin, 1983)

2. Stafford, P., *After Alfred: Anglo-Saxon Chronicles and Chroniclers 900–1150,* (Oxford University Press, 2020), p.26

3. Ibid., p.39

4. Ibid., p.41

5. Ibid., p.51

6. Ibid., p.52

7. Ibid.

8. Ibid., p.82

9. Ibid., p.81

10. Ibid., p.87

11. Ibid., p.99

12. Ibid.

13. Ibid.

14. Bachrach, B.S. and Fanning, S. (ed. and trans.), *The Annals of Flodoard of Reims, 916–966,* (University of Toronto Press, 2004), location 125

15. Ibid., location 182
16. Ibid., location 164
17. Ibid., 19B
18. Montpellier BIU H 151 (late 10th C, the most important witness, but not an autograph); Vatican Reg. lat. 633 (early 11th C); Paris BnF 9768 (*c*.1000). The Vatican and Paris manuscripts derive from a version that was slightly revised around 976–978, about a decade after Flodoard's death. Personal email from Dr Edward Roberts, Senior Lecturer in Early Medieval History
19. Campbell, A. (ed.), *The Chronicle of Æthelweard: Chronicon Æthelweardi*, (Thomas Nelson and Sons Ltd, 1962), p.ix
20. Ibid., xii
21. Stafford, P., *After Alfred: Anglo-Saxon Chronicles and Chroniclers 900–1150*, (Oxford University Press, 2020), p.49
22. Winterbottom, M. and Lapidge, M. (eds.), *The Early Lives of St Dunstan* (in Latin and English), (Oxford University Press, 2011), p.ixiv
23. Ibid., p.xv
24. Lapidge, M., 'Byrhtferth and Oswald' in Brooks, N. and Cubitt, C. (ed.), *St Oswald of Worcester, Life and Influence*, (Leicester University Press, 1996), p.65
25. Whitelock, D., *English Historical Documents: c.500–1042 – Volume 1*, First Edition, (Eyre & Spottiswoode, 1955), p.839
26. Lapidge, M., 'Byrhtferth and Oswald' in Brooks, N. and Cubitt, C. (ed.), *St Oswald of Worcester, Life and Influence*, (Leicester University Press, 1996), p.73
27. Whitelock, D., *English Historical Documents: c.500–1042 – Volume 1,* First Edition, (Eyre & Spottiswoode, 1955), p.841–3. It is believed that this annoymous work was written at Ramsey from 995 to 1005, and is now assigned to Byrthferth.
28. Ibid., p.832
29. Lapidge, M. and Winterbottom, M. (ed. and trans.), *Wulfstan of Winchester The Life of St Æthelwold,* (Clarendon Press, 1991), p.70
30. Whitelock, D., *English Historical Documents: c.500–1042 – Volume 1*, First Edition, (Eyre & Spottiswoode, 1955), p.833
31. Lapidge, M. and Winterbottom, M. (ed. and trans.), *Wulfstan of Winchester The Life of St Æthelwold,* (Clarendon Press, 1991), p.70
32. https://www.bl.uk/collection-items/life-of-st-dunstan

33. Sawyer, P.H. (ed.), Anglo-Saxon Charters: An Annotated List and Bibliography, rev. Kelly, S.E. and Rushforth, R., (2022). http://www.esawyer.org.uk/ S739

34. Ibid., http://www.esawyer.org.uk/ S731

35. Jayakumar, Shashi, and Jayakumar, Sashi 'Foundlings, Ealdormen, and Holy Women: Reflections on Some Aristocratic Families in Ninth- and Early Tenth-Century Wiltshire', *Medieval Prosopography*, Vol. 24, 2003, pp.103–43, p.105

36. Norton, E., *Elfrida: The First Crowned Queen*, (Amberley, 2013), p.191, but *La Vie de Sainte Vulfhilde par Goscelin de Canterbory*, Analecta Bollandiana 32 (1913), p.10–26

37. Van Houts, E.M.C. (trans.), *The Gesta Normannorum Ducum of William of Jumièges, Orderic Vitalic, and Robert of Torigni,* (Clarenden Press, Oxford, 1992), p.xxi

38. C1 London British Library, MS Arundel 41. C2 Paris, Bibliotheque Nationale, MS Latin 15047, C4 Oxford, Bodleian Library, MS Bodley. Van Houts, E.M.C., (trans.), *The Gesta Normannorum Ducum of William of Jumièges, Orderic Vitalic, and Robert of Torigni,* (Clarenden Press, Oxford, 1992), pp.xciv–c

39. Van Houts, E.M.C. (trans.), *The Gesta Normannorum Ducum of William of Jumièges, Orderic Vitalic, and Robert of Torigni,* (Clarenden Press, Oxford, 1992), p.c

40. Greenway, D. (ed. and trans.), *Historia Anglorum*, The History of the English People: Henry of Huntingdon, (Clarendon Press, 1996), pp.307–309

41. Please see Winkler, E.A., 'Æthelflæd and Other Rulers in English History 'in *English Historical Review* Vol. CXXXVII, No.587, 2022, for a thorough assessment

42. Stafford, P., *After Alfred: Anglo-Saxon Chronicles and Chroniclers 900–1150*, (Oxford University Press, 2020), p.107, n.26, specifically referencing Henry of Huntingdon and Gaimar

43. See introduction Priest, D. (trans.), *William of Malmesbury: Gesta Pontificum Anglorum – The Deeds of the Bishops of England,* (Boydell Press, 2002)

44. Mynors, R.A.B. (ed. and trans.), completed by Thomson, R.M. and Winterbottom, M., *William of Malmesbury: Gesta Regum Anglorum – The History of the English Kings,* (Clarendon Press, 1998), p.189

45. Ibid., p.187

46. Ibid., p.199

47. Ibid., p.225–7
48. Ibid., p.207
49. Ibid., p.211
50. Ibid., pp.199–201
51. Ibid., p.203
52. Ibid., p.207
53. Ibid., p.213
54. Ibid., p.217
55. Ibid., p.219
56. Ibid., pp.257–9
57. Ibid., p.261
58. Ibid., pp.265–7
59. Priest, D. (trans.), *William of Malmesbury: Gesta Pontificum Anglorum – The Deeds of the Bishops of England,* (Boydell Press, 2002), note to the translation
60. Ibid., p.198
61. Ibid., pp.115–16
62. Ibid., p.202
63. Ibid., p.109
64. Ibid., p.124
65. Ibid., p.125
66. Ibid., p.135
67. Ibid., p.126
68. Ibid.
69. Ibid., p.127
70. Ibid.
71. Hardy, R.D. and Martin, C.T. (trans. and ed.), *Lestorie des Engles Solum la Translacion Maistre Geffrei Gaimar*, (Cambridge University Press, 2012), p.ix
72. Ibid., p.x
73. Ibid., p.128, line 4054
74. Darlington, R.R. & McGurk, P. (ed.), *The Chronicle of John of Worcester – Volume II: The Annals from 450 to 1066*, (Clarendon Press, 1995), p.xvii
75. Ibid., pp.xxi–lix. These are Oxford, Corpus Christi College 157. Evesham Almonry Museum s.n. Dublin, Trinity College 502. London, Lambeth Palace 42. Cambridge, Corpus Christi College 92. Dublin, Trinity College 503.

76. Darlington, R.R. and McGurk, P. (ed.), *The Chronicle of John of Worcester: Volume II – The Annals from 450 to 1066* (Clarendon Press, 1995), p.373 [916]
77. Ibid., pp.379–80 [919]
78. Ibid., p.405
79. Ibid., p.409
80. Ibid., p.421
81. Greenway, D. (ed. and trans.), *Historia Anglorum*, The History of the English People: Henry of Huntingdon, (Clarendon Press, 1996), p.299
82. Ibid., p.301
83. Ibid., p.303
84. Ibid., p.307
85. Ibid., pp.307–309
86. Ibid., p.309
87. Fairweather, J. (trans.), *Liber Eliensis: A History of the Isle of Ely from the Seventh Century to the Twelfth*, (Boydell Press, 2005), p.xiv
88. Ibid., Book II, 39, p.135
89. Electronic Sawyer, and Macray, W.D. (ed.), *Chronicon Abbatiae Ramesiensis*, (Cambridge University Press, 2012), although the manuscript names listed there have since changed. For transcripts BL, Harley 311, ff. 14v–20v, (s.xvii) and BL, Stowe 938, ff. 3–75v, (s.xviii)

Chapter 11: The Royal Women of the Long Tenth Century

1. Foot, S., *Athelstan (*Yale University Press, 2011), p.74, n.46
2. Yorke, B., 'Edward as Ætheling', in *Edward the Elder, 899–924* Higham, N.J. and Hill, D.H. (ed.), (Routledge, 2001), p.25
3. PASE Wulfthryth [2]
4. See Keynes, S. and Lapidge, M., *Asser's Life of King Alfred and other Contemporary Sources*, (Penguin, 1983), p.235, n28, for details, and Key, M.J., *Edward the Elder*, (Amberley, 2019), pp.75–7, for a discussion
5. There is an argument that Ælfflæd may have been the daughter of Æthelred I, and therefore Edward's cousin. This theory has been

discounted on the uproar such a union might have caused with the church. However, perhaps it should not be dismissed. In the teeth of unhappiness, Alfred's brother married his stepmother, which would have been against canonical law.

6. Swanton, M. (ed. and trans.), *The Anglo-Saxon Chronicles*, (Orion Publishing Group, 2000), p.93

7. Ibid., p.95

8. Ibid.

9. Ibid., p.96

10. Ibid., p.97

11. Ibid., p.98

12. Ibid., p.103

13. If William of Malmesbury's identification of him is correct.

14. Swanton, M. (ed. and trans.), *The Anglo-Saxon Chronicles*, (Orion Publishing Group, 2000), p.104

15. Ibid.

16. Ibid.

17. Ibid., p.105

18. Ibid., p.104

19. Macray, W.D. (ed.), *Chronicon Abbatiae Ramesiensis*, (Cambridge University Press, 2012), 11 and 53 (index)

20. Swanton, M. (ed. and trans.), *The Anglo-Saxon Chronicles*, (Orion Publishing Group, 2000), p.61

21. Foot, S., *Athelstan*, (Yale University Press, 2011), p.259

22. Like much in this period, the location of Brunanburh has proved elusive. It is widely believed to have taken place either on the Wirral or in the North East of England.

23. Swanton, M. (ed. and trans.), *The Anglo-Saxon Chronicles*, (Orion Publishing Group, 2000), p.111

24. Ibid., p.110

25. Ibid., p.111

26. Ibid., p.110

27. Ibid., p.112

28. Ibid.

29. Ibid.

30. Ibid.

31. Ibid., p.113

32. Ibid.

33. See Downham, C., *Viking Kings of Britain and Ireland: The Dynasty of Ivarr to AD 1014*, (Dnuedin, 2007), pp.115–120, for a detailed discussion of the identity of Erik/Eirik

34. Macray, W.D. (ed.), *Chronicon Abbatiae Ramesiensis, (Cambridge University Press, 2012)*, 11 and 53 (index)

35. S593 Sawyer, P.H. (ed.), Anglo-Saxon Charters: An Annotated List and Bibliography, rev. Kelly, S.E. and Rushforth, R., (2022), http://www.esawyer.org.uk/

36. Jayakumar, S. 'Eadwig and Edgar', in *Edgar, King of the English, 959–975*, Scragg, D. (ed.), (Boydell Press, 2008), p.85, for a full discussion

37. Swanton, M. (ed. and trans.), *The Anglo-Saxon Chronicles*, (Orion Publishing Group, 2000), p.113

38. Ibid.

39. Ibid.

40. Ibid.

41. Jayakumar, S. 'Eadwig and Edgar', in *Edgar, King of the English, 959–975*, Scragg, D. (ed.), (Boydell Press, 2008), p.85, n.12

42. Norton, E., *Elfrida: The First Crowned Queen*, (Amberley, 2013), p.42

43. S675, S676, S676a, S677, S678 Sawyer, P.H. (ed.), Anglo-Saxon Charters: An Annotated List and Bibliography, rev. Kelly, S.E. and Rushforth, R., (2022), http://www.esawyer.org.uk/

44. For a discussion of this topic see, Jayakumar, Shashi, and Jayakumar, Sashi. 'Foundlings, Ealdormen, and Holy Women: Reflections on Some Aristocratic Families in Ninth- and Early Tenth-Century Wiltshire', *Medieval Prosopography*, Vol. 24, 2003, pp.103–43, which attempts to trace the noble families of Wulfthryth and her cousin Wulfhild, the two women who Edgar both tried to marry, and did marry.

45. Ealdorman Leofwine of the Hwicce begins to attest Æthelred II's charters from 993. His son, Earl Leofric began to attest to the king's charters from the late 1020s. It is possible that Leofwine's father fought at the Battle of Maldon, is commemorated in the poem, and thus, the family may have been connected to that of Ealdorman Byrhtnoth.

46. Barrow, J., The Chronology of Benedictine 'Reform' in *Edgar, King of the English 959–975*, (Boydell Press, 2008), p.223

47. Norton, E., *Elfrida: The First Crowned Queen*, (Amberley, 2013), p.88

48. Ibid., p.90

49. Rumble, A.R., 'The Laity and the Monastic Reform in the Reign of Edgar' in Scragg, D. (ed.), *Edgar, King of the English, 959–975*, (Boydell Press, 2008), p.245, S1242

50. Stafford, P. *Queen Emma and Queen Edith*, (Blackwell Publisher, 1997), pp.139–40

51. Hollis, S. (ed.), 'St Edith and the Wilton Community', in *Writing the Wilton Women* (Turnhout, 2004)

52. Fairweather, J. (trans.), *Liber Eliensis, A History of the Isle of Ely from the Seventh Century to the Twelfth*, (Boydell Press, 2005), Book II, 39, p.135

53. Stafford, P., *Unification and Conquest*, (Oxford University Press, 2002), p.57

54. Ibid.

55. Swanton, M. (ed. and trans.), *The Anglo-Saxon Chronicles*, (Orion Publishing Group, 2000), p.123

56. Ibid., p.122

57. Whitelock, D., *English Historical Documents*: *c.500–1042 – Volume 1*, First Edition, (Eyre & Spottiswoode, 1955), p.841–3. It is believed that this annoymous work was written at Ramsey from 995 to 1005, and so in the lifetime of Æthelred, and indeed, his mother.

58. Keynes, S., *The Diplomas of Æthelred 'the Unready' 978–1016*, (Cambridge University Press, 1980), p.168

59. Norton, E., *Elfrida: The First Crowned Queen*, (Amberely, 2013), p.114, but Stubbs, *Osbern's Life of St Dunstan*

60. Whitelock, D., *English Historical Documents*: *c.500–1042 – Volume 1*, First Edition, (Eyre & Spottiswoode, 1955), p.549, (130)

61. Ibid., p.857, although Æthelred's name is not included in all of the manuscript versions

62. Ibid., p.841, (236)

63. Keynes, S., *The Diplomas of Æthelred 'the Unready' 978–1016*, (Cambridge University Press, 1980), p.168, for a discussion of the later sources

64. Stevenson, J. (ed. and trans.), *Simeon's History of the Church of Durham*, (Llanarch Press, Facsimile reprint, 1993), p.671

65. Sawyer, P.H. (ed.), Anglo-Saxon Charters: An Annotated List and Bibliography, rev. Kelly, S.E. and Rushforth, R., (2022), http://

www.esawyer.org.uk/S834 and S835, Keynes, The Diplomas of King Æthelred the Unready, p38

66. PASE and Sawyer, P.H. (ed.), Anglo-Saxon Charters: An Annotated List and Bibliography, rev. Kelly and S.E., Rushforth, R., (2022), http://www.esawyer.org.uk/ as well as Keynes, S. *The Diplomas of Æthelred 'the Unready' 978–1016*, (Cambridge University Press, 1980)

67. See Keynes, S., *The Diplomas of Æthelred 'the Unready' 978–1016*, (Cambridge University Press, 1980), p.237, for a discussion of his categories for the surviving charters

68. Swanton, M. (ed. and trans.), *The Anglo-Saxon Chronicles*, (Orion Publishing Group, 2000), p.131 997 (E)

69. S835, S840, S842, S843, S845, S849, S876, S878, S879, S888, S891, S896, S904, in receipt of S877, and acts as witness on S1454

70. PASE S1454 dated between 990 and 992

71. Norton, E., *Elfrida: The First Crowned Queen*, (Amberley, 2013), p.172, with reference to S1503 and S904, both of which mention the land after Elfrida's death

72. Swanton, M. (ed. and trans.), *The Anglo-Saxon Chronicles*, (Orion Publishing Group, 2000), p.124

73. Ibid.

Chapter 12: Conclusion

1. Foot, S., *Athelstan*, (Yale University Press, 2011), p.51

Index